When Good Dogs Do Bad Things

Also by Mordecai Siegal and Matthew Margolis

Good Dog, Bad Dog

Underdog: Training the Mutt, Mongrel & Mix-Breed

Also by Mordecai Siegal

The Good Dog Book

The Mordecai Siegal Happy Pet/Happy Owner Book

The Good Cat Book

The Simon & Schuster Guide to Cats

Happy Dog/Happy Owner Book

A Dog for the Kids

Also by Matthew Margolis

The Dog in Your Life (with Catherine Swan)

Some Swell Pup: Or Are You Sure You Want a Dog? (with Maurice Sendak)

The Liberated Dog

When Good Dogs Do Bad Things

Mordecai Siegal
Matthew Margolis

LITTLE, BROWN AND COMPANY
Boston • Toronto • London

Library of Congress Cataloging-in-Publication Data

Siegal, Mordecai.
    When good dogs do bad things.

    Includes index.
    1. Dogs—Behavior.   2. Dogs—Training.
I. Margolis, Matthew.   II. Title.
SF433.S58   1986   636.7′08′8   86-7411
ISBN 0-316-79008-7

10 9 8 7 6 5 4

HC

Design by Patricia Girvin Dunbar

Published simultaneously in Canada
by Little, Brown & Company (Canada) Limited

PRINTED IN THE UNITED STATES OF AMERICA

For all the dear ones:
Beverly and Jesse Margolis
Vicki, TJ, Ida, and Jasper Siegal

Contents

When Good Dogs Do Bad Things

Problems, Problems, Problems . . . Yours or the Dog's?

Mordecai Siegal

Will Rogers *should* have said, "I never knew a *dog* I didn't like." When good dogs do bad things they are not necessarily problem dogs; they may simply be dogs with problems, and that makes a world of difference. Dogs with problems are the Clark Gables and Joan Crawfords of the canine world. Lovable rogues, they live the lives of good dogs going wrong. We love our rogues and we love them even more when they have mended their ways. This page is the first step in that direction.

It is impossible to anticipate dog problems. Who can predict which sweet and adorable puppy will become a barker, a biter, or a destroyer of furniture? There is nothing more depressing than your new "best friend" developing a taste for your couch or leaving something on your carpet for you to step in.

Sooner or later every dog has a problem. Even the owners of obedience-trained dogs will need help. The need may be immediate or in the near future. Unfortunately, some dogs may be pure gold for years and then suddenly create an unpleasant situation for the family. Housebreaking failures are among the most common problems that come back to haunt us, along with barking, howling, and destructive chewing. The most critical problem is biting, which requires immediate attention and serious consideration.

It is altogether possible that a dog and its owner are ready to talk to their lawyers. Maybe the dog keeps dragging sacks of trash into the living room or peeing and dumping everywhere but outside. The disenchanted dog owner may be trying to cope with all-night howling or chewed-up furniture legs. Perhaps the dog bit someone. The family pet may be hiding under the bed to avoid the obscenities and broomsticks flung in his direction. But dogs and their owners do not divorce. When things go sour, the dog is simply thrown away. The frustrated owner takes him to the pound or tries to situate the animal "on a farm." In any case, he loses his home. A dog removed from his home is emotionally shaken and psychologically harmed. The sight of a dog led away from his home and family forever is a very sad one. When the animal looks back at his owner for the last time, it can break your heart. In many instances he is doomed to an uncertain fate, including the possibility of a lethal injection.

Some dog problems are preventable and many are not. However, once a problem exists your choices are to solve it, live with it, or get rid of the dog. If you feel, as we do, that animals are not objects but are living creatures with feelings and are entitled to kindness and respect, we suggest that you try to solve the problem if you can. We recognize the fact that *not every problem has a solution*. But most do.

DOG TRAINING AS OPPOSED TO PROBLEM SOLVING

A dog that is obedience-trained behaves much better than one that isn't. Let us understand the difference between obedience training and solving dog problems. Obedience training is a teaching process that creates in a dog's mind a set of desired responses to specific commands that are given vocally and with hand signals. This procedure makes life more convenient for people, safer for dogs, and happier for both. A proper training course offers a step-by-step, systematic method of organizing a dog's responses to authority and directs the dog toward obeying various but quite spe-

cific commands. An obedience-trained dog has learned to walk gently in "Heel" at the side of his owner; to "Sit" on command and then to "Stay"; to lie "Down" on command, and "Stay"; to "Come" when called; to obey "Go To Your Place"; and to relieve himself in a place most desirable to humans. This discipline is accomplished by a professional dog trainer or by a determined dog owner with an obedience-training book. (An obedience course for pets should not be confused with obedience training that is taught for the sport of Obedience Trials sponsored by the American Kennel Club, although there are similarities in the basics of the training. Dogs trained for Obedience Trials become highly skilled and advanced beyond the daily necessities of a good house dog. AKC Obedience Trials are an important and enjoyable aspect of the dog sport and highly recommended for those with an ongoing interest in dog training.)

Solving dog problems is quite different from obedience training. Where obedience training teaches a dog to obey specific commands, solving dog problems is sharply focused on changing unwanted behavior, whether a human is present or not when it occurs. Problem solving is also an attempt to change unacceptable dog behavior that has developed over a period of time. Obedience training is conditioning and problem solving is reconditioning. Both are aspects of behavior modification.

Reconditioning techniques and solutions are offered to solve such problems as jumping the fence, digging up the yard, lack of housebreaking, chewing, and all the other unwanted habits. We do encourage you to obedience-train your dog as well. What must be understood is that even an obedience-trained dog might defecate in the house and dig up your yard. You will still have to deal with your dog's behavior problems, and that must become your number one priority.

DOG PROBLEMS/PEOPLE PROBLEMS

Problem behavior appears off and on throughout the life of a dog. The first time is during the growth and development stage of puppyhood. Until they are educated and corrected, all young dogs behave in a way that is troublesome for humans. Grown dogs can become problematic suddenly, without warning, catching you quite by surprise, or gradually, without attracting attention, until the problem reaches a serious stage. Sometimes the owner is unaware of a problem until the neighbors slip a petition under the door asking her to move. It is safe to say that most dog problems are present in the first year of life. It is a crucial time for everyone. However, there are solutions for the majority of problems in the majority of dogs. Success depends upon trial-and-error with the solutions offered here, on the nature of the dog, and on your determination to work patiently until the problem is solved.

Toward that end it would help to understand something about the nature of the most common problems that dogs develop along the way. Although all dog behavior in the home can be understood by comparing it to dog behavior (or wolf behavior) in the wild, it seems to depend on whether it is a dog problem or a people problem. A dog problem is behavior that is not only undesirable but in some way unnatural for domestic dogs. Among such "dog problems" are de-

Loneliness, boredom, and lack of attention are important causes of destructive behavior in dogs.

structive chewing of objects, biting (friend or foe), and begging for food or attention.

A people problem would be behavior that is natural for dogs even though it may be totally unacceptable to humans. Most pet owners would pass out if a dog hunched his body and let go on the carpet in front of dinner guests. That is a people problem. A housebroken dog (one that eliminates when and where you want him to) is behaving artificially for a dog. In the wild, a dog (or wolf) uses his urine and feces to claim territory and establish boundaries, among other things. Although he would not relieve himself where he eats or sleeps, anyplace else or in front of other members of the pack is quite acceptable. The most common "people problems" are housebreaking, barking, and digging behavior.

There is one other important source of behavior problems for dog owners to be aware of. On occasion a dog will develop a physical ailment that could very easily result in unwanted behavior. For example, a bladder infection or bladder stones could cause a dog to urinate indoors. Food changes, water changes, or emotional upset could cause diarrhea, and house training would be very difficult for a dog with this condition. If a dog has a kidney infection, what is the point of setting up a housebreaking program? A dog in pain may snap or bite if touched in the tender area. But dog owners must realize that these behavior problems are unusual and temporary. Once the medical problem has been taken care of, the behavior problem, in all probability, will disappear, unless the behavior has had enough time to become habitual. If that happens, the behavior problem must be dealt with as recommended in this book.

Make no mistake; pet owners do not have to live with problem behavior whether it's natural to the dog or not. The message here is to deal with the root cause of the problem, not merely its symptoms. When trying to solve behavior problems a knowledgeable dog owner not only knows what to do but is more understanding and patient and therefore more successful.

Myths of Dog Ownership

1. *All big dogs need a lot of exercise.* Not true. Breeds such as the Newfoundland, St.

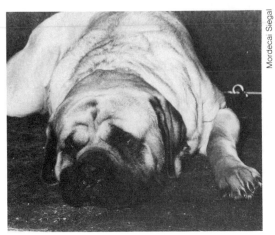

Many large dogs are docile and spend most of the day sleeping.

Bernard, or Kuvasz need some exercise but spend most of their day sleeping.

2. *Small dogs do not need exercise.* Not true. Some small breeds such as the Yorkshire Terrier, Norwich Terrier or West Highland White Terrier have a great deal of energy and require a physical outlet for it.

3. *Small dogs do not have to be trained.* Not true. These breeds require more housebreaking training than others and are incessant barkers.

4. *Dogs behave badly out of spite or jealousy.* Not true. Thinking this is to assign highly complex human responses to dogs. Because many people do not know how or why a dog problem develops, they tend to personalize it. Dogs bring out intense emotions in people for good or bad, and dog owners often believe their dogs are feeling exactly what they are feeling. It doesn't happen that way. Dog behavior is different from human behavior.

5. *Dogs feel guilty when they do something wrong.* Not true. Guilt, one of the most trou-

blesome and complicated areas of human psychology, should not be applied to dog behavior. In humans, guilt is experienced as emotions, thoughts, and intellectualized concepts sometimes caused by or resulting in irrational behavior. What humans mistake for guilty behavior in dogs is really an expression of anxiety. Dogs may hide or cower or get that low-eared, droopy look when you arrive because they have done something forbidden. But that "hangdog" look stems from associating punishment, yelling, or rejection from you with the misdeed. That "guilty" look is the fear of your arrival and not a feeling of remorse. It is the result of your having hit him with a newspaper, chased him under the bed, or gone berserk at him in a previous experience. Wouldn't you lower your ears and hide in the corner under those circumstances? If a dog felt truly guilty, he might regret his misbehavior and attempt to correct himself.

6. *It's cruel to have a big dog in an apartment.* Not true. This myth is usually accompanied by the statement that city life is not good for a dog. If that were true, there wouldn't be millions of dogs living happily in the large cities of this country, as they do. There are probably one million dogs in New York City or Chicago and at least two million dogs living in Los Angeles. Because of the obvious restrictions of city life, city dog owners tend to pay more attention to their pets' needs than in any other circumstance. They walk them in the coldest, wettest, hottest weather, exercise them, rush them to the vet for the slightest ailment, and keep the grooming shops busy and prosperous. Most city dogs have a great life.

7. *You have to hit your dog to control him.*

Not true. Hitting a dog is a terrible thing to do. It doesn't make you or the dog feel good. It can only make your dog fear you and/or teach him to be aggressive. How would you teach or correct your dog if you didn't hit him? The techniques in this book offer a better way.

8. *You have to knee your dog in the chest to keep him off.* Not true. Why would you want to use your body negatively? If you knee your dog ten times you'll probably hit his chest just once, but you may hit his jaw, his right or left leg, or possibly his side. Ask a veterinarian about possible injuries from this technique. How, by the way, would you knee a Yorkshire Terrier? There is a better way to correct this behavior that is not so hard on you or the dog.

9. *You have to step on the dog's back paws to keep him off.* Not true. You could break or dislocate a bone. This technique helps develop aggressive behavior, especially toward you. And then there is the pain that is caused.

10. *Housebreaking involves rubbing a dog's face in his own mess.* Not true. This does not accomplish anything. All it does is scare the dog. Your hands and your angry tone become associated in the dog's mind with a terrible experience. It is an inhumane expression of frustration and rage disguised as a teaching method. If it worked, why would it become necessary to keep repeating it? The truth is that it does not work.

11. *Never spoil your puppy by letting him get away with anything.* Not true. It is a popular misconception that you must constantly discipline a puppy and never let him get away with things. We expect puppies to do everything wrong if they are normal. The dog owner's job is to educate himself and

then educate the puppy. This involves obedience training geared for puppies and correcting *some* puppy behavior that leads to serious problems such as nipping.

12. *A dog has to be free.* Not true. Letting him loose is fine if you want to get a new dog every three months. Dogs need to be restricted for their own safety and out of respect for other people. Dogs cannot be made to look both ways when crossing a street. Many communities prohibit free-roaming because of possible destruction to property a dog may cause or harm he may bring to innocent strangers. An untethered or unleashed dog is also a nuisance. Whether he lives in the city, the suburbs, or the country, a dog on his own has a short life expectancy.

13. *Applying guilt to a dog is an effective training technique.* Not true. One of the great myths of dog ownership is that if you make him feel guilty enough he will stop eating the carpet and knocking you down with his front paws. Saying to a dog such things as "What did you do?" or "You bad dog!" in an accusing tone of voice, may have a punishing effect. It may even have a correcting effect (in some situations), but it does not teach the dog anything. In dog training the animal must first be shown what to do. Then he is rewarded for doing it. After that the dog is corrected when he doesn't obey a command. When a child enters a classroom for the first time, he is never tested before the subject is taught. Why make a dog feel guilty for doing something wrong when he wasn't taught the correct thing in the first place? The reality is that dogs are going to behave in their natural way until we teach them to do otherwise. Guilt is just another form of punishment and it is hardly justified or productive in dog handling.

A PHILOSOPHY OF DOG TRAINING AND PROBLEM SOLVING

We believe that dogs need love and affection. They respond well to it, making dogs and humans feel good. If you rely on this idea for teaching from beginning to end, you will have a happier, more accomplished pupil. Problem solving should not change the positive aspects of the dog's personality. The fun and pleasure of owning a dog do not come to an end because you decide to solve a behavior problem. The solution is achieved by bonding with your dog.

People bond with their dogs by creating a happy environment. Be loving and affectionate verbally by talking to him in the nicest way possible; physically, by touching and stroking him. Even your body language has an effect. You can constantly tower over a dog and overwhelm him or you can occasionally get down on his level and treat him as a pal. Different styles of treatment can make dogs and humans feel good or bad about each other.

It is important to understand what to expect from a dog at various ages. Your feelings change for the better when you learn to expect less maturity from a three-month-old puppy and more from a three-year-old dog. When a three-month-old dog nips we say, "He's only a puppy. He just needs to be corrected." But if a three-year-old dog chews your furniture, it's a serious problem. Each age group requires a separate approach to problem solving. The techniques used may vary from age range to age range, or they may be the same but applied with less or more intensity. The age and the type of problem demand separate ways of dealing with these situations even though both may deal with the dog's teeth.

The key to being a successful dog owner is your emotional relationship with the animal. If you can translate loving and caring feelings into a method of training and problem solving you will not lose the dog's personality or make him feel less wanted. After all, we just want to solve the problem, not remake the dog into something else. When anger, frustration, and rage enter into a problem situation, you may win the battle and lose the war. The goal is to retain the dog's happy disposition and outgoing personality while changing unwanted behavior. That is what most dog owners want to accomplish.

Dogs (and people) need love and affection.

Some Essential Tools and Techniques for Problem Solving

When applying the solutions offered in Four, "A Directory of Problems," you will find many references to items of equipment and to problem-solving techniques such as the *Margolis Maneuver*. The equipment referred to, although easy to obtain, demands an understanding of its proper use. Everyone knows how to attach a leash to a dog. But which type of leash and how long it should be depends on what you hope to accomplish with it. Using your voice as a training tool is another example of the training techniques to be found in the following pages. Everything presented in part Two is of vital importance for using the problem-solving techniques offered in "A Directory of Problems." We urge you to read this entire section carefully and refer to it frequently as you use the book to solve your dog's problems.

Mordecai Siegal

SIX-FOOT LEASH

A leash is much more than a line attached to a dog's collar. It is a birth-control device, an accident preventer, a good-neighbor policy, a wildlife and environmental protection tool, and much more. *In dog training and problem solving it is the primary means of teaching, correcting, and communicating with a dog.*

Leashes can be made of leather, braided nylon, nylon webbing, waxed cotton (Cordo-Hyde), and metal. A six-foot leather leash is the most useful and durable type for training and everyday use. Leather softens with age, making it more comfortable for the dog, and lasts longer than most other materials. It is easier on your hand as well as the dog's body. One can hardly tell when a metal leash is about to break. It is quite apparent when leather begins to wear and develop thin sections. This fact is very important when handling dogs. Metal leashes are made of link chain and come in a variety of widths and lengths. A weak link on a chain leash can go unnoticed and snap without warning, allowing the dog to get away from you. Only welded chain can stand up to a strong dog's pull, but the metal can become a heavy burden for the dog. Metal leashes sometimes develop sharp edges, which can irritate or scratch your dog. Nylon webbing is very popular because of its strength, light weight, and bright colors. However, it does burn your hand if your dog quickly pulls away from you, causing the leash to slide against your skin.

The width of a leather leash is important. Five-eighths of an inch is ideal for medium-to-large dogs. A leash five-eighths of an inch wide, or wider, provides the necessary strength for a large dog and does not overwhelm a fragile dog by being too wide or too heavy. Narrower widths are best for small dogs. Strength and comfort are the main considerations when selecting the proper leash for your dog.

STREET HANDLE

This is a valuable training tool sometimes referred to as a "tab." It consists of a large leather or nylon leash handle without a leash. A metal clip is attached to the base, allowing it to hook onto a collar. It provides the weight of a leash but not the length. In everyday use it is designed for medium-to-large dogs, allowing the owner to maintain close control when walking. For training and problem-solving purposes it provides the

owner with the ability to correct the dog (see part Two, "The Margolis Maneuver") without having to drag his leash around for long periods of time.

SLIP COLLAR

Sometimes this very important tool is referred to as a "choke collar," but that designation is unfortunate. It gives a wrong impression to people who quite correctly are concerned about the wellbeing of their dogs. A slip collar does not choke a dog. When used properly, the leash is tugged to the side, causing the collar to tighten gently around the dog's neck for a split second. It is then instantly released. The purpose of doing this is to communicate to the dog that he did the wrong thing. The slip collar is not a punishment device; it is a correction device. It does not hurt the dog. When solving dog problems you should not think in terms of punishment, which has no teaching value. You must use a "correction," which delivers the message of disapproval. The slip collar is the

Marybeth Eubank

Essential problem-solving equipment: slip collar, shake can, six-foot leash, thirty-foot leash, and street handle.

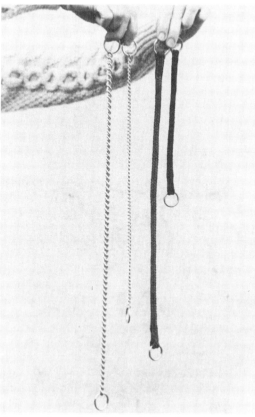

*Assorted steel and braided nylon slip
collars.*

most effective, the kindest, and the most humane training device available. It is easier on a dog than a very harsh tone of voice and far more communicative. Without it you could not train a dog properly or solve many behavior problems. Next to a leash it is the dog owner's most valuable tool.

Although slip collars are commonly used, they do baffle those who have never used one. It is simply a length of small-link chain with a ring at each end. The materials used for the equipment are steel, brass, or various alloys. Slip collars are also made in leather, braided nylon and nylon webbing. One can improvise a slip collar with the hand loop at the end of any leash. Instead of hooking the metal clip to a collar run it through the hand loop making a temporary lasso. Place it around the dog's neck, hold the metal clip in your hand and pull it gently until the loop fits snugly. It works well in an emergency if the collar breaks. Useful for catching a dog that has gotten away from you, it works exactly as a lasso. Please bear in mind that this should only be used as a temporary measure. You will definitely need a good slip collar to implement many of the problem-solving techniques in this book.

We recommend a slip collar made of stainless steel or other smooth but hard metals. The links should be small and welded tightly together with a solid, unbroken ring at each end, since the collar is only as strong as its rings. If your dog has very fine or silky hair, you might consider using a leather or nylon slip collar; a metal collar could rub some of the coat away. Braided nylon slip collars are good for very small or very fragile dogs.

Pay careful attention to the size of your dog's slip collar. A needlessly long collar becomes a heavy burden of metal. But obviously, if it is too short it will not fit around the dog's neck or it may be too tight. Measure your dog's neck with a tape measure or a length of string. Add three inches to that measurement. That's the collar size to ask for.

How to Place the Collar around the Dog's Neck

Hold one end of the slip collar by the ring with your left hand. The collar will fall into a vertical line. Grasp the bottom ring with

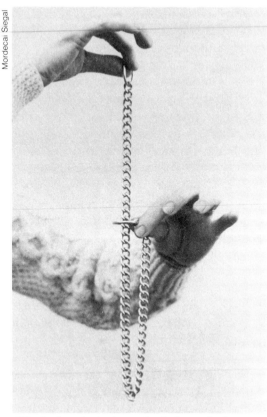

Mordecai Siegal

Work the chain (or nylon) through the bottom ring so that it begins to form a slipknot.

your right hand. Work the chain (or nylon) through the bottom ring so that it begins to form a slipknot. Gravity should help. Most of the chain should drop through the bottom ring, creating a loop that goes around the dog's neck. Remember, your left hand is still holding the top ring and your right hand is holding the bottom ring. Place the loop over the dog's neck properly. The ring in your left hand should point away from the dog's body from his right side. *The collar must tighten around the dog's neck when pulled and loosen when released.* It must slide back and forth smoothly and quickly for the sake of

the dog. This is essential. When placing the slip collar over the dog's head, you are applying it correctly if it looks like the letter P around the dog's neck. When incorrectly placed, the slip collar resembles the number 9 on the left and the number 6 on the right and will not slide back and forth as it should. Refer to the illustration on page 13. You can now attach the metal clip of the leash to the outer ring of the collar. (When the leash is gently pulled, the collar should tighten around the dog's neck and loosen instantly when released.) Once you have done this, you are ready to restrain your dog, walk your dog, or correct your dog. You are in control.

How to Hold the Leash Properly When Correcting Your Dog

Stand next to the dog on his right side, facing in the same direction, so that you are both looking ahead. Open your right hand and hook the loop at the end of the leash onto your thumb, as illustrated on page 14. As the leash hangs from your right thumb, grab the middle of the leash with your left hand, form a loop, and fold it over your right thumb. You will have four straps of leather across the palm of your right hand. Two loops of the leash will be hooked around your thumb. Close the fingers of your right hand around the four straps of the leash so they are pointing toward you. Adjust the length of the leash so that it crosses no more than the width of your body, allowing just a little slack.

For added strength, grip the folded leash with your left hand as well. Place your left hand directly *under* the right so that both hands are holding the leash like a baseball bat (page 16). This gives you enough leash to jerk it to the right effectively when correcting your dog with the Margolis Maneuver. In order to avoid communicating tension to the dog, it is important to maintain a relaxed but firm grip on the leash. While holding the leash keep your hands close to the center of your body, slightly above or below the waist (whichever is more comfortable). The correction is administered by quickly jerking the leash to the right and returning to the original position.

Draw a line with a pen on the middle portion of the leash where it loops over your thumb. This will help you find the right location each time you use the leash. Draw a

second line on the sewn loop at the top of the leash to remind you to hook it onto your thumb. The grip described here will give you absolute control. Few dogs can bolt from an adult woman or man when held with this technique.

The Margolis Maneuver. The Margolis Maneuver is a method of communicating to a dog that he did the wrong thing and must do better. It is the most effective correction available to dog owners. Those who love dogs and wish to use this technique of dog-human communication must understand that it is not a method for punishment but a

The other ring of the slip collar is on the left side of the dog's neck if you are facing him (a). Attach the metal clip to the outer ring (b).

gentle form of correction. It is the closest we can come to a language between us and the canine world. The leash and slip collar work together with the Margolis Maneuver to signal to the dog your displeasure. They are not designed to hurt, scare, or intimidate. The leash and slip collar are meant to work like a telegraph line attached to the dog. Using them properly, as recommended here, is important for problem solving and maintaining a humane code of behavior toward your dog. *It is essential to understand that not all dogs are the same. They vary in temperament and therefore require different approaches to* *physical correction depending on their sensitivity, stubbornness, and so on. Please refer to part Three, "Your Dog's Personality," to learn how to shape the Margolis Maneuver to the needs of your dog.* The Margolis Maneuver is the most important correction technique available for changing a dog's bad habits.

SHAKE CAN

This is an improvised tool that is easy to make and very effective as a corrective de-

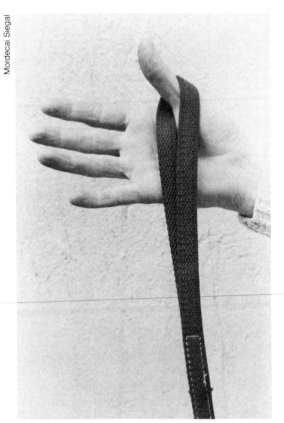

Open your right hand and hook the loop at the end of the leash over your thumb (c). Adjust the length of the leash by gathering up the slack and holding it in your right hand (d).

vice when the dog is not wearing his leash and collar. Take an empty soda can, wash it, and slip ten pennies into it. Tape the opening so the pennies cannot fall out. Now shake the can vigorously. It will make a very loud but commanding rattle similar to the sound of a New Year's Eve noisemaker. This is another way to correct a dog, especially a puppy. It easily gets his attention when shaken loudly and accompanied with a very firm "NO!" It enables you to deliver a correction from across the room without the use of a leash.

YOU

Of all the problem-solving tools there is none greater or more important than yourself. Everything about you is useful for ridding your dog of his bad habits. Your manner, your behavior, and your attitude all count heavily when you are relating to a dog with problems. All dogs require a pack leader. In a domestic situation a human must play that important role. If you are a source of authority, your dog will respond well to the problem-solving techniques offered in this book. Various aspects of your physical persona play a key role in solving dog problems.

The Human Voice

The sounds you make and the words you use are essential tools in problem solving. Your voice, when used properly, is a fine piece of equipment for our purposes. And the precise delivery of exact words is equally effective. Modifying your dog's behavior is accomplished by correcting the dog firmly *as he is in the process of doing something wrong* and

by praising him lavishly as he *stops* doing the wrong thing because of your correction. Of course, the dog should be praised if he does the correct thing in the first place.

The word *no,* when delivered in a commanding, authoritative tone of voice, telling the dog you mean business, is vital to teaching him how to behave. Seems obvious, doesn't it? There's more to it, though. If a dog is ever to learn what he may or may not do, he must accept your authority. That means that you must be able to convince him that you are in control. This is accomplished by your manner when dealing with him. You must have a sense of authority about you. You are not being asked to become a drill sergeant or a police officer, but you are being asked to acknowledge what you already are: an adult who is responsible for the life of a dependent animal. The situation is very much like parenthood. Parents are people who take charge when necessary. The proper tone of voice helps.

Use Your Voice Properly. Nothing amuses a dog more than its owner squeaking out a command in a soft tone of voice or yelling in a near-hysterical scream with endless repetitions like *"Stop. STOP! STOPPP!!!"* Poor enunciation of the command words also earns no response from the dog other than a yawn or a blank stare. It is easy with just the least bit of effort to learn to command your dog in a dominant manner. Most dogs respond instantly to commands spoken clearly in a firm tone of voice. Their doing this does not mean the honeymoon is over. It is simply a realignment of your relationship. Bear in mind that this interaction is not between two human beings. It is a human and a dog, and the dog needs a leader.

Once you get your dog's attention by producing a resonant, authoritative sound, it is essential to have something to say. For the purpose of problem solving, that something is the *vocal correction,* which is as important and precise a tool as anything you will ever use. The vocal correction is simply one word, *no,* said in a firm tone of voice. Anything more than that reduces the impact of the correction. You are not trying to influence your dog or negotiate with him; you are giving him a correction. "Don't you do that. Stop it! Get away from there" are absolutely

useless. You might as well add, "Wait till your father gets home!"

To enjoy the fullest possible effect from the correction "no," you must be able to say it clearly so that the dog can make no mistake about your meaning. The word consists of one consonant and one vowel. A clear, sharp-sounding *n* is accomplished by placing the tip of your tongue on the front part of the roof of your mouth. Allow your cheeks to expand into something like a hard smile. Do not be afraid to exaggerate the expression on your face. Next, form a circle with your lips

Stand next to the dog, on his right side, facing in the same direction. Hold the leash with about three feet of it gathered up in your right hand and draped across your thighs (a). Quickly jerk the leash firmly but gently to the right side of the dog (b).

and utter a very round-sounding o. When these are combined quickly, with the proper deep breath sound added, your dog will turn around and snap to attention. He should stop whatever he is doing and totally accept your authority. You are now in control.

Body Language

When a dog lowers his head, sniffs the ground, and then begins to circle around, we know that he is about to do something. Get out your Pooper Scooper. That is body language. If his hackles are raised and he stands absolutely still, his body language tells us he

Release the tension on the leash immediately following the jerk (c).

is ready to fight. Dogs maintain in their minds an entire catalogue of body language that helps them interpret what is going on in the minds of other dogs. The same is true of humans. Dogs are influenced by the body language of their owners. This can be good or bad, depending on what you are doing. As we said before, in order to solve your dog's problems you must modify his behavior. You cannot even begin to do this unless your dog accepts your authority. Body language is very much a part of the process.

A very assertive or aggressive dog will not defer to a human with a weak grip on a leash or a slouched-over body that gives in to his every move. This style tends to allow the dog to lead when being walked and make the decisions about where and when to go. Human body language can alter much of this. Holding a leash properly (see illustration) with firmness while walking the dog helps. Keeping your body straight and firm improves the situation greatly. Moving in a brisk and determined manner sets the right tone and places authority where it belongs, in the hands of the owner. Do not go too far with this, however.

With some dogs, maintaining an authoritarian body language is counterproductive and creates more problems than it solves. For example, a shy, timid, or very small dog may develop problem behavior because the owner is always towering over the animal in too dominant a manner. In other words, the human is constantly scaring the dog by overpowering him with size, position, and manner.

Small dogs or shy dogs need a little more distance from humans to feel secure, especially if they are attached to a leash. The insecurity may stem from something simple such as the fear of being stepped on or something complex such as the fear of being hit. This type of dog should be kept one or two feet away so he can look up at his owner's face without having to bend his neck at a severe angle.

If a shy, timid, or very small dog is overly dominated, he may develop a wetting problem, a chewing problem, a barking problem, or even a fear-biting problem. Here, a change in body language can be very beneficial. Throughout the course of any day kneel down to the dog's level, eye to eye, and talk to him affectionately. You can even do this at least once or twice when walking such an animal. When going to touch him or pet him, bring your hand up from the ground, palm up. The first stroke should be under the chin. You could even offer your knuckles to his nose. The idea is to make physical gestures that are nonthreatening. If your hand comes down on the top of his head, palm down, you might give the dog the impression that you are going to hit him. A frightened dog will cringe or get a worried look in his eyes. Positive body language is reassuring for all dogs and is a very easy transition for humans to make. Check it out. You'll find that it works.

HOW TO CORRECT YOUR DOG USING THE MARGOLIS MANEUVER

One should never discuss correction without first discussing praise. All dogs are sensitive, although some are more so than others. Because of their instinctive pack behavior, their social attachments, and their need for a leader they thrive on human approval and despair at rejection. Therefore, it is unneces-

sary to punish a dog, physically or mentally, to teach him something. First, he must go through an actual teaching process, which means showing him what, precisely, you want him to do. The teaching and behavior modification techniques that have been established over the years are based entirely on positive and negative reenforcement. One must encourage a dog by praising him every step of the way. Praise is positive reenforcement of the teaching process.

Once the dog has demonstrated that he has learned what you have taught him, it is fair to correct him if he refuses to obey. In training, the dog must respond on command. In problem solving, he must stop his bad habits. If he does not respond properly, the dog owner should give him a mild correction using the Margolis Maneuver. That is negative reenforcement.

In order to correct the dog, the slip collar and leash must be attached to him. It works best when the owner is standing to the right of the dog facing in the same direction. (See "How to Hold the Leash Properly When Correcting Your Dog") Holding the leash with about three feet of it gathered up in both hands, quickly jerk it to the right side of the dog. When jerking the leash, be firm but gentle, so that the collar causes no pain. Release the tension on the leash *immediately* following the jerk. This is extremely important. Do not jerk the leash forward or in any direction other than to the right. The dog feels the correction when the slip collar tightens for an instant around his neck. It is not painful, but it is negative and gives the dog a sense of rejection for his failure to obey. The tug must always be accompanied with a firm *"no"* from the owner. *It is absolutely essential that you praise the dog im-*

mediately following a correction. The theory is that the correction has "encouraged" the dog to stop doing the wrong thing, and the praise reassures him that he is still accepted and loved. Most dogs will then work to earn your praise because it is a reward. Corrections are a form of rejection, but they have a *teaching* effect rather than a punishing effect. Although there seems to be a fine line here, the difference is significant.

To recap the technique: correct the dog by jerking the leash when he refuses to obey or do the proper thing. Say *"no"* in a firm tone of voice. Release the tension on the leash instantly and then praise the dog affectionately. That is the Margolis Manuever, the most useful means of dog-human communication available.

THREE

Your Dog's Personality

Your dog's personality has a great bearing on how you solve his behavior problems. But let's take a close look at the word and try to avoid the usual confusion. "My dog is a manic-depressive," says someone at the launderette. "He is full of vinegar until my husband comes home, and then he flops into a corner of the room and sulks. Do you think he should see a shrink?" There is nothing wrong with this dog. Chances are that no bond has been established between the dog and the man, or the situation may be worse. The dog may, for some reason, be frightened of the man and shrink from his company. But manic-depressive? That's strictly for humans. If you are going to apply psychological jargon to your dog's personality you might as well consult his daily horoscope; it makes about as much sense.

It is interesting and often funny to talk about our dogs as though they were people. Dinner party chitchat is certainly livened up with anthropomorphic dog talk. "She loves me; she loves me not." If you think your dog doesn't love you anymore, try a pork roast. It is bound to renew his interest.

"I always thought Phydeaux was conservative, but he will not stay in the same room with house guests that are stuffy or the least bit upper-class. Do you think the dog is political?" It could be flatulence. May the Force be with you.

"My dog thinks he's a cat but in reality he's an anal retentive with ambivalent feelings toward me." Perhaps he needs more fiber in his diet?

"My dog is sexy." "My dog thinks I'm sexy." Let us pray for guidance. And so on and so forth. These are all personality traits that are best left to the realm of human folly. Just as insect behavior is different from fish behavior, dogs are different from people.

Mordecai Siegal

BITCHES

Personality does play an important role when you are trying to determine how to solve your dog's behavior problems. Our use of the term *personality* is closer to the term *canine temperament*. However, the term *temperament* isn't quite on the mark because it implies a genetic quality that cannot be influenced. Although we are dealing with a shade of gray, *personality* is a more useful term because it encompasses genetically derived behavior along with environmentally influenced behavior, which can, to some degree, be modified.

The personality traits of any dog may possibly come in various combinations of the six types that are formulated below to help you understand your dog and how to correct him. Some dogs will possess the qualities of only one of these described types. Others may possess any number of them and quite possibly all of them. A dog could likely be bright and responsive some of the time, belligerent another time, and stubborn on still other occasions. The question is which is number one. Your job is to determine the most dominant personality type within the spectrum of your dog's behavior. Use the correction methods given in this part of the book for that personality type when working toward a solution to a specific problem.

When dealing with your dog's behavior problems it is extremely useful to understand what has caused your dog to be the way he is. In many cases one can only guess, but even an educated guess will help you. You will be far more sympathetic and patient if you know more about your dog. Patience helps get the job done. Understanding your dog also contributes greatly to creating a bond between you.

There are four elements that shape dog behavior. As well as genetic (or inherited) influences and environmental influences, there are early socialization and dog-owner relationships (handling). These are the basic elements that shape a dog's personality. The genetic influence, of course, has to do with the dog's parents or grandparents. Environmental influences are those things in the dog's background that could have created a problem, such as traumatic experiences like gunshots, auto backfires, or firecrackers. Early socialization is the human handling of the dog as a puppy, during the critical stage between the third and eighth week of life. A dog handled by humans during that period will be much more responsive to humans and dogs than one who was not. And, finally, dog-owner relationships, or how the dog was treated, has much to do with the dog's behavior. Was the dog abused, hit, given affection, related to often enough, left alone, frightened in any way? A puppy shipped by air from a puppy mill in the Midwest who spends several weeks in a small, crowded cage in a pet shop may behave differently from one who came to you from a more pleasant situation. The dog's history will tell you a great deal about his behavior and any possible problems he has. It is a fact that knowing why your dog behaves the way he does helps you recondition his behavior and make him into the best dog you have ever owned in your life.

To implement the solutions for various dog problems you will be asked to use one of the correction techniques previously discussed in part Two. *How* you employ a correction or a solution to the problem is of vital importance because every dog is unique. By misusing corrections, you could create more problems than you solve. It is a matter of degree. For example, a very stubborn dog would have to be dealt with in a much firmer manner than a timid or shy dog; otherwise, behavior problems will simply get worse. If you are overbearing with a very shy dog, he could become vicious. Within the realities of dog behavior, one should know something about the various canine personalities that exist. It is necessary to redefine your meaning of the term *personality* so that it becomes a useful concept for implementing the techniques that exist in our "Directory of Problems."

Once you understand your dog's personality, you will be able to administer the right amount of positive, corrective technique. When correcting with your voice, you'll know when to give a loud, firm "NO" or a very soft *"no."* When using the Margolis Maneuver, how hard should you jerk the

Mordecai Siegal

leash? Softly, medium, or hard? What about the noise factor as a correction? Do you rattle the shake can vigorously, rattle it vigorously and say "NO" in a loud voice, or rattle it softly without your voice? One shake, or two? Your dog's personality determines how to correct him and to what degree. But you must first determine your dog's personality; this is exactly what a professional dog trainer must do before beginning any program. A shy dog requires the lightest form of correction. If that does not get the desired response, the trainer tries the next degree of intensity. In that way the animal is not frightened or abused. If you understand your dog's personality, you can change unwanted behavior without losing his happy disposition. The dog will still love you even though you correct him.

In the "Directory of Problems" some entries will remind you to remain aware of the need to adjust your corrections according to your dog's personality and refer you back to part Three. This is an important and valuable reminder.

One last note concerning the six personality types. These category names were selected so that dog owners would understand

and identify with them in human terms. A more scientific set of names could have been chosen, but it is easier to identify a *hard-headed* dog rather than one that is *dominance-resistant*. Please do not feel that these types are intended as insults against any particular breed. Dogs, like people, have all types of personalities. Everyone knows people as well as animals who possess any or all of these characteristics. It is the combination of traits and behaviors that make them interesting, unique, and quite lovable.

Read the following personality profiles carefully. Your dog is most certainly going to fall into one or more of these categories. After thoughtful consideration and evaluation you should be able to profile your dog's type. Each personality profile will set up guidelines for correcting a dog of that description.

HARDHEADED/STUBBORN

This personality type represents the kind of dog that will eventually do what you want him to, but not without some form of resistance. Hardheaded dogs are unwilling to please you the first time around. They hold out. Very often they "talk back" or bark and even growl when given a command. It is a dog's highly qualified struggle with you for dominance. Such dogs must be convinced that you are the leader of the pack. This is not accomplished through abusive behavior, however. It has more to do with assertion through vocal quality, body language, and a take-charge manner.

Stubborn dogs have been referred to by some owners as strong-willed, spiteful, or even obnoxious. They are capable of making inexperienced dog trainers miserable. Eventually they do respond well to problem solving and training. With persistence, insistence, and patience (and the proper handling), this type of dog becomes a responsive animal. As tough as it is to train or recondition a hardheaded dog, the reward is considerable because greater demands are made on you, increasing the satisfaction for a job well done. Stubborn dogs are usually bright and responsive along with having other positive qualities, once you get past the resistance to your authority. However, you're going to have a hard time with a hardheaded dog. Such dogs are mostly found among the breeds belonging to the sporting, hound, and terrier groups.

How to Correct a Hardheaded/ Stubborn Dog

Noise Corrections. You are going to have to be very vigorous when using the shake can. The dog must be convinced that his response to the noise is more important than his desire to do what he wants. When the can is shaken, it must not only be loud but the dog should see you do it. This correction should be accompanied with a loud, firm "NO." The sound and the gesture combined make a strong correction, especially for stubborn puppies. Praise the dog vigorously after each correction.

Physical Corrections. Although you have the option of executing the Margolis Maneuver in a soft, medium, or hard manner, stubborn dogs require a medium-to-hard jerk on the leash accompanied with a loud, firm "NO." Where some personality types never require a jerk on the leash at all, the stubborn dog almost always does. Praise must immediately follow every correction. This is vital.

Verbal Corrections. Your voice should be firm, robust, and loud. Do not be frightening. The object is not to scare the dog but dominate him. Be authoritative. A stubborn dog wants to do what he wants, when he wants to do it. Your voice, your words, and your manner must convince him that he cannot have his way. In the beginning, verbal corrections are given with either noise or physical corrections. After a while, the dog will respond properly to your verbal correction alone. Praise the dog after each correction.

LAID-BACK/SEDATE

We have all met this type of dog. You know a laid-back/sedate dog when you see one: he is usually sound asleep. For him, life is in the slow lane. "Hey, have a nice day . . . see you later." Nothing seems to matter to such a dog.

Sedate dogs are lethargic but lovable, quiet but responsive if handled properly. There is an absence of exuberance when they express their affection, but the feelings are definitely there. They constantly nap, and when they are awake they are interested in food, which tends to make them sleepy and ready for another nap. Many of them are named Louie or Goofy or Droopy Drawers.

On the plus side, laid-back/sedate dogs usually have none of the common puppy problems such as jumping, nipping, chew-

ing, or excessive barking. How could they? They train well and recondition well, but listen to the beat of a different drummer. They move at a slower rhythm than other dogs. In fact, sometimes there is no rhythm at all.

Dogs that are sedate can be found in some of the giant breeds such as St. Bernards, Newfoundlands, Great Danes, Mastiffs, or Great Pyrenees. Others might be found in breeds that are traditionally considered sedate such as the Basset Hound, English Setter, Clumber Spaniel, Bloodhound, English Toy Spaniel, and Tibetan Terrier.

How to Correct a Laid-back/Sedate Dog

Noise Corrections. It is probably not necessary to correct this type of dog with a shake can or by popping balloons. The mild problems that dogs of this type develop, plus their sluggish responses, require a more gentle, patient teaching approach. We very rarely find a sedate dog with a chewing problem, for example. If the dog is not housebroken, some form of correction will be necessary, but noise correction is the wrong technique to choose.

Physical Corrections. These are rarely, if ever, needed. Sedate dogs do take longer to respond to training or reconditioning than other types. The reconditioning process will require greater patience from you and more repetition of teaching techniques. Do not mistake their slower rate of response to you as stubbornness or an inability to understand you. They simply require more time than most dogs to respond properly. Jerk the leash in a soft-to-medium manner accompanied with a soft or gentle "no." Lavishly

Mordecai Siegal

praise the dog after each correction. Praise is the dog's reward, and it must be given enthusiastically to have the effect of positive reenforcement for what has been learned.

Verbal Corrections. Maintain a soft tone of voice. Your dog may be very sensitive in addition to being laid-back/sedate. A harsh verbal correction may depress him or alter your relationship in some negative way. It is easy to assume that this type of dog is stubborn when in fact he is just slow. Remember the tortoise and the hare? Well, you may have the tortoise under your roof, and you simply have to be good at waiting. Concentrate on the problem and not the symptom. Verbal corrections should be given when necessary but in only as firm a tone as necessary. A sedate dog will respond properly to a verbal reprimand but will

slink away with hurt feelings if you are too harsh. Praise the dog lavishly after every correction.

EXCITABLE/NERVOUS

This is a personality type that can be considered outgoing but on the overbearing side. Excitable/nervous dogs are pacers and panters who never sit still. They are the ones who will jump on you even when they are on leash with their owners. It is difficult to get them to respond to commands. They strain on the leash and will run to the horizon from your backyard if given the opportunity. They chew everything. Nervous dogs whine or bark when left alone. They bark at the slightest intrusion on what they consider their territory (which could include all of Chicago). This is especially true of apartment dogs. Anyone walking through the public hallways of an apartment house will certainly catch hell from a nervous dog on the other side of a door. Neighbors hate this.

Because nervous dogs are easily distracted, they are difficult to recondition or train. They do not concentrate on their handler. Their high energy level makes them excitable and far too responsive to the slightest bit of attention you might give them. Praise given after a command must be subdued. They are constantly on the move and may even, in extreme examples, develop a glassy-eyed stare, focusing on nothing at all. It is difficult to get an excitable/nervous dog to obey you.

However, excitable/nervous does not have to be a negative personality type. Through proper training and handling, that nervous energy can be channeled to create an incredible working animal. Many behavior problems can be avoided with this type of dog with early obedience training.

Dogs of this personality type can be found among such breeds as Doberman Pinschers, German Short-haired Pointers, Irish Setters, Vizslas, Weimaraners, Black and Tan Coonhounds, Norwegian Elkhounds, some Boxers, Pulis, Fox Terriers.

How to Correct an Excitable/Nervous Dog

Noise Corrections. It will be necessary to be quite firm with this type of correction. When popping balloons for a nervous dog you may have to be very close to the dog to achieve the proper response. Using the shake can requires several loud, vigorous rattles in full view of the dog. This should be accompanied with a very firm "NO." Do not be surprised if even this fails to get the proper response. Praise the dog after each correction. However, do *not* increase his nervous and excitable behavior with prolonged or lavish praise. Be positive, brief, and subdued in your praise.

Physical Corrections. The most effective correction technique for dogs of the nervous type is the Margolis Maneuver. It must be firm and hard, or it will have little or no effect. Jerk the leash quickly with vigor, and in a loud, firm voice say, "NO." Even though you want to make an impression, you must bear in mind that you are sending a message and not punishing the dog. Do not be abusive with the leash and slip collar. How hard you jerk the leash has to do with age, size, breed, and tolerance. A four-month-old puppy must be corrected in a far gentler manner than a two-year-old dog, even if he is

excitable/nervous. The individual dog's needs must be taken into account when determining how firm to be when using the Margolis Maneuver. Consider whether to jerk the dog in a hard, medium, or soft manner. You are the best judge to make that decision. Give the dog quick, quiet, and subdued praise after each correction. This is especially important with the Margolis Maneuver.

Verbal Corrections. Your tone of voice must be sharp, resonant, and loud. It is important that you never sound hysterical or out of control. Verbal commands are of a one- and two-syllable nature and must be enunciated clearly. Nothing gets a dog's attention better than a well-articulated *"no"* spoken clearly in a firm tone of voice. Some other verbal corrections are *"out," "off,"* and *"cut."* However, *"no"* is the one recommended. Always praise your dog after each correction. Praise for an excitable/nervous dog should be given quickly, quietly, and positively. If you are too exuberant with your praise, the dog becomes excited and forgets what the praise was for.

TIMID/SHY

Rarely are dogs of this type going to jump fences or dig up your yard. But they could have housebreaking problems. They could develop barking problems. And some shy dogs become biters. This has a great deal to do with their insecurities and fears. Timid dogs are not quite as fearful as shy dogs. One could almost say that they are sensitive rather than fearful and that they exhibit caution when dealing with new people or situations. Timid dogs are frightened by loud noises or sudden moves. But they are not afraid of strangers if they are mild-mannered and affectionate. It is possible to have a timid dog that is quite friendly and outgoing on his own terms.

Shy dogs are more withdrawn and completely lacking in self-confidence. Fear rules their lives. A shy dog will feel secure with his owner but no one else. He hides from strangers and unfamiliar sounds. He is afraid of noises and runs away when you pet him. Everything makes his ears go down, his head droop, his tail hide between his legs. And yet some shy dogs adjust perfectly to their families and have very pleasant lives. The timid/shy personality appears in dogs as an inherited characteristic, a breed trait, or because of early traumatic experience or bad handling. Unfortunately, it could have been caused in some dogs by all of these factors. Timid/shy dogs can be found among some of the toy breeds such as Chihuahuas, Italian Greyhounds, Papillons, and Poodles (toy). Some Cavalier King Charles Spaniels and some Bernese Mountain Dogs are timid-to-shy along with some Afghans, Borzois, Greyhounds, Salukis, Whippets, and Shetland Sheepdogs.

How to Correct a Timid/Shy Dog

Noise Correction. None is recommended for this personality type.

Physical Correction. None is recommended for this personality type unless absolutely necessary. The Margolis Maneuver should be given very gently if at all. Jerk the leash softly and say "no" in a gentle tone of voice. Praise the dog with enthusiasm after each correction. It is essential.

Verbal Correction. Correct this type of dog with a soft tone of voice only. Start out very softly in tone and work your way up in intensity until you discover which tone gets the proper results without frightening the dog. Loving, affectionate praise must always follow a correction. This is especially important with a timid/shy dog.

A shy dog is the one who always hides, turns his back, or tries to avoid contact. In young puppies shyness is almost always an inherited trait.

RESPONSIVE

On the surface it would appear that everyone would want a responsive personality in a dog. But that is not necessarily true. Like members of the family, dogs appeal to individual people for individual reasons. A shy or timid dog brings out the parental instincts in some, while an aggressive dog acts as an alter ego for others. The nervous/stubborn personality is exactly what some dog owners admire most about their favorite companion animal. A responsive dog is not necessarily the right dog for every person or every family. Not everyone wants a dog he considers smarter than himself or one that gives absolute obedience.

The primary virtue of a responsive dog is the luxury of easy training. Dogs of this personality type are eager to learn, willing to please, and quick to understand. It makes obedience training smooth and fast. That is fine if getting the job done is all you are interested in. However, there is no great challenge involved when training such a dog unless you become involved with American Kennel Club obedience trials. There, the training is quite advanced for the purpose of winning dog obedience competitions and obedience titles such as C.D. (Companion Dog) or U.D. (Utility Dog), from the AKC. Some dog owners enjoy working with difficult dogs because there is greater satisfaction in accomplishing the task. It is a matter of interest as opposed to need.

The responsive dog is a curious, energetic animal who loves his family and never hesitates to express his needs or desires. Sometimes the dog's sharpness works against the family when they try to limit his activities or restrict his movements. Only an obedience command will inhibit his attempt to follow his heart's desire. This type of dog cannot be outsmarted. These are happy, outgoing dogs.

Some breed examples of this personality type are German Shepherd Dogs, Standard Poodles, Golden Retrievers, Labrador Retrievers, English Springer Spaniels, Dachshunds, Bernese Mountain Dogs, and West Highland White Terriers.

How to Correct a Responsive Dog

Noise Correction. Use the shake can with moderation. A vigorous rattle works best with puppies. If the rattle is not quite

Mordecai Siegal

enough accompany it with a firm *"no."* The shake can is probably not necessary for adult dogs. A verbal correction should stop him from whatever wrong thing he is doing. Always praise your dog exuberantly after each correction.

Physical Correction. Use the Margolis Maneuver when called for in the "Directory of Problems," but jerk the leash in a soft or moderate manner and accompany it with a firm *"no."* Do not jerk the leash more than is necessary or you may alter the dog's easygoing personality. A responsive dog should not be overcorrected. It is not necessary to do so, and it upsets the animal. Unnecessary corrections tend to erode the dog's self-confidence. They also make him suspicious or hesitant with his owner. It is of vital importance that you praise your dog with warmth and affection after each correction using the

Margolis Maneuver. It gives him exactly the right reward to work for. Praise also maintains his trust in you and reassures him that you are not upset.

Verbal Correction. Do not use a harsh tone of voice. A clearly enunciated correction spoken firmly should suffice for dogs of this personality type. The correction "no," projected with good breath control (see part Two, "How to Use Your Voice Properly"), gets the job done. These are normal dogs with normal problems and do not require anything but soft-to-moderate corrections of any type. Verbal corrections are usually used in connection with noise and physical corrections. Eventually, verbal corrections alone will be all that is necessary. Lavish praise after each correction is absolutely essential. Do not forget to give it. Both you and the dog will be rewarded.

AGGRESSIVE

Of all the canine personality types, this is the most problematic because of the possibility of danger to humans, young and old alike. Dogs in this category are at the least annoying and unpleasant, if not always dangerous. Theirs is a category of negative dog behavior that represents a wide range of intensity that, although not necessarily dangerous, has the potential for dangerous behavior.

An aggressive type could merely be hostile, one that threatens people or other dogs with barks or growls or maintains an impervious attitude when commanded. Hostility in dogs is their way of dominating those they live with or encounter. It is how wild dogs or

An aggressive dog will threaten anyone about to violate his territory, even if it is a car. Sometimes the issue is dominance and sometimes it is simply fear of the intruder. The confines of a car can upset the nicest dogs.

wolves become the leader of the pack. The Alpha wolf (or leader) must fight aggressively to gain his position, and then he behaves with hostility and belligerence toward the lesser pack members in order to maintain his position.

Some aggressive dogs are belligerent and actually attempt to bully others by running at them and then stopping, by placing their bodies in such a way as to block a person's path, by pushing or slamming with shoulders or hips, by using all available means of intimidation to get their way. Dominance is the issue.

A full-blown aggressive dog is one that does not inhibit his behavior. He will attack a person or another dog because of territorial intrusion, fear of being attacked, or generalized antagonism. It is dominance with a vengeance. Aggressive warning behavior involves various forms of body language such as direct stares, raised hackles, raised ears, snarling mouth showing teeth, arched body, and a tail that is pointing upward or downward in a straight vertical line. The bite may range from a warning snap to a nip to a full bite as he shakes his head from side to side, which is meant to do as much damage as possible. In addition, an aggressive dog may chase, spring, pounce, or jump upon his target.

Aggressive dogs are either dominant-aggressive or fear-aggressive. The behavior of a dominant-aggressive dog is much more dangerous and is based on his desire to boss and bully all those around him. Fear-aggressive behavior is less dangerous but frightening; it stems from the dog's anxiety about someone or something.

Within every breed there are individual dogs that are more aggressive than all the rest. Usually they have inherited aggressive behavior qualities from one or more of their parents or grandparents. Some dogs, however, are made aggressive by their experiences in the world. Abusive human behavior, for example, can most certainly create an aggressive dog.

How to Correct an Aggressive Dog

Noise Correction. Shake cans and popping balloons are effective for aggressive puppies and full-grown dogs that are *not* the dominant-aggressive type. A loud rattling sound with the shake can in full view of the dog or puppy should get his attention and deliver the message that he did something wrong. Always accompany this correction with a loud, firm "NO."

Physical Correction. The Margolis Maneuver will require a light-to-medium jerk on the leash, accompanied with a loud, firm "NO" for all dogs of this type *with the exception of the dominant-aggressive personality.* Always give lavish praise after every correction; it is extremely effective. By praising the dog after each correction, you are setting up a desire in him to work for that reward.

Dogs that are dominant-aggressive require a very hard jerk in addition to a loud, firm "NO." Here again, remember to praise the dog greatly after each correction. *Sometimes dominant-aggressive dogs react to a hard correction in a wild or dangerous manner by biting the leash or biting the person giving the correction.* If you are getting such signals in response to your corrections, do not wait for a catastrophe. See a professional dog trainer. If such a dog is one year old or older and weighs over thirty pounds and is intimidating you or any member of your family, by all means get professional help.

Verbal Correction. All corrections should be given in a loud, firm voice. Use of the correction "NO" is usually given with a noise or physical correction. However, the dog will eventually respond to a verbal correction alone. Always praise the dog lavishly after every correction. This is an important element of the reconditioning process.

FOUR

A Directory of Problems

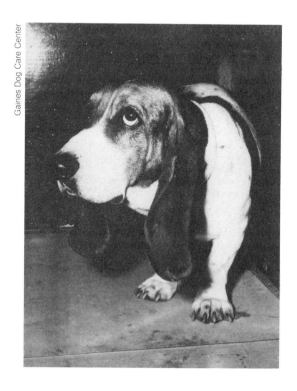

Gaines Dog Care Center

This directory consists of entries about the 31 most common but vexing problems dog owners experience at one time or another. The problems are taken up in separate articles, each independent from the others. They are presented in alphabetical order for the sake of convenience. Each entry is complete and deals thoroughly with its subject. Additional help may be available in other article entries. When these are applicable, the reader will be directed to them.

The format for each article is presented in four sections. The first, "Origins of the Problem," delves into natural aspects of dog behavior, to give the reader a more sophisticated understanding of the problem in question. The second section, "Reasons for the Problem," offers the dog owner a wide variety of possible causes stemming from the dog's environment or living conditions. The third section, "Solutions," is sometimes subdivided into "Environmental Solutions" and "Reconditioning Solutions." "Environmental Solutions" suggests methods of changing the dog's external conditions. "Reconditioning Solutions" offers ways of dealing with the dog's behavior in a direct and sometimes dynamic manner. The directory will offer as many approaches as possible to turning the dog's behavior around. The last section of each article is "Prevention Tips," offering important advice to the owner on how to stop the problem from becoming worse or to prevent it from beginning. This section is useful for all dog owners whether a problem exists or not.

BARKING (Excessive)

With few exceptions, all dogs bark. Barking is a problem only when a dog barks exces-

Bob Wortham

Fence fighting is an irritating form of barking and snarling that upsets everyone, including the dogs.

sively. It is maddening to be forced to listen to the dog next door who barks himself hoarse. Human anger turns to frustration and frustration turns to rage. There have been neighbors and landlords who have made life miserable for those who kept a dog that never stopped barking. The barking problem must be solved for the sake of being a good neighbor and for the security of your lease. Many court cases involve frazzled people seeking relief from the annoying sound of a dog that barks excessively.

Because most barking takes place when the owner is not home, you have no choice but to believe the neighbors. If you are re-

ceiving complaints from your neighbors but your dog has never barked excessively in your presence, it is not unreasonable to give the dog the benefit of the doubt just one time. Send him to a local boarding kennel for several days without letting anyone know. Obtain a signed receipt from the kennel for the dog's whereabouts on those days. Ask those who are complaining if they heard the dog bark on the days when he was away. If the neighbors complain about the dog even though he was not there, you do not have a dog problem, you have a neighbor problem. Get a lawyer.

Excessive barking is common and is not difficult to verify. Leave your house as you always do but return quietly after a short period. If your dog is a barker he will start up if he is not aware of your presence. In that case you *must* stop this undesirable behavior.

Origins of the Problem

Barking consists of a series of short, piercing sounds that vary little in tone or variety. Monotonous and repetitious, it is a noise few humans can tolerate for long. Barking indicates aggressiveness, anger, loneliness, playfulness, or a demand for something. *It is always a means of communication triggered by a state of excitement.* When considering dog behavior in the wild (or wolf behavior), we understand that barking serves several functions. In the wild wolves do not bark as much as domestic dogs do. However, they often do it for the same reasons as their city cousins. Protecting territory, asserting dominance, and expressing need are the fundamental triggers involved in barking. The dog that is born an excessive barker will initially begin because of external stimulation such as the arrival of a letter carrier or meter reader. However, the barking may go on long after the intruder has gone because the sound of the dog's own barking may stimulate him into an escalating frenzy. It is like chasing his own tail because he has no idea it is connected to him.

Dogs are pack animals, not emotionally suited for isolation or being left to themselves for long periods of time. They make strong social attachments within the pack structure and function as a group. It is an important part of their survival mechanism. Dogs and wolves hunt as a group and then divide all pack responsibilities. When they live with humans, the family becomes their pack. When left alone they may bark, growl, howl, whine, whimper, or bay in an effort to communicate with the dominant member of the pack, which could be you. Excessive barking is an exaggeration of their natural behavior and can be eliminated only by giving them what they want or by reconditioning them with problem-solving techniques.

Reasons for the Problem

Improper Confinement. Excessive barking often begins in puppyhood, when the untrained dog is not housebroken and has other problems such as chewing. The owner unwisely places the small dog behind a closed door when she or he must leave the house or apartment. Improper confinement will definitely cause a barking problem in addition to any other behavior problems. If the housebreaking or chewing problem had been dealt with properly, the barking problem would not have developed.

Tethering. Indoors or outdoors, a tethered dog will sooner or later become frus-

trated and begin to bark to communicate his displeasure.

Crating. Using a dog crate is usually an effective, positive tool for housebreaking and other aspects of behavior control. But some dogs react adversely to the confinement of a dog crate and try to bark and claw their way out. This is especially true of a hyperactive animal.

Outside Distractions. These comprise major causes of excessive barking. When a dog is kept outside he is likely to bark excessively at kids who tease him, at a steady stream of strangers (working and hunting breeds become very vocal in this situation), at a variety of street noises, including auto backfires, firecrackers, and lawnmowers, at free-roaming dogs (strays and neighborhood dogs), at the dog next door (who can create barking conversations).

Mechanical Noises. Excessive barkers may very easily begin their vocal racket at sounds like elevators, slamming doors, telephones, doorbells, vacuum cleaners, or blenders.

The Time of Day. Some dogs will not bark during the day because they have become accustomed to the daily noises. In the warmer states many dog owners keep their dogs out overnight to avoid hygiene and grooming problems inside the home, such as shedding fur and dirt. Leaving them out is also a way of avoiding training and behavior problems. However, such a dog is quite likely to start barking at two in the morning at the slightest sound, movement, or noise.

Environmental Sounds. The sounds of thunder, lightning, and even rain can start some dogs off on a rampage of excessive barking.

Separation Anxiety. Owners can cause a dog to bark by making too big a fuss when they leave the house. In an attempt to avoid upsetting the dog (and possibly to alleviate their own feelings of guilt) they become overly exuberant, loving, and affectionate just before walking out the door. The problem is that they create an even bigger vacuum when they leave. The dog hungers for more attention than he would have needed. The result is anxiety and frustration, triggering chewing and barking behavior.

Hunger. This sounds simple, but the dog's barking mechanism can be triggered from an inadequate diet or a meal that his owner forgot to give him.

The Dog's Previous Home. The source of the dog may have been a major influence in creating excessive barking behavior. Whether he came from your neighbor's backyard, a pet shop, or a breeder's kennel, the dog may have been allowed to bark from lack of attention or may have been encouraged to bark and may even have been rewarded for doing so. If such a dog has been barking excessively every day of his life for 18 months, the problem may not be solvable.

Overaggressiveness. All aspects of the aggressive dog's behavior can stimulate a long siege of unpleasant barking.

Strong Territorial Feelings. If there is no restraint or limitation placed on this type of dog, he will bark excessively whenever a stranger enters your property whether you're there or not, whether it's an invited guest or visitor on lawful business.

Temperament. Dogs of extreme temperaments will express their feelings by barking. Nervous, fear-ridden, and, in some cases, shy dogs will bark excessively at the slightest stimulation.

Lack of Exercise. Excessive barkers may not be getting enough exercise and may release their pent-up energy by barking, digging, chewing, and so on.

Genetics. Excessive barking is probably related more to inherited behavior than to anything else. Not all dogs bark at the same things nor will they all do it with the same intensity. Some breeds are barkers, and certain individual dogs within any breed (including mongrels) are born with the instinct to bark excessively. Excessive barking can be a trait passed from one generation to another genetically. However, even a dog with an inherited need to bark excessively does it when some external element triggers it. One must learn to recognize such a situation and then do what can be done to correct it.

Solutions (Environmental)

Barking Outdoors. If your dog is separated from your neighbor's dog by a chain-link fence, and the pair participate in "fence fighting," it is important to prevent them from seeing each other. This can be accomplished by running pliable slats through the links, boarding up the fence completely, covering the fence with green, fine-mesh tennis netting, or placing the dog on the quiet side of the house in a newly constructed dog run.

You can purchase a portable dog run, a tie-out stake, or a clothesline run that operates like an overhead trolley. Attach a clothesline 8 or 10 feet off the ground to the side of your house and to a tree. Run the clothesline through the loop of a leash and attach the clip to your dog's collar. Be sure the leash is long enough to allow him to lie down. This run prevents the dog from gaining free access to that portion of the yard where he engages in barking duels with the dog next door. At the same time it gives him some freedom to move about the yard.

You might calm a barking dog by appealing to his denning instinct with a doghouse. One can easily be built or purchased. Check the various mail-order catalogues or talk to your hardware store dealer.

Perhaps your dog barks because he is thirsty or hungry. A hungry, thirsty dog will certainly complain in the only manner he knows. He'll bark or he'll chew. Reevaluate the dog's feeding schedule. If you're not home, perhaps a friend or neighbor could feed the dog a little later in the day. Be certain that no other animal is eating his daily food ration. Stray dogs, cats, squirrels, chipmunks, or even birds will eat any food they can find. Hunger or thirst would certainly be the problem if the dog has the habit of turning his bowl on its side and spilling the food onto the ground. Use a heavy, weighted bowl or feed the dog indoors, making certain he has eaten his fill before going out in the yard on his own. You could purchase a self-feeder, which provides dog food automatically with the help of a mechanical timer. You may provide cold water all day with a product called Lixit, which attaches to your outdoor faucet.

Do not keep a dog outdoors in order to avoid behavior problems such as lack of housebreaking or chewing. You may be trading another behavior problem for barking. Take the time to housebreak your dog or solve whatever problem he has. See the appropriate entry in this directory.

Barking Indoors. Sometimes a sudden sound or noise will start a dog barking as if a switch had been turned on in his brain. A telephone ringing with no one to answer it will certainly do it. In that case unplug the phone or hook it to an answering machine. Doorbells, door chimes, and door knockers used by strangers when you're not home very often start a chain of barking that could go on for ten or fifteen minutes. Try to arrange for deliveries to be made when you're home or shift them to a neighbor's house.

Some dogs feel more secure when trained to use a dog crate when the family is away for a few hours. Depending on the dog, the crate can be left open and used as an indoor doghouse or have its wire door closed to confine the dog. A wire dog crate appeals to a dog's denning instincts. It looks like a cage but to your dog it can be a cave, the core area of his territory. In the wild, a dog would take possession of a small cave, dig a large hole in the ground to hide in, or nestle in the hollow of a log. It is a sanctuary where he can get away from it all. It makes him feel secure to have a "den" where he can rest or sleep without worry. A large variety of dog crates is available in mail-order catalogues and at pet supply stores.

When you do not wish to use a dog crate, restrict a dog's access indoors with a puppy gate. This is a common device found in most hardware stores. It is not recommended that a dog be shut away behind a closed door, a practice that can actually encourage barking. Closed doors not only create a barking and whining problem, but can negatively alter a dog's personality. A puppy gate is made of plastic mesh screening on a wooden frame that is wedged between two doorposts or a metal gate that wedges between the doorposts. Both types are effective. The little dog sees out but remains confined in one room. The kitchen is best for this purpose. It is a fine alternative to a crate and less expensive.

Solutions (Reconditioning)

Approach the problem like a detective to determine what you think might be the cause. Is it the dog's environment? Perhaps it's something you are doing or something you are not doing. It could be inherited behavior, but barking is usually triggered by something external. Barking is the symptom. Something you are doing *may* be the problem. There can be no permanent solution without awareness of the external causes. Do you make too much fuss over the dog when you leave, thus getting him all excited?

If you do, then he will bark the minute you are out the door. Has he had enough exercise, or does he have pent-up energy and nothing to do with it? If necessary, reread "Reasons for the Problem." Developing an overview will prove very useful. It will help you come across to the dog as the leader of his pack, and that's the final step to solving any dog problem.

Reconditioning your dog to stop his excessive barking will require the proper use of your voice plus the Margolis Maneuver (see part Two, "Essential Tools and Techniques for Problem Solving"). If you permit your dog to bark, he may eventually bark excessively. You cannot tell him "no" in a gentle tone of voice. If you give the dog a very firm, harsh "NO" he will eventually get the message that he is not allowed to bark. The difficult part, however, is getting him to stop when you are not home. The "no" is an extremely important correcting tool. If this is not effective — and it isn't with some dogs — then you must employ the Margolis Maneuver. It is a physical correction given with the help of a six-foot, leather leash attached to a slip collar. Bear in mind that the Margolis Maneuver involves tugging the

Fence fighting can be corrected with the Margolis Maneuver. (a) Allow the dog to get to the end of the leash. (b) Grip the leash with both hands. (c) Jerk the leash

leash in a jerking motion. How you do this and to what degree depends on the age, size, and personality type of your dog. Please refer to part Three, "Your Dog's Personality," before using this physical correction. It is a teaching device and not a punishment. The *improper* use of it can create more problems than it solves.

Barking After the Owner Leaves the House. To solve this problem you must teach the dog that barking is not permitted. For the purpose of problem solving, place the slip collar and leash on the dog five or ten minutes before you are going out. Pretend you are leaving. Do not deviate in any way from your customary departure habits. You do not want the dog to suspect that you are not really going. You might even consider using a room deodorizer to kill your scent, since a normal dog will smell your presence outside the door. Now leave. Jiggle the lock with your key, as you always do, but do not lock the door. Walk away. Quietly return so the dog does not detect your presence. Wait. Do not do a thing until the dog goes into a full cycle of barking. Open the door sud-

denly, take hold of the leash quickly, and jerk it as indicated in the Margolis Maneuver. As you do this say "NO!" in a very harsh, meaningful tone of voice. The dog should be completely surprised. Wait five seconds for the message to sink in and then praise the dog for having stopped barking. The praise is absolutely essential and must be considered an integral part of the reconditioning technique. Repeat this procedure several times on the same day and for as many days as necessary to end the problem.

Each time you go out lengthen your distance from the door and the time you rush in to correct the dog. Go down the hall (if you live in an apartment). Go out the front door. If the dog can hear it, you might even go so far as to start your car and drive away. The dog will never bark if he knows you are still around, and therefore you will not be able to recondition him. Each time you lengthen the distance and the time you correct him you extend his ability to refrain from barking. Eventually he will stop barking excessively. Otherwise he will only learn to stop barking for brief periods. *Although a dog cannot as-*

Bob Wortham

Bob Wortham

hard and shout "NO" in a harsh tone of voice. (d) Praise the dog and command him to "Sit" (if he is obedience-trained). (e) Praise the dog. Command him to go "Down" and praise him again.

sociate a correction with his misdeed if it is given too long afterward, you still have ten or fifteen seconds to correct him after he stops barking. Any correction given after fifteen seconds is like punishing him for greeting you.

If you wish to go to the expense you may use a training device known as a *handle* or sometimes referred to as a *tab* (see part Two, "Essential Tools and Techniques for Problem Solving"). This useful equipment enables you to correct the dog without his having to drag the leash around all day. It is simply a leash handle (and a clip) without the length of the leash. You may start the reconditioning process with the leash but switch to the handle after the first day.

The *shake can* is another correction device that can be used with the rush-through-the-door technique. If the dog barks when he is not wearing his slip collar and leash, it is still possible to correct him. Now that you are involved in solving the dog's barking problem you should not miss any opportunity to correct him the instant he barks, even though he is not wearing a leash and collar. This can be accomplished with a "shake can" (see "Shake Can" in part Two).

This home-style noisemaker is inexpensive and easy to make. Have several placed around your home and keep one in your pocket or purse when you go out. When the dog barks, reach for a shake can, place it behind your back, and rattle it vigorously, saying "NO" in a harsh tone of voice at the same time. The dog is likely to believe that the sound came from your voice if the shake can is held behind your back. The noise further establishes your dominance and makes the dog more obedient. The shake can may be used anywhere in the house or outdoors.

If the dog barks from within the house once you have gone out, you may rush in as before, shaking the can and saying "NO" in a harsh tone of voice. Or you may throw the can against the door from the outside, saying, "NO!" Let him know that the noise from the shake can is a negative reaction to his behavior. Do not forget to praise the dog after every correction.

A *water pistol* can also be used in place of the leash and slip collar or the shake can. This is yet one more alternative that could work when the dog is not attached to his leash. Squirt the water at the dog and say "NO" in a harsh tone of voice. Immediately praise him. Some dogs will lick the water and think you are playing a game, but others will be startled and will respond properly.

If your dog is left outdoors all day, the same techniques apply to solving his barking problem. However, when you leave you must remain out of sight or scent, or he will not begin a barking cycle. Once he begins barking, you must suddenly appear and correct him with the Margolis Maneuver or any of the other corrections suggested. For the outdoor dog a sudden burst from a *garden hose* can be an effective correction.

Corrections While at Home. Correct the dog every time he barks while you are home. Keep him attached to the leash and slip collar or the handle and slip collar. If the doorbell rings he will certainly bark. Use the Margolis Maneuver to correct him. The same applies when he barks at noises, other dogs, and so on. Here, too, you may use the shake can or the water pistol in place of the leash and slip collar to correct him. If you consistently correct him every time he barks while you are home, it may not be necessary to use the rush-through-the-door technique.

When Barking Is Permitted. It is quite possible that you may want your dog to bark at outside noises or strangers at your door. If you allowed the dog to bark in the past, you inadvertently encouraged him to do it. Now all you have to do is make some rules to bring into focus when he may or may not bark. Is it desirable for him to bark for 10 seconds, 30 seconds, 1 minute, 2 minutes, or not at all? Correct him immediately if he is not allowed to bark at all, or allow a brief period of barking to pass before correcting him. Decide on the barking time and coordinate your corrections with it. The same applies for those things he is allowed to bark at and those things he is not.

If you want your dog to learn to bark for a short period of time, do not use the word *no* with the correction. Use the word *cut*. "No" means he did something wrong. "Cut" tells him to stop barking; he did a good job. It is a very important distinction to the dog, and he will understand the difference if your tone of voice, body language, and attitude are firm but not harsh. Praise, immediately following the correction, is an important part of the reconditioning process. Allow the dog to bark for the desired time period, execute the Margolis Maneuver saying, "Cut," and then praise the dog for obeying.

Soothing Distractions. If your dog does not bark immediately after you have gone but does it later in the day, try soothing him. Sometimes the sounds of the radio or tape-recorded music are enough to create the conditions of your presence. Some dogs respond better to all-talk radio stations, while others prefer FM music. If your dog is accustomed to hearing music that you listen to on a regular basis, such as classical or country-western, then by all means that is the type of radio station to tune in while you are gone. No one knows if a dog has any appreciation for music. Leaving it on is simply an attempt to create the same environment that exists when you are home.

Another possibility involves an answering machine. Most answering devices allow for monitoring the incoming calls over a small loudspeaker. Set up the machine so it is within earshot of the dog and can be monitored by him. Call your dog at intervals based on the times when you think he barks. The answering machine will amplify your voice as you say "No" in a firm but not necessarily harsh tone of voice. The sound of your voice may be enough to soothe and distract him from barking. If nothing else, it will give him something to think about.

A variation of the answering-machine technique is to have a neighbor enter your home at a prearranged time. Call your own telephone number and have the neighbor answer it. Have the neighbor place the telephone receiver next to a small microphone plugged into the amplifier of your hi-fi equipment. The neighbor leaves, and you are now in a position to hear the dog bark over the telephone. When he does, give him the verbal correction "NO" in a loud, harsh voice, which will be carried from your telephone to your hi-fi amplifier and heard on the speakers. This procedure is not as complicated as it sounds and works very well. The only problem may be with your coworkers, who are certain to think you are crazy.

Exercise. Exercise alone will not end your dog's barking problem but can certainly be a valuable part of the solution. Some dogs bark when left alone because they are bored, lonely, and sorely lacking a physical release for their energy. These are the conditions that set the scene for canine mischief and destructiveness. Barking can be the least of the problems for such a dog.

An important answer, in part, is to exercise the dog before leaving him alone. A fifteen- to thirty-minute workout each morning before you leave the dog could eliminate much of his barking problem. A good daily regimen is a brisk morning walk for toileting purposes, a run, a "fetch" session with a ball, a stick, or a Frisbee, and then some playtime indoors. One good indoor game is Hide the Biscuit. Show the dog the treat, place him behind a gate or in his crate so that he can see you hide it. Release him and say, "Go find!" Do it over again several times. If the weather prevents an outdoor workout, the morning is a perfect time to conduct obedience training sessions with the help of a training book. If the dog has already been trained, then practice all his commands, developing them into a routine. Give him quick commands three, four, or five times in a row. Mix them up so that he uses up both mental and physical energy. "Heel . . . Sit . . . Heel . . . Sit . . . Heel . . . Sit," and so forth.

The best thing you can do for your dog is to work him out first thing in the morning instead of just a quick walk for toileting. It will use him up and release his tension. An extra thirty minutes in the morning could make the difference between good relations with your neighbors or having to get rid of the dog.

Chewing Relief. It seems so simple, but the best solutions often are. Before leaving your dog alone, give him a substantial rawhide bone or Nilabone toy to chew on. It not only serves as a distraction but offers a release for the energy and mounting frustration that often lead to barking.

Neighbor Participation. If you cannot be home, maybe your neighbor will help with the corrective process. When the dog barks, perhaps the neighbor will be friendly enough to walk over to your front door with a shake can and correct the dog. Some neighbors will appreciate your efforts to eliminate the barking problem and be grateful for the opportunity to help end the problem. It's better than complaining about the noise.

Not Leaving the Scene of the Crime. Most people with dogs between the ages of seven weeks and one year confine them when they leave the house. Confining a dog to one room is part of a housebreaking routine and is also necessary when dealing with early chewing problems. But that is when the whining and barking begin. Try confining the dog (with a puppy gate or dog crate in the kitchen) while you are at home but in a different room from the dog. He will probably whine and bark to be with you. It is much more convenient to confront the problem while you are at home than to try to deal with it any other way. Every time the dog barks or whines, correct him with the Margolis Maneuver or the shake can, the water gun, or a firm, harsh "NO!"

Changing Your Ways. As discussed earlier in this article, many dogs bark because of the separation anxiety they experience when left alone. This anxiety can also cause housebreaking and chewing problems. A nervous, insecure dog will actually feel worse after you leave if you pay a great deal of attention to him before going out. Stimulating the dog with physical expressions of affection and a great deal of attention just before leaving him alone increases his energy level and raises his emotional pitch. Some owners feel guilty when leaving the dog behind and say such things as "I'm going now. I'll be back. I love you. Don't feel bad. That's a good dog! What a good dog!" This is always accompanied with hugs, kisses, petting, and even some play. After you leave, the dog is left behind standing inside a big "empty." He topples from elation to depression to frustration, and that's when the barking starts. It's as though he were saying "Don't go. Come back. I want more." If this scenario sounds familiar it's because many of us enact it. Modify your own behavior when leaving the house. Do not relate to the dog in any special way in the last fifteen minutes before leaving. It is not suggested that the dog be ignored. Behave in a subdued, calm manner with the idea that you are not going to raise the dog's expectations in any way. Tone things down, be matter of fact, be loving but reserved. It will help him cope. There is no rational reason to feel guilty about leaving the dog for a few hours or even for the length of the working day. Making a big fuss over the dog because of such guilt creates barking problems. Do not leave the house with the dog craving more attention. Reward him with loving enthusiasm when you come home. That is the time for it.

When All Else Fails. As a last resort, try to end your dog's barking problem with the "Time Out" method. Remove him from your environment totally and place him in a boarding kennel for several days. There, he will no doubt bark at the other dogs a great deal. In that situation he can be monitored on a daily basis by professional trainers who will correct him on a regular basis. If a trainer can stop him from barking when he is surrounded by other barking dogs, then he can be transferred to your home free of his problem. There are professional dog trainers who maintain kennels for this purpose and they are usually listed in your *Yellow Pages* directory under "Kennels" or "Pet & Dog Training."

Prevention Tips

Have Your Dog Walked by Someone Else. If you are away from home for eight to ten hours every day, you could hire someone to walk the dog. A midday walk could make a difference. It would help the dog dissipate his energy and relieve his frustration. If you cannot find a professional dog-walker (they are often listed in the *Yellow Pages*), perhaps you can hire someone in your neighborhood to perform the service. In large apartment houses a doorman will perform that service for a tip. Neighborhood kids are always looking for ways to earn after-school income. If the dog is friendly enough and the kid is responsible enough, you may never have to worry about excessive barking.

Confront All Behavior Problems. By solving all of your dog's behavior problems such as lack of housebreaking and chewing, you may prevent a barking problem from developing.

Consult Your Neighbors. Ask if your dog barks during the day. It is far better to get the bad news now before the problem becomes severe.

Do Not Tie the Dog Up. Nothing creates frustration leading to barking faster than tying a dog to a short tether or chain. If your dog must be confined — and many should be — use a wire dog crate or a puppy gate in the doorway of your kitchen.

Provide Food and Water. Be certain your dog is getting his full ration of food. If necessary, use an automatic feeder that works on a timer.

Provide Shelter. Outdoor dogs must have some shelter such as a doghouse or garage. There are special pet doors advertised in mail-order catalogues and dog magazines that allow the dog to enter your house or garage when the weather is bad.

Leave the blinds, shades, or curtains closed when you go out so the dog has no opportunity to bark at people, animals, or moving objects.

Unplug the Phone when You Leave. Some dogs are driven to barking by an incessantly ringing telephone.

Place a "Do Not Disturb" Sign on Your Door. It may prevent tradesmen from ringing the doorbell and setting off a long barking cycle. Have a sign custom-made stating "Do Not Ring or Knock. It Makes the Dog Bark."

Adjust the Lights in Your House. When you leave your dog, he may become mellow in subdued lighting or even darkness. The exact opposite may be true. Experiment with this.

Teach Selectively. All dog owners should be aware that they often teach their dogs to behave in a particular manner without knowing they are doing it. Pats on the head and verbal praise are accepted as rewards by dogs. They teach the dogs to do whatever they did just before the "reward" was given. If you tell your dog he is a good boy immediately after he barked, in effect, you have taught him to bark. This can be useful or counterproductive, depending on your needs. (See *"When barking is permitted."*)

Make a Chart. For one week note the time of day or night each time your dog barks and what makes him bark. This chart will be the most useful aid you can have for preventing excessive barking. It will help you develop the overview discussed at the beginning of this article. Look at it and decide what is desirable for him to bark at and what isn't. With this knowledge, you know when to correct the dog and when not to. Use the chart in conjunction with the techniques in *"When barking is permitted."*

BEGGING

In some homes the best way to cure a dog of begging is to let him taste the cooking. But that isn't always the answer. A dog that begs at dinnertime is not only annoying; he is often obnoxious. Some beggars sit on the floor and look up at you with a pathetic expression. If that doesn't work, they begin to

Bob Wortham

Begging, no matter how cute, is bad for the family and, believe it or not, bad for the dog.

whimper. If you continue to hold out, they just might do anything from standing on their hind legs and twirling to leaping up onto the table and grabbing something off your plate. This may be funny in a Walt Disney film, but if the dog has any aggressive tendencies it could also be dangerous. Try to stop an aggressive beggar once he makes his move and you just might get bitten.

And what about that dinner party: you know the one, where your important business contacts are coming to discuss your future in the company? Can your career stand a guest being stained with saliva, smudged with paw dirt, and covered with fur as your four-legged Gunga Din presents himself as a famine victim? Hardly.

Begging, no matter how cute, is bad for the family and, believe it or not, bad for the dog. In terms of behavior it is at best a nuisance and at a worst a danger. Begging also has an impact on the dog's nutritional needs. Throughout this century canine researchers

working for the pet food industry have scientifically studied the eating patterns and nutritional needs of domestic dogs. The result has been a complete and balanced commercial ration that supplies all the nutrients needed to sustain life and promote growth and good health. If you are clever enough to feed your pet any one of the dozens of premium dog foods available, then you are doing him a disservice by allowing him to beg whenever you are eating something. Food given between regular feedings may upset the nutritional balance provided by your commercial diet and could also cause obesity and other digestive disorders.

Allowing a dog to beg for food encourages him to become more demanding, which leads to bullying and aggressiveness. Have you ever witnessed a large dog jumping on a child who is eating something? It not only terrifies the child but becomes dangerous if he or she pulls the food away. Begging is a behavior problem that is intolerable and should be stopped.

Origins of the Problem

On the surface begging appears to be a simple behavior having to do with your dog's appetite. Though all dogs will beg if encouraged, begging involves more than simple hunger. A dog that has developed the habit will take his position near or under the dinner table even if he just finished eating. Some will leave their own food uneaten and beg once your meal has begun even if they like dog food and dislike your food. This is because begging has little to do with hunger.

In studies of wolves and domestic dog colonies, researchers learned that all puppies and cubs exhibit a set of care-seeking tendencies referred to as *et-epimeletic behavior.*

Care and attention are sought by infant and adolescent dogs from their mothers. The whimpering, whining, and yelping of puppies are et-epimeletic expressions that are mostly connected with hunger, cold, or fear. As the youngsters mature they run to the mother dog on her return to the nest and leap at her in an attempt to lick her face and breast. If the pups are still nursing, they scramble for a teat. If the weaning process has begun, she will disgorge half-digested food for them to eat. This is the first form of "begging" a dog exhibits in its life.

From early puppyhood dogs must impose themselves on their primary source of food, warmth, and safety (mother dog) if they are to survive. It is probably instinctive plus learned behavior. Begging for food is a natural and necessary activity for all puppies and very young dogs. When newborn human infants cry out in the middle of the night, we do not refer to it as begging. We say, "It is time to feed the baby." But the similarity between human infants and neonatal puppies in this respect is significant.

Children must be given their food throughout childhood at scheduled intervals and when they express hunger. Having regular meals with their family is a form of nurturing that they come to rely upon. When they are hungry they speak up. "What's for dinner, Mom?" could easily serve on most family crests. Taking meals together is a family activity that brings stability and security in the lives of most people. Because dogs are pack animals that form social attachments, the same holds true for them. When a dog begs it would appear that he not only wants your food but desires to be included in the social aspects of mealtime.

Some grown dogs appear to beg more than others. When they are pampered like chil-

dren, they are, in effect, kept in a state of perpetual childhood. Begging is a logical outgrowth of that life-style. Such dogs crave the nurturing as well as the food. To insist on a dog's eating from his own bowl and to deny him the privilege of begging is to demand that he once and for all behave like an adult dog. Still, a house dog will never have the tremendous burden of fending for himself. He will continue to live the good pet-life without the unnecessary habit of begging.

Reasons for the Problem

Allowing the Dog at the Table. Most puppies are allowed to play under the table at mealtimes. They smell the food and quickly discover the extended hand offering wonderful tidbits. There is no doubt that they are cute as they cock their heads and lick and munch from loving fingers. It is the first lesson in the school for canine begging. What was cute at four months becomes annoying and irritating by ten months and older. Dogs also hang around at mealtime in hopes that food will be dropped on the floor. It quickly becomes an unwritten law that the dog gets all that is found on the floor. This is especially the case with children at the table. If the dog is allowed to be at the table during meals he will surely become a beggar.

Feeding Food Scraps. The act of giving the dog food from your plates after each meal is enough to instill in him a state of anticipation that eventually turns into begging behavior. This is true even if you scrape the leftovers off the plate and into his bowl. It also encourages the dog to hang around the immediate vicinity of the table. Such a dog can give you more pressure than if he actually came up to your chair in hopes of a handout.

Giving an Inadequate Diet. It is quite possible that the begging dog is hungry. Use a premium dog food, one that is complete and balanced, containing all the nutrients required by dogs in amounts needed to maintain them throughout their lives. Table scraps offer no consistent approach to balanced nutrition. A dog's minimum daily requirement of protein, fat, carbohydrates, minerals, and vitamins has been established by the National Academy of Sciences. Any dog food that labels itself "complete" or "balanced" must, by federal and state regulations, offer the minimum daily requirement of canine nutrition as established by the National Academy of Sciences. Follow the feeding instructions on the label of any quality dog food or ask your veterinarian to establish a proper diet based on your dog's individual needs.

Keeping an Irregular Feeding Schedule. If your dog is fed at different times each day you cannot be certain when he is hungry and not knowing that will keep him primed for begging at your table. From weaning to six months (twelve months for giant breeds) feed your dog three times a day. From six months to twelve months (twelve to eighteen months for giant breeds) feed your dog twice a day. Past one year the average dog will thrive well on one meal a day, preferably in the morning. Try to feed your dog at the same time each day and feed him just before your meal when possible. It must be firmly established in the dog's mind that his feeding schedule has nothing to do with the family's meal schedule. They should be very separate events.

Giving Too Little Attention. It is often felt that a dog begs because he receives too much attention. Paradoxically, a dog could develop a begging habit because he is not given enough attention. As creatures that live socially in packs, dogs crave the company of others. If they are left alone during the course of the entire working day and not paid any attention except for two brief walks, it is natural for them to want to be with the family at dinnertime. Begging for food is a way of interacting with the family.

Solutions (Environmental)

Choosing Now. A decision must be made about begging. You must decide whether it is to be allowed or not. Some dog owners do not consider it to be a problem. Others regard it as a very minor problem. If you have allowed this behavior to go on but do not like it, then resolve that it must come to an end and do what is necessary.

Deciding Where to Feed the Dog. Feed the dog in a different part of the house so there can be no mistake about his core territory. The doggy dining area should be in a place that is distinctly different from yours. Never allow the dog to claim your dining area as his territory. If this has already happened, his thinking on the subject must be reconditioned.

Solutions (Reconditioning)

Correcting the Dog. In comparison to other behavior problems, begging is not very serious nor is it difficult to solve. Whether you live with a little beggar or a big beggar, the solution is the same. Allow the dog to do his worst and at the appropriate time exe-

When correcting the dog with a shake can, be sure to say "NO" in a firm, harsh tone of voice as you rattle the can loudly. Then praise your dog for obeying.

cute a correction. This must be done every time the dog begs for food, no matter where it happens.

Place the leash and slip collar on the dog five or ten minutes before each meal. If you wish you may use a "street handle" instead of a leash (see part Two, "Essential Tools and Techniques for Problem Solving"). Ignore the dog. Serve the meal as you always do and be prepared to correct him. When he begins his normal begging behavior, do nothing until it reaches its peak, which could involve anything from sitting, watching you intensely, whimpering, or actually trying to steal food. At the moment of truth, without warning, grab the leash or the handle and correct the dog with the Margolis Maneuver (see part Two, "Essential Tools and Techniques for Problem Solving"). Before using the Margolis Maneuver read part Three, "Your Dog's Personality," to determine his

personality type. His type will influence the manner in which you use the various corrective techniques.

It may not be necessary to use the Margolis Maneuver. Correcting your dog with a shake can may be enough to do the job (see part Two). If you have several shake cans conveniently located, you can always correct the dog whether he is wearing the leash and slip collar or not. Or you may find it convenient and effective to correct the dog with a water pistol or squirt bottle. Be sure to say "NO" in a firm, harsh tone of voice as you execute any of the corrections, immediately followed with verbal praise for having obeyed you. (If your dog is obedience-trained, an interesting alternative is to use some of the training commands when he starts begging. "Down-Stay" or "Go to Your Place" will do nicely.)

Prevention Tips

The Siegal Dictum. Never feed your dog *anything* from the table. Insist on this rule from all members of your family and dinner guests. Consistency on this point is absolutely vital.

BITING

The most serious behavior problem in dogs is biting. It is dangerous, upsetting, and often costly in terms of medical treatment and lawsuits. It is difficult to love a dog that bites you. And yet many who own such dogs love them dearly and try desperately to solve the problem. Some accept biting as a normal part of life with their dogs, while others ignore it as though it didn't exist, until they experience a disaster. Dog owners must do all

Mordecai Siegal

The maternal instinct in dogs is strong, and many dogs, unless encouraged to be biters, get along very well with children.

that is possible, all that is necessary to prevent their dogs from biting people and other animals. Anything less is gross neglect from both a moral and a legal point of view. Biting as a behavior problem seriously reduces the quality of life for dog owners and all those who come in contact with them. Because of the complexity of the problem the subject has been divided into six separate articles and entered into the directory in alphabetical order. They are "Biting (Children)"; "Biting (Because of Food, Possessions and Objects)"; "Biting (Because of Overprotection of Property)"; "Biting (Because of Pain, Medical Problems, Grooming)"; "Biting (Because of Punishment)"; and "Biting (Because of Shyness)." It is essential that the following information be read carefully before proceeding to the article that applies to your dog's biting problem.

Unless a domestic dog has been trained for guard or attack work, biting is a distortion of normal behavior. Most dogs do not bite unless they have been provoked or they have a serious behavior problem. It is reasonable to

assume the average dog is not a biter. Of the dog population the percentage that bites is small. Still, there are a significant number of dogs who have bitten people (many of them children). Some of the bites have produced grievous injury and in a few incidents caused fatalities.

Although a nip from a puppy is nothing, it can ultimately lead to a major biting problem once the dog matures. Snapping, nipping, and biting behavior must always be dealt with immediately whether it is seen in a grown dog or a young puppy. Because of the serious nature of the problem we categorize dogs that bite into three significant age groups. *These age groups and the information accompanying them must be applied to dogs with any of the six types of biting problems entered in the directory.*

Puppies seven weeks to six months old express their biting behavior in the form of snapping and nipping and are considered easy to correct because of the age, size, and lack of maturity.

Young dogs six months to ten months old are still in a safe, manageable range but demonstrate a different quality and degree of aggression in the form of growling, snarling, and biting. This is a problem no owner of such a dog can afford to overlook. Here, too, we are comfortable with the solutions that are available to those who wish to change their dogs' behavior with the help of this book. A dog with a biting problem in this age group can probably be reconditioned with the solutions offered here.

Dogs ten months old and older who bite are much more difficult to recondition. Sometimes they cannot be changed. *Once a dog is past ten months old and has a biting problem, he is capable of causing serious injuries and therefore requires professional evaluation.* We recommend consultations with a professional dog trainer, an animal behaviorist, or a veterinarian. They can even work together. The problem is too serious for an amateur.

A professional consultant is more objective about a dog with a biting problem and can assess the situation knowledgeably and without emotion. No matter what solution one tries, there can be no guarantee that a mature dog with a biting problem will never bite again. If a dog's biting behavior cannot be changed by professionals, the dog owner must seriously consider removing the animal permanently from the home to avoid possible injuries. The average dog owner cannot determine the seriousness of the situation, the reasons for the behavior, or the best course to take. Should the dog be removed from the home or not? Professionals can only suggest such action. It is a decision that people must make on their own, but not without sound advice from those who should know.

If a decision is made to keep the dog because of strong emotional attachments, one should ask if anyone will suffer physical harm down the road. Dog owners must become aware of the potential danger to their family, friends, neighbors, tradesmen, and, not the least important group, visiting children. Medical costs and lawsuits for the owners of a biting dog are almost a certainty. Most local courts are unsympathetic to dogs that bite and to their owners. The question most often put to the owner is "Why did you wait for things to get this bad?"

The objective party, the professional consultant, will take some of the responsibility for the decision off the shoulders of the guilt-ridden and confused dog owner or parents. If it is determined that the dog has a dangerous, unsolvable biting problem one must face the few options available. They are relocating the dog to a home without children, relocation to a rural setting with fewer people coming in contact with the dog, relocation to a working farm, placement in industry, the military, or a police department for guard work (here, the dog's aggressiveness might be a positive factor), or "putting the dog to sleep" (euthanasia).

Another possibility is to castrate a male dog to help eliminate biting behavior, but doing this is controversial. It takes six weeks after the surgery for the male hormone, testosterone, to clear the dog's body. It is only after that period that the effectiveness of the procedure can be determined. Castration will calm down a very aggressive dog but will not necessarily end a habit that has become established. A castrated dog will still need some form of behavior modification, as is stressed in the "Solutions" section of the directory. Some professionals recommend doing it, while others do not. Altering a biting dog's sexuality has no effect on female dogs at all. Some shrink at the thought of castrating a male dog, comparing doing it to human castration. For some dogs, it is their last best chance. A biting dog that has no potential for adjustment to another home must be euthanatized.

Origins of the Problem

It is only in degree that domestic dog behavior is different from wild dog or wolf behavior. The instincts and social patterns of both animals are strikingly similar. When dogs or wolves bite they mean to injure, throw into submission, or drive away an animal. Biting is an integral part of their survival. Without this ability dogs in the wild could not hunt. Biting is primarily for attacking a prey animal and eating it. It is also the fighting technique of dogs, utilizing their teeth as weapons. Wolves prefer to slash from the rear. When attacking smaller animals they dash in, make a snapping bite, and quickly move away to avoid injury. Some domestic dogs bite in a similar manner but may also attack from the front and keep attacking, disregarding the possibility of being injured themselves. In a natural setting wolves hunt and fight in packs, using various strategies from which the ability to herd cattle is seen in their cousin, the domestic dog. Wild dogs and wolves bite each other in combat over dominance, mating, pack privileges (food, sleeping quarters), and territorial intrusion. When a domestic dog bites a human, the very same issues are involved from the dog's point of view, even though the behavior may be irrational in terms of human reality.

The struggle to maintain territory is the most frequent cause of behavior that leads to biting in wolves and domestic dogs. Aggressive dogs, even if they are not very territorial, maintain a personal space or distance beyond which they will not tolerate anyone's presence. All dogs behave to a great degree according to their natural instincts rather than their environmental influences. Dogs are territorial in our homes because it is instinctive behavior. In the wild, territoriality is vital to survival. Only a limited number can be fed from a delineated area serving as a territory. Wolves understand that a territory provides food and sanctuary. When others cross over their boundaries, the crossing is taken as an invasion, and every effort is made to drive the invaders out. It is in this type of defense that we see the roots of most biting behavior in domestic dogs.

Among wolves and wild dogs there is a natural logic behind biting behavior, having to do with hunting for food, driving off invaders, or fighting for dominance. In our homes, these are not rational issues for a normal dog. If a pet dog continually bites people, he should be considered eccentric or even abnormal. He is certainly atypical.

A Warning. If your dog bites and you are planning to solve the problem with any of the solutions suggested in the following six "Biting" articles, be careful. If you are not alert and on your guard, you can get bitten by your own dog. Maintain firm control as much as possible with the help of the leash and slip collar and the tone of your voice; keep a respectable distance when making corrections; and, most important of all, maintain a strong, Alpha-wolf attitude. A large aspect of solving the problem is gaining dominance over the dog so that he will obey you. This requires a firm manner. You need only go the extra step to gain control. However, do not get bitten in the process.

BITING (CHILDREN)

Children, more than any other group, are likely to be the victims of dog bites. The majority of these incidents are not critical. But there are enough serious bite injuries involving children to warrant a strong caution. Parents do their children a great disservice if they fail to educate themselves about the dangers involved in canine biting behavior. For parents, this could be the most important article in the directory.

Reasons for the Problems

All of the various reasons for biting can be traced to one of four sources: inherited behavior, which can be blamed on those who breed dogs indiscriminately; poor socialization, which means there has been a lack of human contact in the very early, critical stage of a puppy's life; environmental influences (people, places, or things) that have terrified a dog; owner behavior, indicating a lack of friendly relations with the dog, abuse, or isolation and alienation. All of the following reasons for the problem spring from these four general sources.

Inherited Behavior.   Some dogs are born with an aggressive temperament, which has been passed genetically, creating an animal with a predisposition to bite.

Abusive Behavior from Children. Children can hurt a dog without fully understanding what they are doing. They may not know that the bite they received from the dog was in response to something they did. If they pull a dog's tail or leg or ear, he will defend himself in the only way he can, which is to snap or bite. Many kids regard their dogs as play objects whose eyes they can poke or backs they can ride. Sometimes children hit, kick, or jump on their dogs in an effort to release the anger or hostility that has built up from some other source. They are quite capable of putting pencils, toothpicks, and other objects in a dog's ears or mouth. It is not hard to understand why a dog would bite a child under those circumstances.

Inconsistent Behavior by Children. Because children behave inconsistently as they grow and develop, they tend to confuse and

bewilder their pets as they do their parents. Sometimes they are friendly and affectionate and other times explosive and emotional. A growing child is perfectly capable of hugging a dog one minute and then teasing him or yelling at him the next. Very often children play hard and do not give their dogs any opportunity to rest until they are finished.

Unfamiliarity with Children. Some dogs are suddenly thrust into the company of children for the first time and have difficulty adjusting to their size, energy, and play behavior.

Visiting Children.   It is wrong to assume that a dog is going to behave himself with an unfamiliar child. Even though he is good with his own child, he may or may not regard the visiting child in the same way. Visitors are not regarded by the dog as members of his pack. He may even view them as violators of his territory. *It is potentially dangerous for a visiting child to relate to the dog of the house in the same manner as he would his own dog.* Likewise, a dog may not tolerate from a visitor what he does from his own family member, with whom a bond has been established.

Sudden Movements.   Small animals making fast, sudden moves across a dog's vision elicit the instinct to hunt, chase, protect, knock down, or bite. All dogs share to some degree this instinctive response to prey behavior, which also involves the defense of territory. Intense play or sudden spurts of energy from children can bring forth aggressiveness in some dogs. Occasionally, a family member or visiting child will tap into these instincts with his or her play behavior and get bitten by the family dog who is somewhat aggressive or territorial.

The Growing Child. Children between three and five years of age are more likely to be bitten by a dog than any other group. In such cases the wound is usually on the face, because the child and the dog are about the same height. Children in this age group do not understand the potential consequences of their behavior with their dogs and squeeze them with hugs, yell into their face, come up to them from behind, and surprise them with sudden shouts like "Boo!" This kind of behavior can cause the best of dogs to bite a child.

A dog can also become aggressive because of the physical and mental transition taking place in a child. For the first three years (one-fifth of the dog's entire life), the dog has been dominant over the child. During this period he is likely to have viewed the child from infancy to toddlerhood as another puppy or a subordinate member of the family. The child's change in size and newly emerging dominance often represent a threat to the dog's long-established position in the family structure. The child may become much more assertive, where in the past he was very timid. Some dogs do not accept that change very well.

The leader of a wolf pack loses his position if he is successfully challenged in a physical confrontation by a younger member of the pack. If you transfer this idea to the family structure, it is altogether possible for a family pet to bite a growing child just to "keep him in his place."

Medical Reasons. If a dog is touched on a part of his body that is in pain he will snap, and perhaps bite, depending on how much it hurts. It is a natural reflex in all animals and not a personality problem. Dogs that have been injured are quite likely to bite the very person trying to help them. It is simply an involuntary response to pain. The same applies to dogs with bladder stones, infections, arthritis, hip dysplasia, and bone fractures.

Poor Vision. A cataract is a growth over the lens of the eye, causing a loss of transparency. Many older dogs experience cataracts in one or both eyes. Impaired vision has behavioral consequences. This condition creates in the dog great insecurity and nervousness, which can turn into a biting problem. Any eye disorder or impairment of vision creates the same results.

Parental Encouragement. Some parents require two very different functions from their family dog. On the one hand, they encourage their dogs to protect them, and on the other, they want a friendly, gentle companion. Although the idea is a good one and certainly possible, it requires expert training and handling to accomplish. By encouraging the protective instincts of a dog, they may be teaching him to become an indiscriminate biter. Inexperienced dog owners may consider a growling, snarling pup to be a good protector without realizing that in two years he can start biting the children, the neighbors, or anyone else who crosses him. It is a problem that professional dog trainers come across every day and try to undo.

Estrus Cycle. The first six to nine days of the estrus cycle (heat) make most female dogs grumpy. It is then that an even-tempered dog may growl, snap, or bite.

Human Anxiety. Frequently, a dog's behavior is a barometer for human behavior. If there is tension and anxiety coming from the human side of the household, it can be seen in some way in the dog. Unfortunately, it is often expressed in aggressive or a shy type of behavior leading to biting.

Solutions (Environmental)

Checking for Medical Problems. If a dog of any age bites someone, and biting is a departure from his normal behavior, consider the possibility that it is connected with pain. Have the dog thoroughly examined by a veterinarian before proceeding to other solutions.

Altering a Child's Behavior. This could easily be the most important action parents can take to help rid a *young* dog of his biting problem. First, children must be taught about "humane attitudes." Being kind to dogs should not merely be a method of problem solving but rather the result of a moral code. Happily, some problem behavior is eliminated when children stop being abusive. But there is nothing unsophisticated about telling a child it is morally wrong to hurt an animal. Impress children with the fact that a dog is not a toy or an inanimate object without emotions or the ability to feel pain.

In addition to the right and wrong of it, there is the practical side that needs clarification for young children. Dogs bite when they are hurt or very upset. Children must be told they will lose their "best friend" if they treat the dog badly. Of course children are always watching their parents. If the parents are abusive to the dog, then the children will certainly copy their behavior. An adult may be able to hit a dog and not get bitten. But

children will not get away with it, because they are shorter and lack personal authority. If they hit or abuse a dog, sooner or later he will bite them.

When parents educate their children about dog care and dog needs they are automatically teaching the fundamentals of humane principles. Children can be taught to view the situation from the dog's perspective. Would they like to have their tails pulled and twisted, and so on? Involving children with such responsibilities as feeding, walking, training, grooming and playing creates a bond of friendship that makes it more difficult for children to hurt their dogs willfully. Even toddlers can help care for the family pet. This attitude, in turn, makes for a happier, more contented animal who is less likely to snap, nip, or bite.

Removing the Frustration. Children experience a wide variety of emotions in the course of one day. They become jealous, deal with siblings and friends, cope with school and the difficulties of learning new things. If a child has a few bad days it is easy for him to relieve his frustration by releasing his anger at the family dog. A puppy or young dog will take the abuse because he has no choice. But some day, when he is big enough, and his jaws are strong enough, he will fight back with his teeth. If the child is old enough and large enough to dominate the dog, he may be OK. But what about the dog's attitude toward smaller, younger children who may enter the house? The older child will have created in the dog an aggressive attitude toward children that will grow dangerous.

Protecting a Mother Dog and Her Puppies. Never allow children to go near a new litter of puppies by themselves. Parents can avoid biting incidents from the mother dog by supervising visitations to the newborns. No one should handle the infant dogs, certainly not the children, unless it is done with the utmost tact and awareness of the mother's apprehension about letting one go. Children must be calm, cool, and collected around the newborns and not give the mother any cause for alarm.

Solutions (Reconditioning)

Protection or Companionship? Decide. Be aware of the problems involved when developing aggressive behavior in puppies for the sake of protection. It is very difficult to create a dog that will protect you from threatening strangers but at the same time be playful, friendly, and affectionate. There is something abnormal about a dog that raises its lips and growls at a child for coming near his sleeping quarters. Never view this as a good thing because you want a dog with protective qualities. You could be creating a monster by not changing that situation as soon as possible. It is important to decide what is normal and what is aberrant behavior. A normal dog should not snarl, growl, or go after any member of the family. If you want protection from a dog, he should be turned over to a professional dog trainer specializing in guard/companion work. This type of training requires great skill and expertise and cannot be achieved by inexperienced amateurs.

Guidelines for Correcting a Dog Who Bites a Child. If you have a dog *under ten months of age* and he is nipping, or mouthing, or showing any aggressive tendencies toward children such as blocking their path, you may use the Margolis Maneuver as a correction to stop this behavior (see part Two, "Essential Tools and Techniques for Problem Solving"). Puppies and young dogs up to ten months of age should respond favorably to this technique and eventually end this behavior. However, there are no guarantees that anything will work successfully with some dogs, no matter how young they may be.

Children should not be entrusted with the responsibility of correcting a dog with the Margolis Maneuver. However, every adult member of the family should correct a young dog or puppy when he shows any signs of aggression leading to biting. The Margolis Maneuver is the most effective correction, but it requires that the leash (or street handle) and slip collar remain on the dog. The shake can can be used during those times when the dog is not wearing a leash and slip collar. Because shake cans are easy to make and very economical, place them all over your house, particularly where the problem is most likely to occur. Using the shake can is less intense than the Margolis Maneuver but much better than allowing a snapping, nipping, or biting incident to pass without any correction at all.

A biting problem with a dog ten months or older requires professional help. If the problem is very serious, a dog trainer, animal behaviorist, or veterinarian (or all three together) should be consulted. Dog owners using corrections such as the Margolis Maneuver or even the shake can on a full-grown dog with a serious biting problem place themselves in jeopardy.

Prevention Tips

For the dog-owning parent, the prevention factor may be as important as or even more important than the reconditioning solutions. The most useful prevention suggestions can be found by reading "Reasons for the Problem" earlier in this article. That section can make parents aware of those situations that cause dogs to bite children. To know them is to avoid them. In effect, prevention factors are a major solution in themselves because they help parents avoid the pitfalls even if the dog has recently developed a biting problem. In many cases a young dog's biting behavior can be corrected by understanding why he bites and changing the conditions that created the problem.

Extending the Dog's Socialization. Although handling a three-week to eight-week-old puppy every day socializes him and makes him better adapted to humans, there is more that can be accomplished. After a puppy has settled into his new home and has made his adjustments, it is time to expose him to new people and new situations. Assuming he has had all the proper immunizations for his age, start taking him beyond your neighborhood to parks, new streets, and new and friendly people. Help him adjust to traffic. The more people and places a young puppy comes in contact with, the better. Few things will take him by surprise later. This broadening of his world will help make him a more social animal with little fear and no reason to bite.

BITING (BECAUSE OF FOOD, POSSESSIONS, AND OBJECTS)

Some of the sweetest dogs can transform in an instant to vicious monsters when you go near their food. Other dogs might develop this frightening but irrational behavior over a large bone or a blanket they sleep on. Toys, old shoes, or a ball with a bell in it can create in a dog an obsession that will produce dangerous behavior. Some biting behavior can be attributed to an abnormal relationship with possessions. It begins in puppyhood and continues for the life of the dog. Although a nip from a puppy does not hurt, a bite from a grown dog is sure to get your attention. Snapping, nipping, and biting behavior must be dealt with immediately whether it comes from a grown dog or the youngest puppy.

Reasons for the Problem

As pointed out in "Biting (Children), Reasons for the Problem," biting can be traced to one of four sources: inherited behavior, poor socialization, environmental influences, and owner behavior. The following reasons for the problem are more specific.

Natural Predatory Behavior. Wolves and dogs in the wild work hard for a living. In order to eat they must hunt down a prey animal, kill it and feed from it until they hunt again. Food must be protected from other predators. If another animal or member of the pack goes near food that is saved, it will be attacked by the leader, or Alpha-wolf. Nursing mothers also protect the food supply in this manner. Survival is the issue. This behavior is instinctive in all canines. It can be seen in some house dogs who growl from deep within their throats, snap, and even bite when anyone approaches their food bowl.

Territory. When pet dogs guard possessions and objects, they are expressing an exaggerated sense of territory. Such dogs will not allow anyone to go near possessions or objects they have claimed, and threaten those who do with snarls, growls and bites. This behavior is closely related to food guarding. Although it is instinctive and quite reasonable in a natural setting, it is perverse when seen in the home.

The Dominant Dog. An overly dominant dog will assert his "leadership" on issues pertaining to food, possessions, or various aspects of territory. Aggressive behavior involving bullying and threats of biting is the form his assertion takes. This type of dog will not allow anyone near him.

Catching the Dog Off Guard. Dogs with a distorted sense of territory or those who guard their food may bite when surprised while they are eating or savoring their possessions. It is a subtle but distinct variation of exaggerated territorial behavior.

Past Experience. A dog with an unknown past may bite over food and/or possessions. The dog you brought home from the pound may have been living on the street, eating out of garbage cans. These dogs had to compete with other dogs for their meals. Often food is fought over in the street. Such dogs would naturally be possessive about their food.

Encouragement by Humans. Whatever a puppy or young dog is allowed to do at an early age can be considered encouragement for that behavior. If a puppy growls or snaps at anyone going near his food or possessions and is not corrected, he is quite likely to continue this behavior as he grows. It becomes serious as he reaches maturity. *This is tied into the very common misconception that one should never go near a dog when he is eating.*

Humans tend to think feeding is a private time for dogs and they should not be disturbed. Therefore they tolerate the growls and snarls over food. Of course, if someone forgets and approaches the dog, he or she may get bitten. That is the result of applying human values to dog behavior. In the wild canines never eat alone or without distractions. Dogs are very social animals.

Solutions (Reconditioning)

The following reconditioning solutions are to be applied *only* to dogs that already have a biting problem when their food or possessions are approached by any member of the family. Do not use these solutions if the problem has just begun and does not involve actual biting. In that situation see "Prevention Tips." Do not use these techniques if your dog is past ten months of age.

The Setup. This solution applies to a biting problem involving food, possessions, or objects. If the problem does not to apply to food but rather a possession, the same techniques apply whenever the dog is involved with the object of his aggression.

Place a shake can on a table or counter surface near the dog's food bowl. Feed him his scheduled meal and walk away. Get the shake can and hold it behind your back. While he is eating, approach his bowl as though you were going to touch his food. *Avoid getting bitten.* Do not get your face close to his, and be ready to pull your hand away quickly. If he growls or snaps, pull your hand away quickly, shake the can hard so that a very loud noise is produced. Do not give the dog the impression that you are going to hit him with it. At the same time yell "NO!" Praise the dog immediately afterward.

The idea is to startle the dog, impress upon him that growling and biting are forbidden, that you are dominant over him, and he must obey. If the shake can does not get the desired response, try banging two pots together. You might even drop the pots on the floor close to him. If he leaves his food, that is acceptable. Although we do not want to scare him away from eating, biting is a serious problem, and solving it is more important than his hurt feelings. Administer this correction every time you feed the dog until the problem ceases to exist. Repeat it six times during each meal at five- or ten-second intervals.

The same technique can be tried with the use of a whistle. Set the dog up as before but correct him by blowing a whistle loudly and yelling "NO" the instant he growls or snaps at you over his food. If that doesn't work, you can really startle the dog with a compressed-air horn. These are aerosol cans with a small horn at the top. When pressed down, they make an unbelievably loud honk. They are used as foghorns for boaters and as a defense against muggers. This device is so loud it almost always will save you from getting bitten.

The Margolis Maneuver with Two People. This is a variation of the setup, but it requires two people. If the problem does not apply to food but rather a possession, use the same techniques substituting the object or possession for the food bowl.

Before feeding the dog, place the slip collar and leash on him. One person holds the leash while the other places the food bowl on the floor. Once the dog begins eating, try to take the bowl away. If the dog objects in any way, the other person corrects him with the Margolis Maneuver (see part Two, "Essential Tools and Techniques for Problem Solving"). Praise him. This is the firmest correction you have in your arsenal of problem-solving techniques. It should be used on a hard case. *Warning! Be cautious. The person taking the food away is in a vulnerable position to get bitten.* Do not use this technique if your dog is past ten months of age. It is a professional dog trainer's technique, and he or she knows how to avoid a dog bite. If you do use this technique, it is suggested it be done at every meal, at least six times each feeding at five- or ten-second intervals. Maintain this schedule until the dog allows you to remove his food without threatening you.

Prevention Tips

Early Conditioning. If you condition the dog at an early age to have his food or prized possessions handled by all members of the family, you will probably avoid this problem. Everyone who lives with the dog should be involved. It is very important. This conditioning can be done in a similar manner to the techniques used in the "Solutions" above.

There is one necessary difference in the way you handle the prevention and solution situations. Assuming you have a puppy and the problem has not yet developed or is not very serious, the approach should be more of a teaching process than a correcting process. Here we are emphasizing praise and positive reenforcement rather than corrections, which are negative reenforcements. It is the difference between conditioning and reconditioning.

Feed the puppy his scheduled meal or give

him his prized possession and walk away. Return to him a few seconds later and take it from him. Speak in a very happy and friendly tone of voice as you do. Make it seem as if something good were happening. "Hey, puppy, look at this. I'm taking your food. What a good boy. What a terrific dog. Yes, you are." You can talk to him. You can touch him. You can hug him. You can gently play with him. No matter what you do with him it should be OK. The puppy may be puzzled, but at the same time will become accustomed to having his food bowl or other possessions touched and will associate something pleasant with it. Do this every day for two weeks to a month. Touching his food bowl or other possessions should not be a big deal to him. The more conditioning you give him, the more he will accept your presence during his mealtime. Praise and affection are positive ways of preventing the problem.

BITING (BECAUSE OF OVERPROTECTION OF PROPERTY AND PEOPLE)

Those who own overprotective dogs should have a sign posted, "Beware of Dog. Trespassers Will Be Eaten!" Everyone has entered a home at least once where he or she has been intimidated by an aggressive, threatening dog and has had to ask the owner, "Is he dangerous?" To which the owner almost always replies, "He'll be OK . . . if you don't get up or make sudden moves." Who cares if *he'll* be OK?

People feel good about such dogs until someone they care about gets bitten. A very protective dog offers his owner a feeling of security and a sense of power in any situation. There seems to be more involved than protection; perhaps there is an element of machismo. But has anyone considered whether it is good for a dog to live that way? Dogs that are aggressive and dominant beyond the point of reason or safety have few, if any, canine or human friends. They are little better than gas station dogs leading a brooding, alienated existence void of social contact. Only one or maybe two members of their families can influence them at all and life is all business. You can only speculate on what pleasure such a dog experiences, if any.

The problem for the owner and the community in general is the dog's inability to understand the difference between friend and foe. The danger is mostly for the unfortunate stranger approaching such a house on lawful business. However, it is not uncommon for owners of overprotective dogs to get bitten as well. After all, an aggressive dog is one who thinks he is the boss over everyone. Often the dog's owner is faced with a criminal or civil court action involving thousands of dollars plus medical costs. Letter carriers, meter readers, delivery people, and all the rest have a terrible dilemma when confronted by a dangerous yard dog. They are not sure whether to risk entering the property or not. More letter carriers are bitten by such dogs than any other group. Sometimes the Postal Service refuses to deliver the mail where a biting dog is always loose on the lawn.

Dogs of this nature are either born that way or encouraged to behave in that manner from puppyhood on. It is a combination of these factors that creates overprotective dogs. There can be no doubt that genetics plays a large role in producing this behavior. Ideally, an aggressive dog should and can behave as a pet as well as a protector.

Reasons for the Problem

Genetics. Aggressiveness is largely an inherited form of behavior. One must look to a dog's family tree for the primary cause. Shake it, and one or more biters are sure to fall out. Most aggressive dogs are the result of indiscriminate breeding. However, some breeds of dog have been developed over a long period to be more aggressive than others. These dogs were bred to perform tasks requiring aggressiveness, such as guard work or some special forms of hunting. Many of the terrier and working breeds fall into this category. Although environmental influences may be involved in biting, inherited behavior is the major reason.

Owner Encouragement. Quite often people purchase a dog of a breed with a reputation for aggressiveness and do all they can to encourage it. Other owners encourage aggressiveness in their puppies no matter what the breed. Obviously, they want a dog that will protect them and their property. Unfortunately, they create aggressive dogs that are uncontrollable. Developing aggressiveness in a young dog without complete obedience training and discipline is like giving a child a loaded gun. Such owners will praise their dogs for barking, howling, and snarling. When you reward a dog for that behavior, it is only a short step to encouraging him to bite someone, whether you want him to or not. Tug-of-war games played with a puppy and an old sock get the young dog growling and pulling. This sort of roughhouse play brings out the aggressive quality in any dog

and is absolutely deadly in an animal with an aggressive disposition. If the dog is not trained for protection work by a professional, the animal is merely aggressive, overprotective, and far too obsessed with his territory. He is totally unreliable as a house dog.

Inadequate Socializing. Socializing a dog goes beyond the critical stage of puppyhood. All human handling influences dog behavior. A dog that is not treated as a member of the family, or one who lives outdoors in the yard or is constantly yelled at and shooed away becomes alienated, aggressive, and possibly dangerous. This is a dog that knows no loving hand and regards all but those who feed him with suspicion and hostility. Such a dog regards those who feed him as the only other living creatures that matter and will drive off or attack anyone else. This is particularly true of some of the working breeds. It is a grave mistake to establish living conditions of this sort for any dog.

Solutions (Environmental)

Changing Your Attitude. It is a philosophical change that owners must make, more than any one thing they must do. Stop encouraging the dog to scare everyone. Do not reward aggressive behavior with praise of any sort. Try to avoid situations where the dog becomes aggressive toward strangers who do not trespass or pose any threat.

When a dog is permitted to run loose, he expands his territorial boundaries and takes this freedom as encouragement to do so. He may claim an entire neighborhood for himself and go after anyone riding a bike, driving a car, or simply walking through. Be there to quiet him when he barks at someone. Stop him every time. You must use your judgment to determine when aggressive behavior is out of hand. Can the dog be called off once he attacks someone? Do you have enough control to make him stop? Do you have any control at all? Now is the time to stop encouraging the dog to bite people.

Build a Dog Run. If an overprotective dog remains outdoors most of the time, he should have an area where he can be prevented from threatening those who lawfully enter your property or premises. A dog run is the ideal form of confinement for this purpose. It is a reasonably long, narrow strip of space that is separated from the rest of the yard or back lawn by chain-link fencing. Dog runs are custom-built by contractors or constructed by home owners. All the materials necessary are available at a hardware supply store. A very well built run has a thin concrete slab poured on the ground inside the run. This prevents the dog from digging his way out and helps maintain sanitation and personal hygiene. A dog run is the perfect do-it-yourself project for anyone who is handy and likes to improve his own property.

Constructing a dog run and placing a dog inside will not diminish his protective quality in terms of the house. He will still serve as a visual deterrent when he is outdoors and do what is natural for him when he is indoors. This simply keeps him from attacking any and all visitors.

Solutions (Reconditioning)

Obedience Training. With the help of a training book or a professional dog trainer, subject the dog to a complete obedience course. Obedience training will go very far toward solving the problem. It will give you control over the dog and stop any aggressive behavior before it becomes lethal. Dog training becomes the instrument by which this form of behavior can be modified to some extent. It is difficult to change a protective or highly territorial dog from being that way. The best you can do is change the form his aggressiveness takes.

Once obedience-trained, the dog will bark instead of bite or will stand firmly in a stranger's path rather than lunge at him. He will certainly back off if ordered to do so. If the dog is trained, he is then capable of being taught when to bark and when not to bark; who is good and who is bad. It is a necessary process to go through if you want to get aggressive behavior under control.

BITING (BECAUSE OF PAIN, MEDICAL PROBLEMS, GROOMING)

If a dog is touched on a part of his body that is in pain he will snap, nip, and perhaps bite, depending on how much it hurts. It is a natural reflex in all animals and not a personality problem. Dogs that have been injured are quite likely to bite the very person trying to help them. It is simply an involuntary response to pain.

There are many sources of pain. Medical problems are the most common ones. Fights with other animals, abuse from humans, and various injuries all produce pain. Sometimes grooming causes pain if the owner does not understand the dog's body or touches a sore spot. When a dog bites someone because he is in pain, biting should be considered nothing more than a temporary situation. However, it can become habitual behavior if it is tolerated.

Reasons for the Problem

Medical Conditions. Just because a dog has a painful medical condition, he is not automatically going to bite someone. Some tender part of his body must be touched, hugged, squeezed, pushed, felt, rubbed, or irritated in some way, and even then he may just snap with a soft mouth. Of course, the more intense the pain, the harder the bite will be. It is a response to the pain that is uncontrollable. A dog with hip dysplasia, for example, will experience pain when placed in a "sit" position during obedience training. If the trainer puts any pressure on the dog's lower back or haunches with his hands, the dog will bite to stop the pain.

The most common medical conditions that cause pain and result in biting are arthritis, hip dysplasia, bladder stones, infections, injuries, skin problems, disorders of the eye, gastroenteritis, seizures, convulsions, broken bones, pregnancy, whelping, lactation, ingesting foreign objects or household poisons, and some forms of cancer.

Old Age. The average life span of most dogs is between ten and fifteen years. Somewhere in the seventh year the dog's metabolism changes and a slow, gradual aging process begins. Muscles lose their tone and the skin loses some of its elasticity. Cell replacement becomes slower, and organs function with less efficiency. The body's immune system slows down, and the dog's ability to fight off sickness diminishes along with its recuperative powers. Large dogs age faster than small ones.

Older dogs experience minor aches and pains that the owner is not aware of because they do not result from any particular disease. If you accidentally touch a painful spot you may get bitten.

Grooming. There are more snapping and biting incidents during grooming than at any other time. Scissors, electric hair clippers, combs, and brushes can all cause pain that will result in biting behavior.

Solutions (Environmental)

Seek Medical Attention. It is unfortunate that some dog owners remain in a fog of misinformation or no information and then stumble in bewilderment when something happens. Dog bites caused by pain are difficult to stop once a tender area has been irritated unless you move the hand away fast. However, it is quite possible to avoid causing pain and thus not get bitten. If the dog has symptoms of illness take him to a veterinarian quickly. When handling him be careful not to touch a part of his body that is in pain. In that way you can avoid getting bitten.

Use a Muzzle. If your dog has been injured or is obviously in extreme pain, he must not be handled until some form of restraint has been placed on his ability to bite. An injured dog will snap at and bite anyone who touches him, even the ones he knows and loves the most.

All veterinarians and animal professionals know how to muzzle the dog with a temporary, makeshift restraint before attempting to touch or move the animal. Anything that can be tied will do. Gauze bandage, string, twine, adhesive tape, a dog leash, a necktie: all are satisfactory. The muzzle is formed by tying a loop with the string material and slipping it over the dog's snout, halfway up. Place it over bone rather than cartilage. Pull the string gently until it tightens, holding the mouth securely shut. Bring the ends of the string under the jaw, forming another loop. Tie the ends behind the ears as you would a shoelace, making a bow. The dog cannot bite anyone in this position. He is ready to be examined and moved without being dangerous.

Prevention Tips

Grooming Care. Bear in mind that few professional groomers get bitten. They realize that most dogs do not have the patience to sit quietly for hours while they are bathed, clipped, scissored, brushed, combed, and puffed up. While you are trying to groom your dog, use praise, kindness, and an occasional biscuit to keep him calm. Do not hit the dog. If he becomes restless and uncontrollable, give him a break every ten or fifteen minutes. (Use a rubber, non-skid mat that keeps him from sliding around so he feels secure.)

There are many aspects of grooming that are potential sore spots. If the dog is hurt while being groomed he is quite likely to bite the one grooming him. For example, improper nail clipping can hurt. Be careful not to cut the nail at the quick (vein), for that will cause pain and some bleeding. Most dogs hate having their nails clipped and resist it even when it's done properly. Use a sharp instrument, hold the dog firmly, be friendly and reassuring, and get the job done quickly.

Scissoring and clipping the coat has pit-

falls. When working with scissors it is all too easy to nick the skin, pinch it, or pull the hair with a dull instrument. Heat from electric clippers can hurt the dog. And then, there is a skin condition called "clipper burn," which is a painful rash that develops on sensitive areas as a reaction to the abrasiveness of the electric clippers.

Combing and brushing a dog's coat can also be a source of pain that will result in biting behavior. If one does not begin gently, the comb or brush may hit a tangle or mat and pull the hair away from the skin. Spray a commercial coat conditioner on the dog's body before brushing and combing. It makes the brush and comb go through the hair smoothly and helps eliminate tangles. However, if the dog is not brushed often, the hair forms mats that are very difficult to comb out and quite painful when brushed. A mat is a collection of many, many tangles and must be dealt with by an experienced groomer.

When grooming a dog's coat, check for "hot spots," which are circular patches of skin that are red, swollen from infection, and irritated. Sometimes they hurt and sometimes they itch. They may appear on the neck, ears, chest, back, rump, and flanks. They can be caused by flea bites, glandular problems, allergies, licking and chewing, and possibly wet hair trapped next to the skin during the shedding period. Any grooming on a dog with hot spots must be done with the utmost sensitivity to avoid causing pain.

Become Aware of Your Dog's Body. You can prevent biting incidents by developing an awareness of canine medical symptoms and their potential for pain. Pay more attention to the dog on a daily basis. Be alert and responsive to variations in his behavior or bodily functions that might indicate a medical condition. Watch for changed eating patterns, lower energy levels, variations in behavior, digestion and elimination variations, discharges, changes in the texture of his coat, limping, pawing, a distended stomach, diarrhea, vomiting, scratching, shivering, bad odor, sneezing, coughing, fainting, bleeding, squinting, straining, changes in stools, blood in urine, flatulence, foaming at the mouth, weakness, weight loss, wheezing, continual whining. These are but some of the symptoms of illness and disease that can lead to biting. If you are aware of them you may be able to prevent a biting incident.

BITING (BECAUSE OF PUNISHMENT OR HITTING)

When you hit a dog he eventually will retaliate ... with his teeth. Some biting problems are simply a response to being hit. When a dog disobeys or fails in his training, some owners yell at him, hit him, and chase him into a corner. This ill-advised behavior may condition the dog into becoming a "fear biter." (See also "Biting because of Shyness.") When a dog bites the hand that hits him, it is not the result of aggressiveness. Far from it. That form of biting is pure defense, from the dog's point of view.

Reasons for the Problem

Hitting and Other Forms of Physical Abuse. The biting response can be seen in all dogs when they are slapped, punched, kicked, shoved, kneed in the chest, or abusively pushed away. The same applies to

pointing an accusing finger at a dog on a continuing basis. (Do not point your finger too close to his mouth.) Verbal abuse can also provoke a biting incident. When an owner constantly admonishes a sensitive dog harshly with such statements as "Bad dog! What did you do? Why did you do this? No! No! No!" the dog can be driven crazy. He may eventually bite.

Housebreaking Failures. Nothing aggravates a novice dog owner more than coming home to urine or defecation on the floor or, worse yet, the carpet. At that moment he or she experiences an irrational desire for revenge instead of finding out why the dog failed and what can be done to correct the situation. This is when most luckless dogs find themselves on the business end of a broomstick or become the target for every curse word ever thought up. It is fascinating to learn how shocked the novice becomes when the dog starts fighting back. A professional trainer is then called in to solve a biting problem instead of a housebreaking problem (and a human behavior problem).

Chewing. Where a four-month-old puppy will chew up only a small corner of an antique carpet or a tennis shoe, an adolescent dog may consume the baseboards, a suede couch, and a collection of rare first editions. Some folks pass out after coming home to a chewed-up house where thousands of dollars' worth of furniture and personal possessions are destroyed. Once the owner revives and picks himself up off the floor he may go crazy and flail at the dog. In that situation the dog is almost certainly going to bite him. Here again, we are not dealing with a biting problem but a chewing problem (not to mention a need for Valium plus three weeks in a rest home for the human).

Solutions (Environmental)

Rid Yourself of Misconceptions. Dogs, even the smallest ones, will eventually bite those who hit them. It is a common misconception that hitting a dog teaches him something. Hitting is not teaching. Hitting is punishment or the expression of frustration. When the owners (and even some trainers) do not know what else to do, they resort to hitting. Dog training techniques and reconditioning techniques do not require physical abuse or punishment. It is wrong to punish a dog for failing to obey when he was never "taught" properly in the first place.

There is never a reason to hit your dog with your hands, your fists, your feet, a newspaper, a broom, a stick, a leash, or anything. Hitting, slapping, and kicking are forms of punishment. When a dog owner slaps his or her dog it is usually an expression of frustration. This is unhumane and counterproductive behavior. If punishment teaches a dog anything, it is to fear you and your hands (or feet). Hitting a dog you are training is the last resort of an amateur.

Hitting a dog is like hitting a two-year-old child. It makes no sense to use such a negative gesture with your hands when you also use them to pet, hug, and stroke the dog. The dog doesn't know what to expect when you reach down to touch him. Are you going to express your love or your rage? Your hands are also important for teaching. Do not expect a dog that has been hit often to accept hand signals and teaching techniques easily. It is not OK to hit your dog, even if doing it

makes you feel better. Being hit forces him to defend himself in the only way he can. There is no problem more serious for dog owners than that of biting. It is bad enough when it happens because of inherited behavior, but the owner is foolish to create this behavior when it can be avoided.

Solutions (Reconditioning)

Identify the Real Problem. If your dog has a behavior problem that elicits from you an emotional response involving hitting, which in turn has caused him to bite, it is time to do something else. Think it through, determine what the problem really is (housebreaking, chewing, barking, or jumping on furniture). Turn to the appropriate entry in this directory for help. Isn't it better to recondition your dog to end his unwanted behavior than to smack him on the nose because you don't know what else to do? It is a question of solving the problem and not the symptom. If you stop hitting, he's going to stop biting. Your role as a dog owner is to teach, not punish.

Prevention Tips

Never hit your dog!

BITING (BECAUSE OF SHYNESS)

Shy dogs will bite those who frighten them. Such incidents are usually an irrational act of self-defense. These dogs experience fear most of the time. When someone walks into a room they back away. Their tails go down, ears flatten, heads droop; they cower; sometimes they shake. If pursued and then cornered, they may bite. However, not every

The shy dog will not bite until someone elicits that response with his or her behavior.

shy dog bites. These are devoted dogs. They stay close to the ones they love and may be good pets. Shy behavior varies by degree. Some shy dogs simply look cautiously at a visitor, although others may run away and hide under a bed. The dog that runs away and hides will bite an unrelenting well-wisher. See part Three, "Your Dog's Personality: Timid/Shy."

Reasons for the Problem

Genetics.   Most dogs that bite because of shyness have inherited this personality trait. The shy dog that bites could be classified as shy/aggressive. Most shy dogs will not bite until someone elicits that response by his or her behavior. If a visitor with the best of intentions persists in following and cornering a dog that has run away from him, the dog will snap or bite.

Bad breeding causes shy dogs to come into the world. Although no one can know for sure what types of puppies will come out of a litter, the skill lies in selecting the dogs to be mated. Experienced breeders carefully examine the pedigree (family tree) of the male and female, acquaint themselves with the individual dogs in the lineage, and then decide if it's a worthwhile match. Unfortunately, some breeders are impressed by Champion titles in the pedigree and have little or no knowledge of the temperaments of the dogs in the line. When you are purchasing a dog from a commercial source, the pedigree has not even been a factor. It is a genetic grab bag full of surprises, some good, some not so good.

Punishment.   When a shy dog bites it is often a direct response to punishment from its owner. These dogs become suspicious, skittish, and fearful as a result of having been hit or abused in the past. They will bite if the human hand looks as though it were going to hit them. They cannot tolerate punishment. (Some dogs have less tolerance for punishment and rejection than others.) Biting induced by human behavior is avoidable.

Hitting a dog with your hands or a newspaper or constantly pointing at him in anger creates a *hand-shy* dog. The same is true if his face is rubbed in his housebreaking mistakes. Hand-shy dogs flinch or cower when you try to pet them and may even bite.

Yelling.   Constant yelling at a sensitive, timid, or shy dog entrenches him in his behavior and can turn him into a biter. "What did you do? Bad dog! Get out! No! No! No!" Shy dogs become *voice-shy* when severely scolded and drop to the ground and wet when you talk to them. They may even bite.

Fear of the Leash. Some shy dogs have a difficult time adjusting to a leash when being walked. *Leash-shy* dogs may be new to city life, and may never have worn a leash before. The fright may not necessarily be caused by the leash itself but by the combination of outdoor city noises and the sudden movement of street traffic when being restrained. Dogs, like other animals, have a "fight or flight" response and will do one or the other depending on the circumstances and the animal's personality.

Another factor is distance. A shy dog will run if something or someone comes within a certain distance. The *flight distance* is the space between the two; it varies with each animal. A dog restrained by a leash may panic when something or someone gets within flight distance. He will shake, pant excessively, strain to get away, and possibly bite at the leash or the person holding it.

Lack of Socialization. Some shy dogs are afraid of strangers and visitors. They are *people-shy*. They get that way because they have not been exposed to people, have spent too much time in a kennel as puppies, and relate well only to other dogs; live in a yard; or because they are bonded to only one person, with everyone else representing a threat.

When a *people-shy* dog has bonded to a single owner, it is usually because the human wanted it that way. Some people prefer a "one-dog, one-owner" relationship and inadvertently create the *people-shy* dog.

This desire could derive from jealousy of those who might "steal the dog's affection" or from being more comfortable with animals than with people. It could also stem from the owner's misconception that this is the proper way to create and maintain a guard dog.

People-shy dogs get upset around anyone new. When visitors come into the house, these dogs bark, cower, shake, hide behind their masters' legs, lie in a corner and refuse to obey commands, back away, and look fearful. They may also wet and bite.

Dynamics of the Puppy Litter. Shy behavior and resulting biting behavior could be caused by the influence of early litter-mate interaction. The runt of a litter, who was not as assertive or as strong as the others, may have been attacked, bitten, or abused by his brothers and sisters. A shy or shy/aggressive dog may have gotten that way because the bullying incidents were serious and frequent.

In addition, his litter-mates might have denied him immediate access to his mother's teats at mealtime or blocked him from getting enough nutrition from the food bowl during and after weaning. Growing puppies need large quantities of nutrition. They eat more food in ratio to their body weight than at any other time in their lives. Puppies cannot be overfed. A puppy with emotional stress has an added energy demand placed on his body and requires more, not less, food. Stress produced by being bullied and bitten as a puppy, in combination with a lower intake of nutrition, leads to hyperirritability and bad behavior or apathy and depression. These are the environmental building blocks of shy behavior or shy/aggressive behavior. It would explain the behavior of dogs whose lineage shows no history of shyness.

Solutions (Environmental)

Change Your Behavior.   Biting behavior caused by shyness can be ended if you alter your way of relating to the dog. Punishment must not be viewed as a teaching method or even a valid means of changing a dog's behavior. Do your best to avoid behavior that produces a *hand-shy, voice-shy, leash-shy,* or *people-shy* dog. Do not hit your dog or yell at him. Doing this only reinforces his shyness and may induce him to bite defensively. A territorial dog who has been socialized will still be protective. A dog will be uncontrollable and dangerous to everyone, including his owner, unless he has the proper training for protection work.

Get the Dog Out into the World.   Socialize him if he has been denied human company or has not been allowed to enjoy the comfort or companionship of human beings. Get him out of the yard, at least part of the time, and allow him the run of the house. If the dog is not housebroken see Five, "Housebreaking," page 165. Expose him to parks, street noises, shopping centers, anywhere he can confront new people, new places, new situations. Be reassuring, gentle, and sensitive to his fear and desire to get away from it all. Talk to the dog, pet him, stroke him, and start slowly. If the dog is obedience-trained this task will be much easier. Take him into a new situation for short periods of time and work your way up to long socializing walks.

In the Litter.   The proud owner of a litter of puppies should watch for bullies. Feed the puppies individually, because the stronger ones push the weaker ones away when all are fed in a group. During weaning, all puppies should be fed at the same time but in different locations. Puppies should not be given access to each other's food bowls until feeding is over and everyone has had his fill.

Past the seventh week, puppies begin to sort themselves out and develop a social structure according to rank. One or two of the litter will become more dominant than the others. Do not hesitate to stop one dog from seriously bullying another. Traumatic experiences during the first three months can make a dog shy for the rest of his life.

Solutions (Reconditioning)

Obedience Training.   Obedience training a shy dog will definitely avoid biting behavior. Although you cannot turn him into a comedian or a trickster, you can make him more secure by gaining control over his behavior. Obedience training allows the dog to walk calmly with you down the street, sit when you want him to, and stop barking or backing away whenever someone visits. Get a self-teaching book and do it yourself or engage the services of a professional trainer sensitive to the needs of such a dog.

Because of their extreme sensitivity, shy dogs require tender loving care during training. Be gentle when correcting a shy dog; this applies to every command taught. Be firm when giving commands but use a soft touch when making corrections and be sure to lavish praise on the dog. Give immediate praise when he obeys a command and be exuberant. The shy dog should be trained slowly. Take more time teaching each command. Don't look for immediate results.

Obedience Classes. In addition to helping the owner to gain control over a shy dog, an obedience class has the added benefit of socializing him. In a class this dog will meet and learn to work with fifteen or twenty other dogs and that many new people. Obviously, the more a shy dog is exposed to other dogs and people, the more adaptive he will become. The exposure may bring an end to the extreme aspects of his shyness, such as biting or running away.

The Kennel Method. Shy dogs bite because of fear and the defense of their territory. All dogs are more aggressive on their own turf. If a dog is removed totally from his yard, his home, and his owner and placed in a kennel, his need to be aggressive will also be removed along with a portion of his insecurities.

A boarding and training kennel has a large staff of people, most of whom are there seven days a week. A dog boarded there will eventually meet them all and be handled by at least ten to twelve people a day. He will be fed two or three times a day, bathed once a week, exercised and trained once or twice a day. It will have the same good effect that sleep-away camp has for preadolescent children. The attention from so many strangers is like a tonic. The socializing effect is much more thorough than could be achieved at home. The dog will get love, be touched, trained, socialized, and pleasantly forced to adapt. Boarding a dog in a kennel has proven to be an enormously successful technique for improving the behavior of dogs with all kinds of problems, but especially for shy dogs. In this controlled environment the trainers can re-create all the situations that produce problem behavior at home and introduce the dog to them for training and reconditioning. *The dog should remain at the kennel for two to three weeks.* This stay is remarkably effective. The variety and quantity of kennel staff help a shy dog adjust to living in the human world without fear.

Seek out a kennel offering a reliable, professional trainer with experience. Such businesses can be found in the *Yellow Pages* under "Dog Training," "Kennels," and "Pets." Make contact; go out and look at the kennel; meet the people. You must feel certain that they are qualified for this type of program. Do not be afraid to tell them what you want. Show them this entry in the directory. If you are satisfied with the establishment, then sign up and send your dog to camp.

Prevention Tips

Recognize the Behavior. Acquaint yourself with the signs and symptoms of shyness as a behavior problem and look for them in puppies and young dogs. Dealing with shyness properly in its earliest stages prevents it from growing into a full-blown problem leading to dangerous, aggressive behavior.

Discourage Aggressive Behavior. Do not reward your puppy or young dog when he growls, barks, or nips. This applies to dogs of all personalities, but is especially important for shy and aggressive dogs. A pat on the head, verbal praise, food, or even play and laughter are rewards if given immediately after the dog has done something. Bear in mind that a reward can teach bad behavior, too.

Do not clutch the dog or hold him tightly every time someone enters your home and he growls. Do not pet him and say, "Easy, fella. Easy." The dog easily misinterprets such actions as rewards for growling or threatening. The command "No" is all that should be necessary. The obedience-trained dog has learned to associate "No" with a firm correction.

Socialize Your Dog. Expose all puppies and adolescent dogs to various types of people, places, and situations. Do not keep the dog in a yard, kennel, or dog run twenty-four hours a day, seven days a week. Bring the dog indoors as much as possible, and if he is housebroken, give him the run of the house. If he is not housebroken or has other behavior problems, solve them with the help of this directory.

Avoid Punishment. "Negative reenforcement" is an essential element of dog training, but it must never be misconstrued as punishment. Communicating to a dog that he has done something wrong is done with the various forms of "corrections" such as a jerk of the leash (the Margolis Maneuver), a loud noise, or a verbal reprimand with the command "No." Knowledgeable trainers praise a dog immediately following a correction to maintain the dog's confidence in himself and his owner. Hitting a dog to train him is simply inhumane and counterproductive. Punishing a dog that has a shy personality only complicates matters and creates a biting problem.

Buy a Puppy Young. Take your new puppy home when he is seven to twelve weeks old. Puppies that have not been socialized to humans during the critical stage of puppyhood (from three to seven weeks) and that live in a kennel for four or five months are much more likely to be people-shy, a condition that eventually leads to biting behavior. Buying older puppies is asking for trouble. Of course this is not the case with puppies from a good breeder who have enjoyed early handling from the third week of life on. When selecting a puppy, do not allow yourself to be moved by the frightened little guy hiding behind the others.

Selecting a shy dog is difficult to resist. Do not give in to your parental instincts. You could be buying a dog that will turn into one that bites or is already a "fear biter." This is not necessarily the case, but the potential for disaster is there. If a puppy growls or backs away when you go up to him, there is something wrong. He should be eager and happy to see you. Cradle the dog in your arms as you would a baby. Talk to him as he lies on his back in your arms. If he squirms uncontrollably or struggles to be free, whines, nips, or growls, he has the potential for a behavior problem. Select another dog.

BITING (THE FEAR BITER)

Fear biting is an often misused term applied to any shy dog that bites out of fear. It is *not* the correct profile of a fear biter. The fear biter is a dog born with a severe character disorder that is unavoidable and rarely correctable. He is the result of bad breeding.

A fear biter is a scared dog who is insecure and nervous and who barks excessively. When he sees something or someone moving past him quickly, he will give chase. If you keep running, he will bite, but if you stop and approach him, he will back away. However, if you corner him, he will bite you.

In his yard he looks like a killer, barking, growling, and threatening in the most frightening manner. He does that only if you are on the other side of the fence. If you open the gate, he will back off. If you keep coming toward him, he will probably bite. This also happens indoors. If the doorbell rings, the dog barks loudly and backs away. The owner usually keeps the dog close to his or her side, giving him a feeling of security. When the door opens the dog barks, growls, and possibly bites. Praising or rewarding such a dog for what looks like protective behavior is a serious mistake. It encourages negative aggression, which will lead to indiscriminate biting.

One must never trust fear biters, because they are completely unpredictable. It is impossible to second-guess when they will bite. Some bite when provoked and others just explode and attack for no apparent reason. Usually, they have been kept in a yard without any socialization and do not relate to anyone but the owner. A dog living this type of life never has the opportunity to relate to other people, noises, or situations. The world is a frightening place to him. His aggressive qualities are seen on his own territory, where he feels more secure than anywhere else. Punishment does not correct his behavior. It makes it worse.

Unfortunately, a fear biter does not exhibit this behavior until he is one to three years old. He may appear to be a shy dog without the aggression. Not until he has physical maturity and some life experience will he exhibit this irrational behavior. Few people are bitten severely by a dog under ten months of age. Only a dog with mature jaw muscles and the strength to match his size can cause serious injury.

Dog owners must learn to recognize the signs of the fear biter when possible. The dog's irrational, dangerous behavior must

not be allowed to develop into a major biting incident. Look for excessive, irrational barking that ends when a person approaches. If a dog snaps and nips in earnest at a hand extended in love or friendship, the potential is there.

There is little or nothing a dog owner can do to change this behavior. If you think you have a fear biter, get an evaluation from a professional dog trainer. It is a problem that only a professional can handle.

CAR BEHAVIOR (INSIDE THE VEHICLE)

There are dogs that ride in cars so casually it makes one suspect that wolves travel in limos. But it is a rare dog that rides in an auto without disturbing the car and upsetting the driver. A car ride makes most dogs either bark, chew, run around, or jump from the back seat to the front seat when the car is in motion. And then there are dogs who run out the car door the minute it opens and dare you to catch them.

They also poke their heads out open windows and try to catch the wind with their mouths and eyes. Slurping the driver's face

Driving with a dog can present problems.

or sitting in his lap can be a menace. Somehow, it always happens as you strain to see through a drizzled windshield and a tractor-trailer threatens from behind with honking horn and flashing lights insisting that you drive faster. All that's missing is the Highway Patrol signaling to pull over as the dog sticks his head out the window and throws up.

Car behavior problems are annoying, irritating, and upsetting. But the worst part about them is the danger created for those in the car and those others on the road. Dogs who are bad passengers distract the driver and place the occupants in jeopardy. Improper car behavior is a serious problem that must be solved for the sake of auto safety.

Reasons for the Problem

Inexperience. When a dog rides in a car for the first time, his behavior will be unpredictable. He may take the experience in his stride, or he may fall apart and drive everyone crazy. The same applies to a dog who is rarely in the car except when he must be transported to the veterinarian's office. These inexperienced travelers have no car manners. They make poor passengers. If they are nervous or hyperactive, their behavior goes far beyond bad manners. At times they reach a pitch of hysteria, making it impossible to drive. They will run back and forth, bark at other dogs, and out of their fright make desperate attempts to be next to the driver.

Early Indulgence. When a little puppy is allowed to sit on a driver's lap he continues to behave that way even if he grows into a seventy-pound dog. It is common for some drivers to place a puppy in the front seat and

fondle it as they drive. It is a way of comforting the dog and restraining him at the same time. However, it creates a behavior pattern that becomes dangerous in later years. Happiness is a warm puppy when he's in someone else's lap.

Lack of Training. A dog lacking obedience training may behave wildly in a moving vehicle. If the dog is uncontrollable in the house, there is no reason to believe he'll be any better in a car. His behavior is likely to be worse.

Bad Associations with Car Riding. There are dogs who have had a frightening experience inside a car and are never relaxed or comfortable when riding. If the experience was very bad, the dog may refuse to enter the car. Dogs who refuse to get into a car may also have a difficult time maintaining their balance and remember the upsetting sensation involved. This is often the case with dogs who do not like to swim or ride in boats.

Territoriality. Aggressive dogs and fear biters may bark insanely inside a car when anything or anyone approaches. The interior of a car is a small area, making their territorial borders far too small for comfort. They are constantly defending those narrow borders because they are trapped inside. People, other dogs, and vehicles come closer to dogs locked inside the car than in any other situation, violating their "fight or flight" distance. When confined inside a car, such dogs can neither fight an intruder nor run from him. The situation defies strong instincts and creates fear and frustration for the aggressive dog or the fear biter. Dogs with these personality problems will jump from the

Bob Wortham

For dogs with bad car behavior, an open window is an invitation to jump out.

back seat to the front seat and back again, bark and growl in a frenzy, and lunge for any intruder approaching the car. If the window is open a serious attack may take place. This behavior can be extremely dangerous if the car is in motion.

Open Car Windows.   A dog who sticks his head out a car window can be struck by another vehicle or a stationary object. He can also leap out when the car is moving and find himself dazed on a highway filled with vehicles whizzing by. Cars in motion distress some dogs, and others become overly excited by what they see. An open window causes nervous, erratic behavior. Some dogs do not hesitate or even think about the consequences of jumping through. At the least, dogs catch dirt specks in their eyes and insects in their mouths when satisfying their desire to stick their noses where they do not belong. The wind can also give them a nasty eye irritation.

Opened Car Doors.   Far too many dogs dash out of the car the instant the door is opened. An unrestrained or unleashed dog will run out of a parked car if given the op-

portunity. The motion of the car plus the anticipation of seeing a change of scenery or arriving home are exciting events for him. All he needs is an open door and he is gone.

Open-air Vehicles.   A dog riding in an open convertible or in the back of a pickup truck cannot be relied on to behave properly even if he has done so in the past. He may not deliberately jump out as the vehicle moves but if he stands, runs, or jumps he may fall out.

Solutions (Environmental)

The Dog Crate.   There is no finer way to transport a dog in a moving vehicle than to place him in a dog crate. It is a lightweight wire rectangle with a Masonite floor and a door. Dog crates are available in many sizes. They either have straight sides, front and back, for home use or straight sides with a slanted front for station wagons and hatchback cars.

It may *look* like a cage with a door to you, but the dog sees it another way. When you travel with your dog, the crate becomes a portable den providing security, comfort, and safety in a strange place. Depending upon the size, it can fit into the back seat of any vehicle. The crate provides a cozy area for the dog to relax in without poking his head out the window or doing anything to annoy the passengers or distract the driver. Dogs calm down quickly in a crate and feel more secure throughout their car ride, especially if it is a long one. A proper crate should be long enough to permit your grown dog to stretch out when lying down and high enough for him to sit up without hitting his head. It must never offer more space than necessary, or it loses its denlike quality. The dog crate is not only safe; it removes a stressful element for the driver.

Other Restraints. There are dog harnesses designed to hook into the car's seatbelt system. Ask a pet supply dealer or look for advertising in various dog publications. It is also possible to place a standard dog harness on the animal and secure him inside the car with two leashes. Tie a leash to each side of the harness and connect it to a stable portion of the car. Try tying the leashes to the seatbelts. Do not tie them to the door handles. The dog could accidentally open the doors.

Back Seat Driver. It is essential that you always keep a dog in the back seat of a car. From the first moment a dog enters the family car he should be indoctrinated to stay in the back. Do not open the rear windows wide enough for the dog to stick his head out.

Poor Driving Habits. Looking at the problem from the dog's point of view, it is possible that your driving style may be the source of his bad behavior. If you speed, make sharp turns, and start and stop suddenly, the dog may be knocked off his feet. At best, a dog must struggle to stay on his feet in a moving vehicle. But a wiggling, wobbling car, lurching in short, quick bursts, or one making a mad dash to beat a traffic signal can drive a dog insane as he tries to avoid falling off the seat.

Solutions (Reconditioning)

Young Puppies. The objective here is to end erratic or annoying behavior inside a car

and prevent resistance to getting into a car as a grown dog. Here is a technique for indoctrinating a small dog to proper car behavior from the start. You will not require a dog trainer, a behaviorist, or even an assistant. Only one person, one car, and a dog are required.

Wait three to six hours after the puppy's last feeding before taking him into the car for his reconditioning sessions. Give him an opportunity to relieve himself before starting. Make each session a short period of time. The car should remain parked for the first part of the session. Put a leash and slip collar on the dog before getting into the car. Take a rawhide bone, a dog toy, or his favorite possession into the car and put it on the back seat. Place the puppy on the back seat, get in, close the door, and sit with him. Offer the dog his toy and encourage him to play with it. Make it a fun time with a gentle, playful manner and a happy tone of voice. Do not get the puppy too excited. Talk to him. Tell him he's a good boy. It is important for the dog to develop a happy association with the car during these sessions. Do not yell at him or punish him and avoid trips in the car to the veterinarian during this period.

Walk the dog in and out of the car (on the leash) five or ten times so that he becomes accustomed to the idea. If he is too little to walk in and out of the vehicle on his own, then lift him up. However, it is important that he wear the leash and slip collar.

The next step is to place the dog in the back seat, close the door, and leave him there. Start the engine and return to the back seat. Sit with him and do what you did before. Talk to the dog and make it a pleasant event. He should adjust to the sound of the engine quickly. Once he does, take a short trip around the block with him in the back seat and you up front, driving. After your short ride, reach over the front seat and grab hold of the leash. Open the door. The puppy will probably try to leave. If he does, administer a gentle leash correction (see "The Margolis Maneuver" in part Two) and say "No" in a firm tone of voice. Keep the puppy in place with the leash. Tell him "Stay" and slide out of the car when holding him in place with the leash. If he tries to leave, correct him again with a mild tug and a firm "No" and "Stay." Always praise the dog lavishly after each command and after each correction. A correction communicates that he did something wrong. Praise tells him he is doing the right thing.

If your puppy has been obedience-trained or is currently being trained, the commands "Sit" and "Sit-Stay" work well here. Repeat this routine once or twice a day until the little dog rides in the car knowing how to behave himself.

With this simple routine you will get the puppy used to the car for short periods of time, get him to behave happily but properly in the *back* of the car as it remains parked; familiarize him with the engine sound, get him to sit without fear or excitement as the car moves, and not leave the car until you give him permission.

The Grown Dog. Obedience training helps enormously. Once a dog has been trained he will be more secure and self-confident in most situations. He will calm down, which makes car riding with him much easier. If your dog is obedience-trained, try several commands when he is in the back seat of a moving car. Tell him "Place" and

"Stay." "Sit" and "Sit-Stay" are also effective commands for car behavior. The command "Heel" will help you get a resistant dog to walk to the car.

Try these reconditioning techniques if your dog has not been formally trained or if you have no interest in having him trained. If the dog hates getting into the car, he must be convinced that it is a pleasant thing to do. Place the leash and slip collar on and walk him to and out of the car several times. As you do, talk to him in an enthusiastic tone of voice. Get him excited with praise and affection. Once inside, give him a hug or an ear scratch.

Solving poor behavior when inside the car requires a second person who drives. After the leash and slip collar are on the dog and he is sitting with you on the back seat, have your helper start the engine and drive off. When the dog barks, chews, runs around the car, or misbehaves in any manner, correct him firmly with the Margolis Maneuver, saying "NO" in a firm tone of voice (see part Two, "Essential Tools and Techniques for Problem Solving"). Stop the car and reverse roles with your helper. You drive with the helper sitting in the back seat, holding the leash. When the dog misbehaves, the helper corrects the dog (using the Margolis Maneuver) *but you must be the one who says "NO" firmly as you drive.* This teaches the dog to obey your verbal corrections from the front seat although he remains in the back seat. You will then be able to control the dog as you drive.

This reverse technique makes you the dog's leader even though it is your helper jerking the leash for the correction. If you do not have a helper you can correct the dog as you drive with the shake can (see part Two,

"Essential Tools and Techniques for Problem Solving"). This tool is most useful for puppies and dogs with milder personalities and less severe behavior problems. A whistle or an aerosol horn is extremely loud and will effectively correct a hard case.

Prevention Tips

To Ride or Not to Ride. That is the question. Whether it is wise to place an untrained, uncontrollable dog in the back seat of a moving car for an extended period of time is for the driver to answer. Until the dog has been reconditioned to behave himself, it may be safer for you and happier for the dog to leave him home.

Start Proper Car Behavior During Puppyhood. Riding in a car should always be viewed as a pleasant, happy experience for the dog. Do not wait until he has grown to full size before indoctrinating him to proper car behavior. Good behavior must be shaped during puppyhood. Follow the rules: keep him in the back; do not open the windows very much; give him a riding command such as "Place" or "Sit" accompanied with "Stay"; make sure car rides are happy experiences.

Buy a Dog Crate. Use it.

CAR CHASING

The car chaser stays deep within the core area of his territory, lying in wait, usually out of sight. He could be in his doghouse, behind a bush, or in the garage. At the first sound of an engine, his ears twist around to-

Courtesy of Sporting Dog Specialties, Inc.

The slant-front crate was designed to fit in the rear of most cars and station wagons. It works well in the home and on the road and prevents most car behavior problems.

ward the source of the sound as adrenaline is manufactured and secreted into the bloodstream. His heart pumps faster. He springs to his feet as the offending enemy first crosses his vision like the breaking of an electronic beam. Sometimes he doesn't see more than a blurred vision of metal in motion. Experienced car chasers respond to the sound of an engine.

In action, the car chaser runs parallel to the moving vehicle as though he were bringing down a caribou. He barks furiously and comes dangerously close to the rolling wheels. Most cars speed away, leaving the dog standing in the middle of the road glaring at the outrage, his honor satisfied and his machismo intact. The situation becomes complicated when one dog leads a small group of neighborhood car chasers. Like satellites, they run on both sides of the vehicle and unnerve drivers trying to avoid hitting them. Car chasers are a nuisance and a danger to everyone, including themselves. This is one more form of problem solving that performs a community service.

Origins of the Problem

Portrait of the car chaser as a young dog: keen vision (Whippet, Greyhound, Afghan Hound, Russian Wolfhound, Basenji); aggressive and territorial (German Shepherd Dog, Komondor, Akita, Doberman Pinscher, Airedale, Rottweiler, Boxer, Weimaraner); sharp hunting instincts (spaniels, retrievers, setters, pointers, some hounds and terriers); and mutts and mixed breeds possessing combinations of these qualities.

Running after cars as they pass through a neighborhood is the dog's response bubbling to the surface from its ancient genetic history. One of two instincts is thrown into gear. The first is the need to defend territory and attack or drive off intruders. This instinct is greater in some dogs than in others. (See "Biting: Origins of the Problem.")

The second instinct involved in car chasing is hunting behavior. Bear in mind that all dogs must hunt to survive when living in the wild. This is especially true of their cousins the wolf, fox, hyena, and jackal. Wild dogs

Car chasers are a nuisance and a danger to everyone, including themselves.

and wolves normally hunt in packs and pursue big game such as moose, caribou, and all manner of large and small hoofed animals. Their technique is to pursue a herd until they find a young, disabled, or aging straggler and separate it from the rest. The pack separates once they have chosen a specific prey animal. Several of them chase it from behind, running alongside, snapping at its flanks. The luckless creature is chased and herded to the rest of the canine pack, which is waiting to attack from the front. The technique is effective but requires participation from the entire pack. It is one of several canine maneuvers that would be the envy of any military strategist. Hunting is an instinct performed with skill and zeal. It is what dogs do best . . . when they must.

Domestic dogs have few if any opportunities to express these instinctive behaviors. Like a dormant virus, the desire to hunt or defend territory lies in the canine mind waiting to be aroused by predetermined stimulation. What sets it in motion is never known and must be attributed to the dog's mystery. It could be a tug-of-war game in puppyhood or an early threat to a food bowl or a pain caused by something in motion. Once started, car chasing becomes a chronic habit that does not end on its own, not even when the dog becomes old. To that type of dog, cars resemble threatening intruders or big game just asking to be brought down. If only one could talk to a car-chasing dog and explain the futility and irrationality of his behavior to him. But a car in motion creates an electrochemical connection between him and the primitive dog trapped beneath his skin. When a domestic dog chases a car down the street it is like watching a shadow from his primitive past.

Reasons for the Problem

Chasing the Owner's Car.   Some dogs learn to chase cars by running after their owners. Being left behind can be frightening to some dogs, even if they are allowed to roam free. Not wanting to be left alone, they will chase the family car as it drives away. This eventually becomes a habit, and all cars are chased.

Lack of Exposure.   Many dogs are kept in the backyard or in the house and are never around street traffic. When they are exposed to it for the first time, they are often overwhelmed with fear and feel threatened by the moving vehicles. They will bark and move aggressively against one or more cars. The same can be true of bicycles, running children, or strangers on foot passing through a neighborhood.

Instinctive Behavior.   As discussed in "Origins of the Problem," chasing cars can be a manifestation of territorial behavior, hunting behavior, or herding instincts.

Hyperactivity.   A highly energetic, nervous, or high-strung dog with a great need to run will chase cars as an outlet for his energy.

Boredom.   If dogs are living out a monotonous routine, day after day, compounded by a lack of exercise and human contact, they might chase cars for relief.

Lack of a Leash.   In rural areas, suburban areas, and some cities, such as Los Angeles, dogs are rarely kept on leashes or confined in any way. They are given free run of their property, which to the dog includes the sidewalks and streets of his neighborhood. Their owners believe that all dogs should be allowed to roam freely, either because it is natural or because the owners feel protected that way. Unfortunately, permitting this gives the dogs every opportunity to become car chasers if they are so inclined, form neighborhood packs, and get themselves into all forms of trouble.

Solutions (Environmental)

Confine the Dog.   The dog cannot chase cars if you deny him access to the street or road. Build a *dog run* made of chain-link fence sitting on a slab of concrete or buy a portable *dog run* at a pet supply store, hardware store, or at a fence company. Be certain it has a gate that can be securely shut with a locking mechanism.

A tie-out stake will also confine the dog to your property (assuming he is not extremely powerful or obsessed). You can also use a clothesline run, which operates like an overhead trolley. Attach a clothesline 8 or 10 feet off the ground from the side of your house to a tree. Run the clothesline through the loop of a leash attached to your dog's leather or nylon collar. (Never use a slip collar or choke collar on the clothesline trolley.) Be sure the leash is long enough to allow him to lie down. The clothesline trolley will not stop a strong dog determined to get free. For those dogs, keeping them in a fenced-in area or indoors is the only way to prevent them from running out to the street in pursuit of cars.

Solutions (Reconditioning)

Correcting the Dog On-Leash.   A dog that has been obedience-trained should know the command "Heel." It is useful for reconditioning a car chaser. If you take the dog outside and walk with him in "Heel" you can administer a firm correction if he bolts toward a moving vehicle. Use the Margolis Maneuver (see part Two). Deliberately walk the dog around the edge of your property in the "Heel" command in anticipation of his going after a car. When he does, correct him with the Margolis Maneuver firmly and then praise him immediately afterward. Do this as often as necessary until he is no longer interested in chasing cars. The obedience commands "No" and "Come" are also valuable for ending this problem. If your trained dog responds to your commands (as he should), they may someday save his life.

The Long Line. If your dog has not been obedience-trained, you can change this behavior with the help of a long leash (or clothesline), about 15 to 30 feet in length, attached to his slip collar. Take the dog outdoors and expose him to the street traffic. If he goes for a car, allow him to run to the end of the line and then jerk it hard as you walk in the opposite direction. As you jerk the line shout "NO!" If you are hesitant about jerking the dog hard, bear in mind that if you do not end his car chasing, his life will always be in jeopardy. It is an extremely effective correction. If the dog is really a hard case you might consider tying the end of the line to a tree and walking away. When a car comes he will run for it as usual, but the line will stop him abruptly as he reaches your property line. He will in effect correct himself.

Boundary Training. It is possible to instill in your dog the idea that he is never allowed to go into the street. You do this by walking the dog around on a leash. Walk close to the curb with the street to your left,

Jerk the long line as hard as you can and shout "NO" in a harsh tone of voice.

and the dog on your left side. Place him on the street side so he can be tempted by cars and other distractions. Every time he attempts to step off the curb you say "NO" in a firm tone of voice. After several minutes slacken the leash and say, "OK," and lead the dog into the street, under your strict control. The idea is that he may never go into the street without your permission. Do this ten or fifteen minutes a day as often as you can. In one or two weeks the dog should understand what you want and comply.

Immediately following the correction, walk in the opposite direction. If you do not end the dog's car chasing, his life will always be in jeopardy.

You can reenforce boundary training by playing "fetch" with the dog outside your house. Attach the long clothesline to his slip collar and throw a ball, a stick, or a Frisbee to him. A tossed ball not only helps reenforce the concept but it lets you know how well your reconditioning is working. Establish a distance beyond which the dog may not go. The border surrounding your property is an ideal cutoff point. As he approaches the boundary line, correct him with a jerk, using the Margolis Maneuver and a firm "NO." Do not fail to praise the dog after each correction. It is an important part of the process. Afterward walk the dog around the boundary line and say "NO" whenever he steps past the line. If your "NO" is not effective, try a whistle or an aerosol can with a horn at the top. Compressed-air horns are extremely loud and are sure to stop the dog in his tracks. Continue these reconditioning sessions until you are satisfied the dog has mended his ways.

Reconditioning the Dog from the Car. You will need the help of two friends. One should drive the car slowly past your house while the other sits in the back seat with the window rolled down. When the dog begins chasing the car the person in the back seat corrects him with a severe blast from a compressed-air horn, popped balloons, or shake cans (see part Two) rattled loudly. The shake can may be thrown to the ground near the dog's feet to startle him (but never thrown at him).

Prevention Tips

Obedience Training. A trained dog can easily be taught not to go into the street. The commands of obedience training are useful for this purpose. They can be employed to teach boundary training as described above. This means the dog must never be allowed in the street unless he is attached to a leash and given your permission to be there.

Exercise. A potential car chaser may never develop the habit if he is given enough exercise to release his pent-up energy. A good run plus a game of "fetch" once or twice a day may do the trick.

Confinement. When confining the dog, be sure to lock both the front and rear gates. Gates with self-locking features close securely and are valuable preventive measures. Be certain that your fences are high enough and strong enough to keep him from jumping or digging his way out. Stretching tennis netting across a fence to block the dog's vision often works. If he doesn't see the movement of a car he may not respond to the sound it makes as it drives past.

Restricting a dog's movement must not be misconstrued as a violation of his natural state. The natural state for house dogs is to obey human commands, stay within the confines of the owner's property, and remain in a closed environment with the gate locked securely. Giving a dog the freedom to roam the neighborhood and chase cars, bicycles, and people is to make him a horrible element in everyone else's life. It also places the dog's life in danger from street traffic.

Nothing prevents the problem of car chasing as well as simply closing the gates. Make sure that you and everyone in the family, especially the children, remember. How can a confined dog chase anything?

CAR SICKNESS (MOTION SICKNESS)

There can be no mistaking this problem. If your dog experiences car sickness you will be the first to know. The signs of car sickness are drooling, nausea, and vomiting. A dog in this state shows uneasiness, yawning, and pleading looks bordering on despair. Car sickness is like seasickness. It upsets the dog and the occupants riding with him in the car.

Reasons for the Problem

Car Movement. Dogs experience motion sickness because of the abrupt or swinging motion of moving cars. It is similar to the forward and backward rocking motion of a boat as it also slides from side to side. When continued or repeated in short intervals, the motion will act on the acoustic nerves, which are two sensory nerves in the cranium. The sway of the car as it moves forward impairs the sense of balance in dogs, children, and some adults. Other contributing causes may be visual disorientation (when the scenery in the windows seems to be moving instead of the car), engine fumes, temperature (hot or cold), and a lack of ventilation. Most dogs feel the need to stand as they ride. But if the car is moving fast, it may be impossible to remain standing or even sitting. Determined dogs persist in trying to stand even when they cannot, and then suffer motion sickness.

Emotions. The excitement or fright of a first car ride may bring about motion sickness.

Inexperience. Lack of experience in cars can create anxiety resulting in nausea. There are dogs who never ride in cars or get into one only when going to the veterinarian or to a kennel. For such dogs the infrequent car ride can be a physical and emotional wrench.

Negative Associations. Many dogs expect something bad or painful with car riding. For some, the only time they ride in a car is when they are in stress. Trips to the veterinarian or a boarding kennel are perfect examples. If a dog experiences a traumatic event in a car, he will become upset when placed in one and then get carsick. Such events would include pain from sickness, injury, or physical abuse.

Solutions (Environmental)

The Dog Crate. Nothing solves the problem as well as a dog crate, described on page 73. Dogs in crates are less likely to experience motion sickness because they cannot slide or fall very much. The sense of security offered by a dog crate has a calming effect, removing the emotional aspect of car sickness. Dogs are more likely to keep their sight on the horizon, which helps them maintain balance and orientation.

The Harness. A dog harness looks like an elaborate leather collar, except that it does not fit around the neck. The front paws and head are slipped through the harness, which is secured around the upper torso with one or two buckles. It is then possible to slide a seatbelt through the top or the bottom of the harness, securing the dog in place and restraining him for the duration of the trip.

There are harnesses designed for auto travel made of nylon, using Velcro fasteners instead of metal buckles, designed for auto travel. Check the ads in the various dog magazines.

Solutions (Reconditioning)

Creating a Pleasant Association. If given half the chance, most dogs become deliriously happy when riding in a car. It is a stimulating opportunity to share an experience with the family. There are dogs who leap with joy when their owners say, "Let's take a ride." They do not get carsick and they do not sink into the depths of depression and despair. Those who do have never been properly introduced to the doggish art of motoring. The following procedure applies to young puppies who have little or no car experience and to dogs of all ages who have a motion-sickness problem.

A dog who often suffers from motion sickness will definitely vomit in the car if he is fed before a trip. This is especially true of dogs with a predisposition toward gastrointestinal ailments. A puppy should have his last meal the night before his car session. Begin early in the morning and then feed him afterward. He will consider his meal a reward for behaving in the car properly. A grown dog should not be fed for eight to ten hours before his reconditioning in the car. Always consider a dog's feeding schedule when taking him in a car. When the reconditioning technique is employed, the puppy or grown dog may get nervous or sick. If he does, stop the car, turn off the engine. Tell him he is a good boy and give him as much verbal reassurance as possible. The key to success with the following reconditioning

technique is establishing a happy, verbal communication with the dog.

The objective is to get the dog to enjoy car riding and believe it is a wonderful thing to do. Place the leash and slip collar on him. Take out your car keys and jingle them while beginning a happy patter of talk that not only gets the dog's attention but also his interest and enthusiasm. The jingling of the keys should become an introductory sound that begins the pleasant association of riding in a car. Open the door and entice the dog to walk in with you, allowing him to hop onto the back seat. If he is too small, lift him in. Sit with him. The doors may be left open if there is no traffic danger. Allow the dog to examine and sniff all he wants. Talk to him, pet him, praise him. Give him a toy, a bone or even a tidbit. If he wants to leave the car, let him do it (maintaining some semblance of leash control). Try to steer him back into the car gently with the leash and praise him every time he returns. Attract him into the car with your voice. Do this many times each session and conduct several sessions a day.

Once the dog is comfortably seated in the back leave him and move to the front. Start the engine. As you do, turn to the back and talk to him. Tell him what a good boy he is and pet him. Build his enthusiasm and excitement with the tone of your voice and the touch of your hands. Turn off the engine. Praise the dog and pet him. Turn on the engine. Praise the dog and pet him. Do this five or ten times.

Take hold of the leash and walk the dog out of the car, talking to him all the time. Allow him to relieve himself, and then steer him back inside. Place him in the back seat and sit with him for a short time. Move to the front seat and start the engine as you keep talking, praising, and petting. Slowly drive off. Although you must not take your eyes off the road, continue to praise the dog, making the ride something special for him. Drive around the block and return home. Park and lavish praise and petting on the dog. Talking to him is the most important aspect of this reconditioning process. It not only reassures the dog about his relationship with you but helps create a pleasant association with car riding.

Prevention Tips

Early Indoctrination. Introduce the techniques described above in "Solutions (Reconditioning)" to a puppy at the earliest age possible.

Feeding. You can prevent a dog from getting sick in your car by not feeding him for a good many hours before a trip. When going to get a new puppy, call the breeder and ask him or her not to feed the dog that day.

Keep Him Happy. Always make the car experience a pleasant one.

Secure the Dog. Use a dog crate or a harness.

Medical Help. The symptoms of motion sickness can be prevented with various drugs and tranquilizers, but these only put off the need to condition the dog positively. Tranquilizers tend to calm a dog (or make him drowsy) if prescribed by a veterinarian in the proper dosage. If the dose is too great for the dog's body mass, he will become woozy, as if drunk, and become disoriented. An overdose of such medication can be dangerous. Never give your dog tranquilizers meant for humans. Because some dogs may suffer a severe weight loss after a long trip, it is advisable to consult a veterinarian about using medications. Never use them without first talking to your vet.

CHEWING

Chewing should be called the "Surprise Problem." When walking into your home and looking at your destroyed furniture, shredded clothing and gnawed appliances, you'll swear you heard someone shout, "Surprise!" just before you fainted. Even when you are revived and the ringing in your ears subsides, it will take some time to recover from the shock that such a sweet adolescent dog, the one whose head cocks to the side so cutely when you talk to him, could have devastated all your personal possessions. It is only funny when discussing *someone else's* little Genghis Khan. There is no humor to be found when discovering that your dog has devoured the baseboards in your house along with half a wall. It is a surprise lying in wait for most novice dog owners. Curiously, many experienced dog owners are caught unaware, too, by a dog that eats wall-to-wall carpeting and the legs off Queen Anne furniture. All dogs chew when they're young.

Origins of the Problem

To understand why dogs chew destructively, you must first understand the concept of behavioral patterns and systems. According to the psychologists and animal researchers Dr. John Paul Scott and Dr. John L. Fuller, in their book *Dog Behavior: The Genetic Basis,* canine behavior patterns fall into nine groups, each one being a complete "behavioral system" containing many behavioral patterns serving some function in the life of a dog (or wolf). The nine groups, or "systems," are sexual behavior, eliminative behavior, epimeletic behavior, et-epimeletic behavior, ingestive behavior, shelter-seeking behavior, allelomimetic behavior, agonistic behavior, and investigatory behavior.

When performing a function, all dogs must use an entire series of behaviors to complete it. This series is called a behavioral pattern. To eat, a dog must lap, chew, swallow, gnaw, and possibly hold his food with his paws. His tail may go out or down. His feet and head may assume a specific position. Each behavior pattern within a system is a separate set of behaviors and has a different function, but they all have a common general function and bear a loose relationship to each other. Destructive chewing is an activity that represents behavior patterns from more than one system.

Because chewing is an activity closely associated with eating, the *ingestive behavior system* is involved. This system includes chewing and swallowing, lapping, gnawing, holding food with paws, eating grass, sucking, pushing with the head, alternately pushing with the forepaws, and pushing with the hind feet.

Physiologically, dogs are meant to live the lives of hunters existing on a diet of meat from prey animals. In the wild, dogs and wolves cannot eat (exercise their ingestive behavior system) unless they catch something to eat. That means engaging their *agonistic behavior system,* which is a set of responses involving conflict with another animal. Hunting, for example, involves agonistic behavior. The system includes chas-ing, biting, snapping, pawing, snarling, growling, barking, playful fighting, pouncing, springing, tossing (small game into the air), and herding. Logically, these two systems relate to each other in bringing needed nutrition into the dog's body. It appears that both systems are involved in chewing behavior. But so are others.

Epimeletic behavior is the giving of care and attention to puppies and some self-care. It involves shelter building, turning around before lying down, digging, scratching (self), rubbing, biting fur, shaking, bringing food, and caring for puppies in general. Some forms of epimeletic behavior always accompany chewing behavior and also cause great damage to human possessions. Digging may be employed, or pawing carpets, wood floors, and furniture. Dogs in a state of stress will respond in this way, not because they intend to damage their owner's home but because it is their only way of dealing with their inner condition.

Et-epimeletic behavior is a system of seeking care that puppies and stressed dogs use to satisfy their needs. It involves whining, yelping, tail wagging, licking the face or hands of a person, and touching with paws. Sometimes these behaviors accompany destructive chewing.

Dogs (and wolves) are highly social animals. It is emotionally and physically stressful for them, especially when they are puppies or adolescents, to spend long periods alone. In most cases, destructive chewing happens when young dogs (or adult dogs who have developed this behavior as a habit) are left alone. It is a rare dog that chews in front of his family. When destructive chewing is a symptom of emotional stress, it is one way a dog has to express his intense feelings and ease them.

Dogs do not behave this way to anger their families or damage their homes deliberately. It is not abnormal or illogical dog behavior. On the contrary, it makes sense for dogs to chew (whatever is available) when they are in a state of anxiety, fear, frustration, or loneliness. Ingestive behavior (chewing, licking), et-epimeletic behavior (whining), epimeletic behavior (digging, rubbing, shaking), and agonistic behavior (biting, pawing, pouncing) are all responses to the dog's emotional needs. Chewing probably makes them feel better. They do it because they have a need to do it. It is their nature.

Reasons for the Problem

Puppyhood. All puppies, like all babies, are born without teeth. Within three weeks puppies grow their first set, which are called *milk teeth* or *deciduous teeth*. There are 28 of them. In the third month, these start dropping off and in most dogs are replaced with 42 permanent teeth. This process can take seven months and is called *teething*. Baby teeth fall out or are absorbed by the larger, permanent teeth, which as they erupt from the gums cause soreness, itching, and some drooling. The molars, found in the rear of the mouth, are the last to come in and can be the most troublesome. Occasionally, the milk teeth do not drop out, the permanent teeth grow in out of alignment, and there are dental problems. This process contributes to a puppy or adolescent dog's need to chew.

During the teething period, chewing alleviates the dog's discomfort and pain. Puppies will chew anything, including boards, fingers, couches, furniture, shoes, and socks. Chewing because of teething and early dental problems can continue for two years.

Improper Confinement. A dog shut away behind a closed door, left alone, will chew as a means of escaping. He will gnaw away at the bottom of a door, the baseboards, or the wall itself. Because dogs are social creatures it takes time for them to adjust to being left alone. During this period of adjustment they may become anxiety-ridden or frustrated and chew to alleviate their emotional state.

Diet. Destructive chewing can be an expression of hunger or an imbalance in the diet. Canine nutrition involves a specific amount of protein, fat, carbohydrates, vitamins, and minerals blended in a complex set of proportions. These are necessary to meet the need for calories and to build and maintain good health. When elements of nutrition are missing, any number of diseases can begin. Chewing behavior can be the first sign.

Lack of Exercise. Certain breeds require much more exercise than others. Hunting breeds, hound breeds, dogs of great energy like the terriers and working breeds need to run, jump, and play. Some dogs will chew any object available if left behind in a small apartment for nine to ten hours a day while their owners go off to work. If they are not getting enough exercise before the owners leave and they do not live in a fenced-in yard, they may chew because they are frustrated. They must have some way to burn off their vigor. Chewing alleviates some of this need.

Personality. No matter what the breed, some individual dogs are nervous or excitable and express their emotions by chewing.

Fear. When a dog becomes frightened, he can chew as a displacement behavior. Displacement is an unconscious defense mechanism that transfers emotional reactions from one object to another. It is a way of discharging tension. Outside noises such as sirens, backfires, or people shouting can cause a dog to panic and then chew to alleviate fear. Something inside the home can also set it off.

Anxiety. There are significant differences between fear and anxiety, although both are emotional states that are often expressed by destructive chewing. Fear is a response to a direct, external danger such as a loud noise or a physical attack. Anxiety comes from an internal, unrecognized source of danger such as frustration, competition, or immediate associations with painful past experiences. A *frightened* dog may run away from the source of fear or stay and fight it. An anxiety-ridden dog may simply mope about in depression or experience feelings of dread or apprehension. Anxiety is the worse of the two conditions because the danger is hidden and therefore less solvable by the dog. Both states create physical reactions, including accelerated heartbeat, rapid breathing, muscular tension, and other danger-related responses.

Anxiety is a slow, worried condition that comes from such sources as a change of environment, change in daily routine, prolonged confinement, improper confinement, or mounting tension. This is a major reason for chewing behavior.

Boredom. Dogs will chew objects until they are destroyed when there is a lack of mental and physical stimulation in their

Gaines Dog Care Center

lives. Boredom is a mental and emotional condition that tires a dog with a dull, tedious routine and is the result of human neglect.

Frustration. If a dog wants to fulfill a need such as getting to another dog he hears outside his home and is blocked by a barrier, he will experience the mounting tension brought about by frustration. This can cause him to chew. He will chew first to effect an escape. When that fails, he will continue to chew to relieve his feelings of frustration. When a dog is frustrated it means that he has been stopped from gratifying a strong need or desire. The consequences can be any number of undesirable actions, including destructive chewing.

Teaching a Puppy to Chew the Wrong Things. Unfortunately, new dog owners (and some who should know better) give puppies various inappropriate objects to play with and chew on. The most common is an old tennis shoe or bedroom slipper. Socks, pot holders (watch out for ingested asbestos), towels, and used clothing are all items unwisely given to young dogs as playthings. Because he is teething or playing, the little dog will chew on the object as a puppy and develop the habit of going for another version of the same item when he is older. People theorize that if a dog is given an old shoe he will not chew a new one. But a dog has no way of distinguishing between Charles Jordan and Adler shoes. New, old, expensive, cheap — a shoe is a shoe for all that and tastes mighty good to the munching puppy.

Solutions (Environmental)

Proper Confinement. New puppies and dogs with chewing problems are either given the run of the house when no one is home or shut away in a small room, behind a closed door. Neither of these solutions helps solve a chewing problem, and both can create even greater problems. These are environmental mistakes.

Proper confinement is an important part of solving a dog's chewing problem. *However, this environmental solution must be used with the reconditioning solution.* Puppies and adult dogs with a chewing problem must be confined in one space when they are left alone until the problem of chewing no longer exists. A medium-sized kitchen or a large-sized bathroom is ideal. If puppies or adult dogs are left alone in a room with a closed door, they feel as if they have been locked out of their home. Such dogs become

insecure, and the chewing syndrome begins. Chewing in this instance is an attempt to escape.

When confining a puppy or a grown dog, do not use a closed door to keep him in the room. Buy a puppy gate. There are many types available at hardware or pet supply stores. The best type is a removable gate, sometimes called a pressure gate, made of metal or plastic, that jams against both ends of a doorway. It allows the dog to see the rest of the house but prevents him from entering it and chewing up the furniture. Just being able to see out of the room keeps him from becoming anxious or frustrated. *The dog must remain in his confined space when there is no one home to keep an eye on him.* Give him the run of the house whenever someone is home.

Clothesline Trolley. There are other ways to confine a dog when you are not home. If you have an outdoor area that is not fenced in, create a clothesline trolley. Attach a clothesline eight or ten feet off the ground from the side of your house to a tree. Run the clothesline through the loop of a leash. Be sure the leash is long enough to allow the dog to lie down. Never use a slip collar or any other training equipment with an overhead line. This homemade device allows the dog to run back and forth but keeps him confined.

Tie-Out Stake. Another way to confine an outdoor dog is to use a tie-out stake, which is a device that screws deep into the ground. Attach one end of a chain or strong rope to the dog's *leather* collar and the other end to the metal top of the tie-out stake. Most of these stakes work on a swivel, giving the dog the ability to move around without twisting the tether. His movements are limited by the length of the chain.

Dog Run.   You may also confine a dog outdoors with a portable chain-link-fence dog run, which can be installed anywhere around your house. It is a high-quality piece of equipment available from mail-order catalogues, pet supply outlets, and fence companies.

Some apartment dwellers are fortunate enough to have a balcony or patio that makes an excellent confinement area during the day. When using a balcony or patio, be certain the dog cannot jump off or get out in any way. You may have to use chicken wire to prevent the dog from slipping through the balcony railings, bars, or other types of opening.

Familiar Sounds.   When leaving the dog alone in the house, turn on a radio and play it softly. Music and talk shows can have two effects: first, they are soothing; second, they are associated with your presence and may give the impression that you are somewhere about. You might even experiment with a video tape recorder. Video tapes can run from two to eight hours. Seeing your image or hearing your voice might keep your dog from chewing.

Solutions (Reconditioning)

Supply Acceptable Chewables.   Small puppies have a need to chew throughout their first year. There is no escaping this form of behavior. The trick, to avoid damage and destruction to property and personal possessions, is accomplished by controlling what the little dog is allowed to chew. Give your puppy the following chewables: rawhide toys, Nilabones and hard-rubber toys with no squeakers or bells in them.

The most inexpensive chew toy you can give a puppy is also therapeutic for his sore gums. Take six washcloths, soak them in cold water, twist them, and put them in the freezer. When they are frozen, give them to the puppy one at a time. Each one will stay cold for about one and a half hours. As he chews each one, the coldness will numb his gums and ease the pain of teething.

Adjust the Diet.   Be certain your dog's diet is adequate and properly balanced. Consult a veterinarian or feed the dog a high-quality commercial dog food that is complete and balanced. Read the label. Chewing behavior is sometimes related to inadequate nutrition.

If your dog does not eat an adequate ration he may be sick, he may dislike his food, or his feeding schedule may not be the right one for him. Have him examined by a vet. Experiment with various commercial dog foods. Try a self-feeding (ad-lib.) program. If a dog eats when he wants to, he usually matches his food intake with his energy and growth needs. Letting him do this removes the guesswork. To let a dog self-feed you simply fill a bowl with high-quality cereal-type dog food and make it available twenty-four hours a day, along with a bowl of water. When the food runs out, fill the bowl. Rarely does a dog on a self-feeding program overeat. Having food available to your dog all day long could make the difference between chewing and not chewing.

Exercise.   There are dogs that have chewing problems because of inadequate exercise. This is usually the problem for city dogs whose owners leave for work early in the morning and do not get home until the evening. The solution is to arise earlier than usual each morning and give the dog a long walk, a run, and a play period with a ball or a Frisbee. A fifteen-minute play period can be very important to a dog. Exercise him again when you come home from work. If this is not possible, then hire someone to come to your home in the middle of the day and give the dog a long walk. There are always willing teenagers who want to earn a few dollars a week. Dog walking has become a business in some communities. Such services can be found in the *Yellow Pages* under "Pets." Just thirty minutes of attention each morning can make the difference between ending a chewing problem and sustaining thousands of dollars worth of damage to your home.

Obedience Training.

If your dog is obedience-trained, practice every morning all the commands he has been taught. Emphasize the "Heel" and "Come when called" commands. Running through an obedience session each morning gives the dog a form of personal attention and exercise that is physically and mentally beneficial.

The command "Place" is good for helping to solve a chewing problem. If the dog must be alone much of the day give him the "Place" command before leaving the house for work. It will help him establish his own area where he can feel comfortable during the long day by himself. Although no dog is going to remain in one spot for eight hours, having a "Place" of his own can help avoid the anxiety associated with being alone. An untrained dog does not understand right from wrong. An obedience-trained dog has had his mind and body structured and conditioned, so that chewing problems are easier to solve. Training gives you tools to correct the dog. It gives the dog an understanding of what to expect. You are accepted as his pack leader and the one with control over his behavior.

Bad Taste.

An effective method of getting the dog to stop chewing your possessions is to make them taste unpleasant. There are commercial sprays available for this purpose or home-made aversion substances to use. The most effective of these products is Bitter Apple. But you can use Tabasco sauce, red pepper, Chinese mustard, alcohol, or vinegar (sprayed from a bottle). They should keep some dogs away from the household items they love to chew. A most effective home-made mixture is a paste made of alum powder and water. Spread it over the dog's favorite chewing objects, such as the leg of a table or the end of a carpet. Alum is extremely bitter and has a puckering effect on the sensitive tissues inside the mouth. Use this paste sparingly to avoid upsetting the dog's stomach. Reapply the alum every two days until the problem has stopped.

Here is an effective way to use the bad-taste aversion technique. If the dog has a taste for books or record albums bait an expendable one. Smear it with any of the bad-taste substances such as Bitter Apple, alum paste, or Tabasco sauce. Leave it where the dog can find it easily but in the general locale of the books or records. Go away from the house for at least an hour. If he chews, licks, or even smells the object, he is not going to like it. There may be some damage to the book, but not much. On the next day bait the same book again and leave it in the same place next to an unbaited book. With luck, the dog will not chew either of them. On the third day, leave two or three books in the same place but do not bait any of them. The dog should now be conditioned to believe that all books taste bad. You can use this technique on just about any object that your dog likes to chew.

Mousetrap Method. If your dog's favorite chewing object is the arm of a couch or an upholstered chair and he must hop up to get to it, try this reconditioner. Set four or five small-size, spring-snap mousetraps on the couch. Hide them with a thick layer of newspapers, taped to the couch. Be careful not to set them off. Leave the house. The dog will probably hop onto the couch and set off the traps beneath the paper so that the penetrating sound along with the vibrations will startle him. Do this several times. It should create an aversion to going near the offending piece of furniture. To complete the lesson, have a chew toy strategically placed in his bed or corner of the room.

Balloon Method. Another aversion technique is the balloon method. Blow up two balloons with as much air as they will hold. Pop them with a pin close to the dog so that he is startled. Do it once again one half hour later. If the dog was startled, blow up several more balloons and tape them to the area he likes to chew. It should keep him away. There is a danger of the dog's popping the balloons and swallowing the rubber, which can be harmful to his system. Do not use this technique if you think *your* dog might chew and then swallow the broken balloons. Do not use this technique unless the dog has a

chewing problem. It is not meant to be a preventive measure.

Shake Can Method. Place shake cans all around your house, especially in the areas where your dog chews your possessions. (See part Two, "Some Essential Tools and Techniques for Problem Solving.") If you can catch him in the act of chewing, rattle the closest shake can loudly and shout, "NO! NO! NO!" Remember, the idea is to create an aversion to the object he is chewing. It's not supposed to be pleasant. Praise him the instant he stops chewing and give him something acceptable to chew like a rawhide bone or an ice cube. Once he takes it in his mouth praise him again. What you are doing here is correcting him for chewing the bad thing and rewarding him for chewing the good thing. It is the basic teaching principle for all animal training and reconditioning.

The Margolis Maneuver. WHEN ALL ELSE FAILS. Of all the aversion techniques, this is the *most* effective but also requires the most time and trouble. It demands your being able to catch the dog in the act of chewing and correcting him with a firm jerk of the leash as described in part Two, "Some Essential Tools and Techniques for Problem Solving."

Days before the technique is to be used, drill a hole in the door closest to the area where the dog does his damage. Install a glass peephole device, sold in all hardware stores. You must be able to observe the dog without his knowing you are there. Also buy a spray can of room deodorizer.

On the day of the lesson leave your home as you always do. The dog must remain behind with one other person. Say good-bye and go through your usual routine of leaving. Shortly after you have left, the other person should place the slip collar and leash on the dog and take him out for a walk. After they have left, return to the house. Spray the outside of the peephole door with the room deodorizer so that your presence cannot be detected. In an area that can be observed from the peephole, leave an object that you know the dog will chew. Go into the next room, close the door behind you, and wait. By prearrangement, the other person and the dog should return in a matter of minutes. The other person must leave the slip collar and leash on the dog. He or she says goodbye to the dog and leaves. When you hear the door close go to the peephole and watch. Be patient. It may take an hour but eventually a chronic chewer will go to work on the object you left as bait. Let him get involved in chewing for at least two or three minutes. Then burst open the door. Shout, "NO! NO! NO! NO!" Grab the leash with both hands and administer the Margolis Maneuver, jerking the leash. Immediately after the correction, praise him in a loving way. Let him know you are still friends, and give him a chew toy, a rawhide bone or an ice cube. Get him to take it in his mouth. When he does, lavish him with praise.

Destructive chewing is a problem that causes dogs to lose their homes. Once a dog has lost his original home, his future is uncertain. If this technique is all that you have left to try, please remember you may be saving the dog's life by doing it. Do it for the dog as well as yourself.

Prevention Tips

Puppy Gate. Confine the dog behind a gate that allows him to see into the rest of the house. Being able to look into the other rooms will make him less likely to try chewing his way out.

Chew Toys. Keep the dog occupied with plenty of toys that can be chewed when you are not home. Rawhide bones, Nilabones, ice cubes, frozen washcloths, and hard-rubber balls are ideal along with anything recommended by a veterinarian or dog breeder. Pet supply stores offer a wide variety of manufactured toys. Look for those made of solid,

Chew toys are important for preventing chewing problems. Unless you allow the dog to have his own couch (some owners do) it is best to teach your dog to keep off. See "Jumping on Furniture," page 124.

hard rubber. They are best. Do not give your dog a chew toy that resembles any real object in your house such as a shoe, a sock, or a pork chop.

Exercise. Take the dog out for as long as you can before leaving him alone. Help him expend his excess energy.

Keep the Dog Outdoors. Chain-link dog runs (permanent or portable) keep the dog confined to your property but allow him the pleasure of being outdoors in the sun, getting exercise when you are not home. A clothesline trolley, as mentioned earlier, serves the same purpose, as does a tie-out stake.

Monitor His Early Behavior. Never encourage a puppy to chew an object other than a chew toy, a frozen washcloth, or an ice cube. If he nibbles on a shoe or nips anyone's finger, correct him firmly by saying "NO" in a harsh tone of voice. If he is big enough, use the Margolis Maneuver. Do not play tug-of-war games or any other games involving his teeth.

COPROPHAGY (EATING STOOLS)

Many dogs will eat their own stool or that of another animal if given an opportunity. The habit is more prevalent among hunting, working, and herding breeds. All stools contain some unabsorbed nutrients and digestive enzymes, making them appealing to dogs as food. It is likely that every dog has indulged in this vice at least once in his life. Coprophagy (pronounced: cop-Roff-a-jee) is not known to cause disease when the dog ingests his own stool. However, the possibility of infection does exist when a dog ingests the stool of another animal because he becomes vulnerable to harmful bacteria, viruses, and internal parasites and the various diseases caused by them. The idea of coprophagy is revolting to humans and can seriously alter their attitude toward dogs in general and their own dog in particular. This problem is both unesthetic and unhealthy. It is best to solve it as quickly as possible.

Origins of the Problem

One possible explanation for coprophagy lies in the maternal behavior of dogs toward newborn puppies. During the first three weeks of nursing it is an instinctive objective of the mother to keep her nest free of urine and defecation. It is assumed that the purpose is to prevent detection from predators. Because the motor capacities of newborn puppies are not well enough developed to allow them to eliminate waste from their bodies, it is accomplished by the mother. The process of elimination is stimulated by the mother's licking of the stomachs and lower areas of the puppies. She continues to lick them until they are clean of all urine and defecation. It is the only way the nest can remain free of their waste matter. By three weeks of age, the puppies are able to stand, crawl, see, and hear. They begin to leave the nest independently and eliminate elsewhere. It is possible that the tendency toward coprophagy is a behavior connected to maternal care that exists in both male and female dogs.

Another possible explanation for coprophagy may be found in maternal feeding behavior. During the first three weeks of life puppies nurse from their mother's teats. Her milk is their primary source of nutrition.

After the third week the mother leaves the nest for long periods, and when she returns she initiates the weaning process. She discourages the puppies from drawing milk from her teats and teaches them to eat solid food. This is accomplished by vomiting into the nest a recent meal, which is meant for the litter to eat. It is in this manner that puppies make the transition from maternal milk to solid food. They eat with relish the meal that the mother provides in addition to water or milk when she makes it available. Weaning is a transitional process from milk to solid food that lasts from one to three weeks depending on the size of the litter, the condition of the mother, and whether there is human help.

Although it is only an unproven conclusion, it is possible that the habit of coprophagy is linked to the puppy behavior involved during the weaning process. Eating partially digested food from a nursing mother must firmly set in a puppy's mind the desirability of food that has already entered and left the body. That would make coprophagy a learned behavior. It is also possible that grown dogs who eat stools find some comforting throwback to the memory of puppyhood through this behavior. Many of the dogs involved with coprophagy are submissive, timid, or extremely playful, indicating a lack of maturity.

Reasons for the Problem

Food Intake. A hungry dog given access to its stool will develop the habit of coprophagy. Dogs who spend most of their time outdoors are the most likely candidates. The same is true if the dog's ration is somehow incomplete, lacking in some of the important

nutrients. Some researchers have theorized that some cases of coprophagy are caused by an enzyme deficiency. Others believe it can be caused by vitamin and mineral deficiencies.

Another diet-related reason can be overfeeding. If a dog is eating more than he can metabolize or digest, his stool will contain a larger quantity than usual of unprocessed nutrients, making the stool seem more like food. Overfed dogs can also become obsessed with eating as a form of behavior and satisfy themselves with stools containing undigested food.

Parasites. A dog infected with internal parasites (roundworm, hookworm, whipworm, tapeworm) will experience some nutritional deficiency. As a result, such dogs, especially puppies, will eat their own stools.

Reaction to Punishment. Dogs who have been severely punished for housebreaking mistakes may eat their stools as a way of hiding the evidence.

Boredom. Dogs who spend a large part of the day alone, especially outdoors, may play with their stools and eventually eat them. It is also true of dogs who receive little human attention.

Breed Characteristics. Various hunting breeds, particularly retrievers, will become involved with their own stools as a means of relieving the need to do the tasks inherent to hunting, such as carrying things in their mouths.

Poor Hygiene. Improper kennel management will help start this habit. If the stools are not removed quickly, the dog is given the opportunity to become involved with them.

Emotions. Coprophagy can be a response to emotional stress. Lonely or frightened dogs may develop this behavior. If a dog is given excessive attention and "babying," he may experience a severe emotional letdown when left alone. Coprophagy could be the result of separation anxiety.

Solutions (Environmental)

Making the stool taste bad. By mixing something with the dog's food it is possible to alter the taste of the feces. This often solves the problem of coprophagy as a self-correcting technique. Glutamic acid added to the dog's ration will change the flavor of the feces and has been recommended by veterinarians. Other additives to the dog's food recommended by veterinarians are various meat-tenderizing products (unseasoned), monosodium glutamate (MSG), oil of anise, and sauerkraut. There is a commercially prepared product for this purpose called Forbid. Whenever you add something to your dog's diet it is wise to consult your veterinarian to be sure it is not harmful.

Solutions (Reconditioning)

Relieving Boredom. There are many ways to enrich a dog's day. Exercising the dog before and after he is left alone can be a good tonic. Spend more time with the dog and relate to him with affection. Establish play times. Get him chew toys, rawhide bones, Nilabones, or a hard-rubber ball. Take him out with you as often as possible. There are many errands on which the dog could accompany you. It is essential for his mental health and happiness to meet

people and see new places. A happy, stimulated dog may forget the nasty vice of coprophagy.

Corrections. You may wish to recondition the dog by correcting him with the Margolis Maneuver or with the help of the shake can. (See part Two, "Some Essential Tools and Techniques for Problem Solving.") Put his leash and slip collar on him before leaving him in the area where his habit is indulged. Watch him without his being aware of your presence. When he begins to get involved with his stool, rush out and correct him, using the Margolis Maneuver or a shake can. You must shout, "NO! NO! NO!" Praise the dog the instant he stops what he is doing. He must never feel that his relationship with his owner has been impaired.

Prevention Tips

Maintain Good Hygienic Practices. Clean all stools from the kennel or yard as quickly as possible.

Assure Proper Diet. Consult your veterinarian about a complete and balanced diet for your dog. Feed your dog a good quality diet, nutritionally adequate for his specific age and life-style.

Housebreak Rather Than Paper-Train Him. If you paper-train your dog, his stools will be left on the papers for a given amount of time. You may prevent coprophagy from developing as a habit by housebreaking the dog, which means that he urinates and defecates outside the house at an established location. In many communities a dog's feces must be cleaned off the street by the owner immediately, and their absence totally eliminates the problem.

Have Regular Veterinary Check-Ups.
Frequent examinations by a veterinarian can
help. Insist on stool analysis for internal
parasites (worms). Always bring a stool
sample to the veterinarian's office for that
purpose.

DIGGING (IN THE YARD)

A dog's digging holes in a lawn or backyard
is a problem dog owners living in a house
face. Few if any apartment dwellers have experienced the frustration and rage created
by finding their lawns or gardens ruined
with a series of potholes dug by the family
dog. Coming home to D-Day in your backyard is an aggravating experience. The problem must be solved quickly, before the local
block association gets up a petition.

Origins of the Problem

Wolves and wild dogs have a shelter-
building pattern of behavior that can be seen
in domestic dogs when they dig up their
yards. These shelters or dens are primarily
used as nesting places for pregnant females
who are close to whelping a litter of cubs or
pups. The den is where the litter will be born
and then reared for the first three to twelve
weeks of life. The nest is usually located
near the route of travel through pack territory. It may be established within a soft
stone bluff or under a shelf of rocks to give a
commanding view of the surrounding area.
Sometimes a hollowed log becomes the nest,
sometimes an existing rabbit or badger hole,
or a fresh hole dug by the female with some
help from the male.

Some wolves dig several nests besides the
one to be first occupied. These may be five to

*Digging behavior is natural for most dogs.
Once it begins, it is difficult to stop.*

ten miles or less than several yards apart,
with more than one entrance to each one.
The holes are large enough for the adults to
ease in and out but never large enough to
permit entrance when the animal is standing
upright. It must crawl to get into the nest or
den. Wolves and wild dogs have been known
to dig tunnels as long as thirty feet from the
entrance. The dirt is flung in one direction
with their forepaws when they dig their den
holes, and a mound is formed. Because
wolves and wild dogs have one litter a year,
the holes are dug in early spring when the
female gets ready to whelp.

The digging behavior of wild canids (dogs
and doglike animals) is also related to marking territory shortly after defecation. Unlike
cats, the dog does *not* do this to bury the
feces but to scratch a visual signature on the
ground for all to see.

Wolves, wild dogs, and domestic dogs all
bury food by digging into a soft surface. In
the wild it is buried around the den to pro-

vide a food reserve for the pups when they are born. During cold weather hungry animals such as the various meat-eaters, and birds as well, cannot get at their supply.

Reasons for the Problem

Temperature. Dogs will dig holes to get into them and cool off when the weather is hot. Some of the northern breeds, such as the Siberian Husky and the Samoyed, will dig holes to keep warm. The reason can be determined by the climate, your area of the country, and the time of year when the digging happens.

Dog Breed. All dogs will dig if given the opportunity, although there are some breeds that tend to do it more than others. They are most of the breeds from the Sporting Group, the Hound Group, the Terriers, and some of the Working Group. Breeds most noted for digging are the Siberian Husky, Alaskan Malamute, Samoyed, Fox Terrier, Airedale, Cairn Terrier. Afghan Hound, Dachshund, Weimaraner, Golden Retriever, Labrador Retriever, Cocker Spaniel, and Doberman Pinscher.

Nervous Energy. Nervous, high-strung dogs have excess energy and will dig from frustration and boredom.

Scent Chasing. Dogs left to their own devices in a backyard or lawn will become attracted to smells that indicate something lies just beneath the surface. They may smell a gopher, a buried bone, or even fertilizer. The scent stimulates their curiosity, their hunting instinct, or simply their hunger and starts them digging.

Burying Feces. Dogs may dig holes in which to bury their stools.

Creating a Den. Digging a hole may be for the purpose of creating a den. If the dog does not have a cool, shady resting place, he may dig one. It is instinctual to create a den as the core area of a territory.

Burying Bones. Cartoons, stories, television, and movies all show dogs obsessed with burying their treasured bones. Although fiction exaggerates, some dogs do become obsessed with this activity in reality. It is behavior based on the instinct to create a food reserve for the expectant mother and for times when food becomes scarce. When dogs are permitted this behavior, it can become generalized and habitual with no meaning or purpose.

Lack of Exercise. Dogs that are never given the opportunity to expend their excess energy may express this need by digging.

Attraction to Plants, Flowers, and Vegetables. The odors coming from the various plant growths around your house can be compelling to your dog and trigger the desire to dig in them.

Solutions (Environmental)

A Doghouse. Sometimes the simplest solutions are the most effective. If your dog digs up the yard because he needs a den or a cool place to rest, build him a doghouse or buy one from a hardware store or pet supply outlet.

A Dog Run. For the same reason build a dog run made of chain-link fence resting on a slab of cement. You can buy a portable chain-link fence from a pet supply outlet, a hardware store, or a fence company. This will satisfy the dog's denning instinct and at the same time prevent the digging.

A Wading Pool. If your dog digs up the yard to create a cool place for himself during the hot months, get him a child's wading pool. The small plastic container is just the right size for any dog to lie in the water and cool himself. Most breeds love to splash around in water, although some do not.

Get Rid of Gophers. If a dog digs up the ground because he is after gophers, then the best course would be to get rid of them. Hardware stores have many commercial products designed to end gopher problems. Be sure to keep the dog away if you use any poison or devices that could hurt him.

The Whole Hole. There are dogs that dig one hole and just keep redigging it and there are those that dig many holes. If there is more than one hole, fill them with the same dirt, packing it down tightly with a shovel, but do not put dirt in his favorite. Fill it with water and keep filling it at every opportunity. Most dogs do not like that and get discouraged. They do not like getting their feet wet. Some breeds, such as the Golden Retriever or Labrador Retriever will love the water, but most will not. Try another solution for water-loving dogs.

Between a Rock and a Hard Place. Place a large rock in your dog's favorite hole. Pack it loosely with dirt. (All other holes should be filled in and packed tightly with a shovel.) When he begins digging again the rock will have a built-in correction waiting for his paws and will discourage him. A variation of

A rock in his hole plus a chicken wire covering offer a built-in correction when he digs again.

Hitting a hard surface when digging is very discouraging.

this technique is to place chicken wire, gravel, crushed pebbles, or aluminum foil (or combinations of all four) in the hole instead of a rock. They are just as unpleasant for a dog to dig into. If the hole is wide enough you can place a metal or plastic lid from a garbage pail halfway down and cover it loosely with dirt. Hitting the hard surface and hearing the noise his paws make against it should discourage him.

Nasty Business.   It is possible to discourage a dog from redigging the same hole by placing his stool in it and filling the rest of the hole with dirt. He will not like it.

Solutions (Reconditioning)

The Corrective Squirt.   An effective method of correcting a dog when he digs holes is to catch him in the act and squirt him with a garden hose. He must be taken by surprise or the correction will be unsuccessful. Dig a narrow, shallow trench from the edge of your dog's favorite hole to a water faucet that is out of sight. The trench does not have to be longer than six feet. The point is to hide the presence of the hose in the hole. Place the nozzle of a garden hose in the side of the hole four or five inches down and point it upward. The dog must not see the nozzle or any part of the hose close to the hole. Lay the rest of the hose in the trench. Cover the trench with dirt. The dog must not be able to see the water faucet.

Bait the hole by placing food inside. Cover the food with a thin layer of dirt. Allow the dog access and leave. Station yourself at the water faucet. Turn the water on the instant he begins digging and let him have a full squirt.

Bob Wortham

Bury the hose and wait for him to dig. A squirt in time saves nine.

Go to him quickly and shout, "NO! NO! NO!" Once he has been corrected, praise him as a matter of reassurance. If you cannot see the dog from the faucet, have someone watch from a window and give you a quiet signal. Repeat as often as necessary.

Balloon Aversion Technique.   Blow up several balloons and pop them close to the dog so that they will startle him. The objective is to develop an aversion to the balloons. Go to the dog's favorite hole and fill it with one or more balloons tied to a small rock. If the balloon aversion was developed properly, the dog should stay away from his hole.

Bad Taste. Place newspaper at the bottom of the hole. Generously sprinkle alum, cayenne pepper, and Tabasco sauce all over the paper. When the dog returns to continue digging, he is bound to taste or whiff the three unpleasant substances. He may get them on his paws and lick them. The taste or scent should deter him from continuing his project.

The Margolis Maneuver. This is the simplest and most effective correction available. (See part Two, "Some Essential Tools and Techniques for Problem Solving.") Place a slip collar and thirty-foot training leash (or clothesline) on the dog and allow him access to the area in which he digs. Somehow you must observe him without his being aware of you. Wait until he becomes so involved with digging that he stops looking in all directions. At that moment rush out, grab the leash, and jerk it hard (see part Three, "Your Dog's Personality" to determine how hard to jerk the leash for your type of dog). As you jerk the leash shout, "NO! NO! NO!" Repeat this every time the dog digs up the yard. It should end his problem behavior.

Prevention Tips

The most logical way to prevent a digging problem is to avoid giving your dog access to the areas he can dig up. A dog run is the best way to keep the dog outdoors without giving him the ability to dig.

If you have a puppy, correct him with the Margolis Maneuver (see parts Two and Three) if he begins to scratch the dirt in your

presence. Corrections given early in a dog's life establish you as his leader and also pattern his behavior in a desirable way.

DOGFIGHTING

When dogs fight, the image of Lassie, Benji, and Snoopy go into the dumper and out of nowhere come Fang and the Devil Dogs. Next to being bitten, it is the worst experience of dog ownership. Dogfighting is a frightening, destructive activity and in most cases entirely avoidable, but once a fight has started, it is difficult if not dangerous to stop it.

In cities and in enlightened communities it is against the law to allow your dog to roam free or to be walked without a leash. Leash laws make it possible for dog owners to prevent one dog from attacking another for any reason. The problem is greatest when a dog off-leash approaches your dog, who is hooked to a leash. Both dogs become extremely tense, and a fight is possible. The knowledgeable and determined dog owner

When dogs meet on the street they become tense, and a fight is possible. It can be a terrible experience.

has several options to avoid injury to people and dogs.

Origins of the Problem

Fighting behavior in wolves has to do with attacking prey animals for food, dominance and subordination, mating privileges, and the assertion of territorial rights. The issues are the same for domestic dogs but the circumstances are different. Because they live with families of people instead of packs of their own kind, all other dogs they meet (with a few exceptions) are viewed suspiciously as strangers and interlopers.

Although it is commonly thought that only males fight other males, this is not always the case. Some males will not fight each other. Occasionally a male and a female dog will fight, and so will two females. Dogs that are socialized to other dogs as well as to people are less likely to attack another dog. What will happen when two dogs meet for the first time is impossible to predict. Only the dog owner can make an intelligent guess about his or her own dog.

Two dogs meeting each other for the first time on neutral territory approach with great caution and intensity. Their tails will go up and wag slightly. A process of investigation begins by touching noses and each sniffing the other's anus and genitalia. It is after this initial ritual that anything can happen. Even the friendliest dogs may reject each other and attack or they may simply go their own ways or begin a friendship.

The bases for most domestic dogfights are the issues of dominance and subordination and the assertion of territorial rights. When dogs fight for dominance they are usually two males and the fight can happen any-where. Females tend to fight each other over territory and (in the home) personal locations and possessions, although there are no absolutes here. Few dogs, male or female, will defer to visitors in their own homes, but neutral territory may have to be fought over for possession as well.

Domestic dogs fight more than wild dogs or wolves because of the distortion of natural canid behavior in domesticity. In the wild, fighting behavior is limited to resolving matters about the social order within the pack. Fights break out to establish a leader, who eats first, and who is allowed to mate. Once these matters are resolved they rarely become an issue again. But pet dogs find themselves in the peculiar position of resolving these matters each time they meet a new dog because they do not travel with a pack. They are imprisoned by a behavioral instinct that is functional only in a true dog-pack social structure. When this behavior is expressed in the human world, it is completely irrational and without purpose. Dog-fighting is a genetic hangover.

Reasons for the Problem

Territory.   When a dog enters another dog's backyard it is an encroachment of territory and a dogfight is likely to ensue.

There is another form of territorial expression that novice dog owners do not expect: it has to do with dogs on leashes. An aggressive or highly territorial dog hooked to a leash becomes possessive about the person at the other end. The human walking such a dog is considered to be a personal possession, and the dog will fight over it. That is why two leashed dogs can easily get involved in a vicious fight even though they are away from their homes.

ce. The issue of dominance is ~~~ght over by two male dogs and ~ anywhere at any time if the ~~are correct. Dogfights of this ~~from the absurd, with growls, ~~es, and urination on objects, to ~~g, with snarling and biting ~~rt and maybe kill. When two ~~eing walked on leashes meet ~~rom opposite directions, condi- ~~able for a fight over dominance.

ocialization. Dogs that have ~~osed to other dogs very often ~~ididates for a dogfight.

Living Together. When more than one dog lives in the same home, fights can break out because of owner mismanagement. If they are fed in the same room, at the same time, and from the same bowl, the conditions are set up for a constant series of dogfights. The same applies to possessions such as toys, bones, or even food treats. When humans raise dogs together from puppyhood, the humans assume they will always get along. It is rarely the case.

Solutions (Environmental)

How to Break Up a Dogfight. It is extremely difficult to stop two fighting dogs without getting bitten. Pouring water on them can end many dogfights instantly. However, water is rarely available where and when you need it.

Pulling a dog away by the tail is dangerous but effective. Lift him off the ground first to confuse him and then drag him away. Some dogs, such as Doberman Pinschers, have little tail to grab, and lifting a dog up by the hind legs is dangerous and not recommended.

If your dog is on a leash, then turn around, jerk the leash, and walk swiftly and forcefully in the opposite direction. If your dog is obedience-trained, give him a hard jerk, using the Margolis Maneuver (see part Two) and shout, "NO!" in a firm tone of voice. Then give him the command "Heel," turn, and walk away in the opposite direction.

Throwing a blanket or even a large garment (such as a coat) over the aggressor dog's head will stop the action long enough to remove your dog from the situation. If you can, break the contact, then hurry away with your dog.

Try asserting your dominance over both dogs with strong body language and a loud, firm tone of voice. Often shouting "NO" or "STOP" or a whole string of such commands will get their attention and break the action. You can try to startle them by throwing objects close to them, especially things that make noise, such as metal pots. There is really little else to be done. It is foolish to attempt to break up the fight by placing your hands anywhere near either dog's head or shoulders or even hindquarters. You are certain to be severely bitten. In the heat of combat, your own dog will not recognize you. He will bite you if you touch him, just as the other dog will.

Prevention is the most important element in dogfighting. Skilled dog owners know how to avoid dogfights and do all in their power to avert such incidents.

Prevention Tips

Obedience Training. An obedience-trained dog will always respond to your commands to some degree even in the heat of battle. It is much easier to prevent a dogfight involving a trained dog than a fight be-

If your dog is obedience-trained, correct him with the Margolis Maneuver (a).
Place him in the "Sit" position (b).

tween two who are not. If your dog is one that fights other dogs or belongs to a breed known for its dogfighting such as the Akita, Bull Terrier, Rottweiler, Puli, Doberman Pinscher, Samoyed, Airedale, Bullmastiff, or Alaskan Malamute, it is essential that he be obedience-trained by a professional trainer.

Learning the Signs of Aggression. When another dog approaches your dog with caution, he may be a challenger or may simply want to get acquainted. If he is trying to look larger than he really is, then he is getting ready for a fight. He will make direct eye contact with your dog and stare hard. The hairs on his neck and back, down to his rump, will stand away from the body. He may lower his head and extend his neck. All four of his legs will be stiff and spread apart in a dominant stance. The aggressive dog may raise a hind leg and urinate and then scratch the ground. Low, throaty growls may be heard as the tail is held straight up in the air or arched slightly forward. At this point the dog may begin investigating your dog (an act that will surely end in a fight) or wait for him to make the first move. If you move forward, the opposing dog will attack. He may also attack if your dog turns his

back The best course of action is to back away slowly and cautiously, lengthening the distance between the two dogs, and then turn around and walk in the opposite direction.

Avoiding the Aggressive Dog. Become aware of the dogs in your neighborhood, learn which are the fighters, and then avoid them. It is not cowardly to stay away from potential dogfights. If you see a strange dog off-leash, avoid it. Be discriminating about which dogs you allow to come up to yours, even if they are held on a leash. At the first indication of trouble, leave the scene. If the dog follows, discourage him with a dominant tone of voice but exercise caution.

EXCESSIVE WETTING

Excessive wetting is a problem that confuses many dog owners. The dog urinates small quantities at inappropriate times and in inappropriate places. Young puppies, nervous dogs, excitable dogs, and frightened dogs are almost always the ones with this behavior problem. The wetting takes place on any surface, including wooden floors and carpeting. What causes confusion is that the wetting is not a housebreaking problem and it is totally unrelated to digestive elimination. Excessive wetters are emotional dogs who may be perfectly housebroken in every other way.

Origins of the Problem

Dogs and wolves living in a natural setting, within a pack order, instinctively accept a social structure based on dominance and subordination. Subordinate dogs and wolves are subject to the demands of the dominant members of the pack; urinating a small quantity is an act of submission and sometimes fear, especially for puppies and cubs. When a young dog encounters an older one, the usual physical investigations take place, leading into a slight tussle. The larger of the two dogs knocks the other over on its back and places one paw near the throat. The smaller dog then urinates into the air, and the encounter is over. The puppy's urination is a signal of submission.

Because human beings have brought dogs into their homes, they have taken over all the caretaking responsibilities that mothers and other members of the pack would normally handle. This human caretaking continues for the life of the dog. The result is that a house pet is kept in a state of perpetual childhood. Add to these conditions the element of inherited or environmentally created shyness, timidity, or excitability, and the result could easily be an excessive wetter.

Reasons for the Problem

Too Much Water. Puppies and young dogs may drink too much water and lose urinary control because of the immaturity of the sphincter muscles that open and close the urethra.

Fear of Punishment. A dog that is yelled and screamed at or physically abused may become permanently fearful of those who do the yelling or abuse. The fear would be expressed in wetting in that person's presence. It is the equivalent in human terms to wetting your pants.

Fear of People. Dogs that are frightened of people, especially strangers, may have been born with a shy personality or they may have been made shy. A lack of early socialization with different people in various localities would create this problem in a dog.

Excitability. There are dogs that are just so excitable that they cannot contain themselves (or their urine) when they see their owners.

Nervousness. Although nervous dogs are similar to excitable dogs, there are differences. The excitable dog generates emotion based on pleasure, but the nervous dog acts on suspicion. (See part Three, "Your Dog's Personality.")

Illness. There is always the possibility that a dog who wets uncontrollably may have a medical problem. Kidney disorders, prostate problems, bladder stones, and many other ailments all can cause excessive wetting.

Housebreaking Mismanagement. Puppies and young dogs (and even some mature dogs) will wet excessively if they are not walked often enough. Dogs' needs vary from one individual to another.

Solutions (Environmental)

See a Veterinarian. The first thing to do is to rule out any medical problem. See a veterinarian and explain the wetting behavior. It could be the first symptom of a serious illness.

Control Water Intake. If you have an excitable puppy, it may be better to take up the water bowl shortly after each meal. By restricting the dog's intake, you may stop the wetting. If the dog has drunk water several times a day, it is not necessary to leave it down for him all twenty-four hours. Ice cubes make an excellent thirst quencher without bloating the dog with water. Consult your veterinarian.

Choose Where to Say Hello. When greeting an excitable dog, do so in the yard, on a porch, in an outer hallway. Avoid soiling the home with urine. It will have a good effect on you and the dog. Doing this also prevents the dog from creating territorial marks or scent posts. Dogs as a rule return to the odor of their urine spots (only they can smell them) and then urinate on top of them. Use an odor neutralizer to obliterate the scent.

Use Body Language. Try not to intimidate the dog with your posture. Do not lean over the animal in a towering manner. Timid or frightened dogs would be placed in an extremely subordinate position and might uncontrollably wet the floor. When you talk to a dog that has this problem, kneel down to eye level and let him make contact. When petting a shy or frightened dog, do it with the palm of your hand upward. This avoids the impression that you are going to hit him.

Solutions (Reconditioning)

Dealing with Other Behavior Problems. If your dog chews, barks, soils the house, or any other behavior problem, you must deal with it in a manner prescribed in this directory. Do not raise your voice or handle the dog in any emotional way. *Do not hit your dog.* When you do, you are compounding the original problem with excessive wetting. (See part Three, "Your Dog's Personality.") Abusive behavior toward the dog will not solve any behavior problem; it creates more. If your dog chews the carpet and you yell at him, you will not only have a chewed carpet but a stained one.

Socialization. The more people your dog meets, the less frightened he will be with strangers, and gradually there will be less and less wetting. Help your dog become adaptive, tractable, and easygoing with new people and situations by giving him plenty of exposure and socialization.

Your Voice. Use your voice in a gentle, loving tone.

Praise Level. If you praise your dog enthusiastically he may become excited and wet the floor. The excitement level of such dogs is geared to the tone of voice of those who relate to them. If you are excited, your dog may get so excited that he will roll over on his back and urinate upward. A shy dog, however, is just the opposite and needs more enthusiasm than usual when being praised. Praise the dog on the basis of his personality. Tone down your voice for an excitable dog and increase your enthusiasm for a shy or frightened one.

Exercise. Several long walks each day or extended play periods with a ball or a Frisbee can reduce nervousness or excitement and have an important influence on the severity of the problem.

Obedience Training. Obedience-train the dog with the help of a book or with the services of a professional trainer. When your dog wants to jump, which brings on excessive wetting, give him the commands "Sit," Stay," and "Down," in that order. Dog training is the best method for ending excessive wetting.

Prevention Tips

All the environmental and reconditioning solutions offered above also serve as prevention techniques for excessive wetting.

GARBAGE RANSACKING

When your king of the burgers is rooting through the garbage pail looking for chicken McBones be grateful if he doesn't find them. They can do him great harm. Getting into the garbage is no joke. There are many bits of food debris, such as bones and packaging materials, that can cause serious blockage in a dog's throat. Eating leftovers from your dinner can cause diarrhea in many dogs. And of course there is the esthetic consideration involved when dogs eat garbage.

A dog with bits of eggshell and coffee grounds on its nose seems cute only in photographs. When you turn the lights on in the middle of the night to find your dog surrounded by orange rinds, steak bones, and

Am I too late for the garbage?

empty cans of tomato sauce, the charm of it all is ever-so-elusive.

Origins of the Problem

Wolves and wild dogs who must hunt to live follow the herds of plant and grain eaters such as deer, wild sheep, caribou, elk, and even moose. Hunting is a cooperative effort targeted at those members of the herd that cannot keep pace with the rest: the weak, sick, or young animals. The hunters are successful in making a kill about 7 percent of the time. There have been periods when canids are known to have gone for seventeen consecutive days without food. However, when they do bring down a prey animal, wolves are capable of eating from ten to twenty pounds of food, mostly meat, in one meal. Over 90 percent of the diet of wild canids consists of meat. The canine stomach can stretch to large proportions for gorging food during times of plenty to offset the many times when there are no prey animals available. According to Scott and Fuller in *Dog Behavior: The Genetic Basis:* "When food is available, they eat rapidly, making little effort to chew their food, they have a large gullet which permits them not only to eat big chunks but to vomit it back easily for the benefit of puppies. The dog is, in a sense, always hungry, but he is not driven to eat."

Reasons for the Problem

Hunger. It is so obvious. When a dog's food ration is inadequate he will constantly be on the hunt for food whenever and wherever he can find it. The garbage pail is the most logical place for him to look for an extra meal. If your dog's nutritional intake is the proper amount, then the number of feedings may be incorrect for his needs.

Because It's There. Few dogs can resist the smell and the look of an open garbage or trash can, available and just waiting for the taking. The habit starts with curiosity. Once dogs get near the can, the smell overwhelms them and they really get into it. The problem begins because the garbage is accessible.

Observation. Night after night some dogs watch the dinner leftovers skimmed into the pail. It is like a school for scraps. They go to it and discover that it is not only interesting but it tastes good.

Solutions (Environmental)

Keep the Garbage Out of His Reach. Try to place the garbage pail out of the dog's reach. Using a smaller pail kept in a cupboard under the kitchen sink is a workable solution. Keep the garbage in a sealed container, outdoors, if possible. Buy and install a garbage disposal unit or a trash compacter. The simplest solution is to keep the nasty stuff out of the dog's reach or put a lid on it.

Solutions (Reconditioning)

Create an Aversion. Place a paper or plastic bag inside the pail. Prepare a paste made of alum powder and water. Spread it around the rim and inside the pail. Bitter Apple is an ideal commercial product for creating an aversion. You can create your own taste sensations with combinations of Tabasco sauce, Chinese mustard, and vinegar. When the dog ingests any of these substances, they will taste awful to him and work as an automatic correction. *Do not place alum or Bitter Apple directly on the food.* Even though these substances taste bad, the dog may eat the food anyway. It is possible to bait the dog in this manner without placing food in the garbage can. If the habit has been established, the dog will poke his nose inside no matter what is or isn't there. To him, the smell is always present.

Balloons. Here is another way to create an aversion to the garbage can. Blow up one or more balloons and pop them close to the dog's face so that he is startled by them.

Not every dog finds balloons on the garbage can. They can spoil his appetite.

Tape one or more balloons to the garbage pail before retiring for the night. They should keep him away.

The Margolis Maneuver. The object is to catch the dog in the act and administer a firm correction to teach him that this behavior is unacceptable. (See part Two, "Some Tools and Techniques for Problem Solving.")

Place a slip collar and leash on the dog one hour before retiring for the evening. Scrape your dinner leftovers into the pail. Go to bed at your normal time and put out the lights. Station yourself at your bedroom door and listen. If it is difficult to hear the dog getting into the garbage, then preset a sound alarm. Simply crumple several sheets of newspapers and place them around the garbage pail. If the dog tries to get to the pail, he must step on the papers and create a slight crackling sound, which is your cue. Give him a few seconds to get his nose deep into the pail. Rush into the room, switch on the lights, grab the leash, and jerk it hard, saying, "NO! NO! NO!" Shortly afterward tell him he is a good dog and pat him on the head. Your praise is his reward for stopping his bad behavior. The praise is necessary.

You may repeat the above technique without using the leash and slip collar, substituting a shake can (see part Two) for the balloons or the collar. The shake can is extremely useful for informal corrections at any time when you see the dog go to the garbage. As he gets his nose inside the pail, rattle the shake can hard and shout, "NO! NO! NO!" Don't forget to praise the dog after each correction. Keep several of the noise-makers at strategic locations around the house. Give the dog a replacement for the garbage pail: after each correction give him a rawhide toy. Or determine if he has legitimate hunger and feed him.

Prevention Tips

Do not feed your dog from the table (see "Begging"), as it is the first step toward the garbage can. Feed him from his bowl or dish only.

Do not allow the garbage can to be accessible to the dog. If there is no inaccessible place for it, place a tight-fitting lid over it.

GROWLING

Growling is a sound that some dogs make, indicating an aggressive, menacing frame of mind. It is a rumbling tone that comes from deep within the throat and sounds just like the word *GGGGROWL*. When dogs growl they usually raise their upper lips into a snarl and bare their teeth. It is a threat or a warning that if you continue your action they are going to bite. Growling is heard from dogs that have been punished, had their food taken from them, or feel threatened by something. When a dog develops the habit of growling, no matter how young or old he is, it must be viewed as a serious problem by the owner. Dogs that growl frequently are dangerous. (See "Biting," page 49.)

Reasons for the Problem

Bad Breeding. Inherited aggressive behavior can be blamed on those who breed dogs indiscriminately. The more popular a breed becomes, the less selective commercial breeders and some amateur breeders are. Instead of refusing to breed dogs of poor temperament or refusing to sell puppies that may have a temperament problem, they breed all dogs who can stand and they sell the progeny, no matter what. It is a matter of dollars and cents.

Poor Socialization. Young dogs that were not allowed to be in the company of humans and other dogs, that were isolated as puppies and allowed to become territorial or overly protective grow up unsocialized. They become aggressive, suspicious dogs that growl frequently and become biters. The socializing of dogs must take place early in their lives.

Environmental Influences. Any number of events in a puppy's life can damage his personality and turn him into an aggressive dog. Negative human behavior, places, and experiences can all terrify and change a dog born with a normal disposition. Gunshots, auto backfires, traumatic traveling experiences, early neglect, and human indifference can all create a growler.

Human Behavior. A major reason for growling and other forms of aggressive behavior is the way owners treat their dogs when dealing with obedience problems. Nine out of ten such owners hit their dogs with a newspaper or with their hands. They confuse teaching with punishment, correction with beating. When dogs are hit, they eventually fight back. Growling and then biting is a form of fighting back.

Unfortunately, some owners praise their dogs for growling and aggressive behavior, thinking that they are raising an animal that will protect them. In reality, they are creating an uncontrollable cur that will become dangerous to all who come in contact with him, including themselves. A dog that growls is a time bomb waiting to go off.

Origins of the Problem

(See "Biting," page 50.)

Solutions

Growling leads to biting and is a serious aspect of dog behavior that must be dealt with whether it is seen in a grown dog or a young puppy. Because of the critical nature of the problem, dogs with aggressive behavior are categorized into three significant age groups.

1. Puppies Seven Weeks to Six Months Old express their aggressive behavior by growling, snarling, and nipping and are considered easy to correct because of their age, size, and lack of maturity.

2. Young Dogs Six Months to Ten Months Old are still in a safe, manageable range but show a different quality and degree of aggression by growling, snarling, snapping, and possibly biting. This is a problem no dog owner can afford to overlook. The solutions offered in the "Biting" entry of this directory are workable for those who wish to change their dog's behavior with the help of this book. A dog with a growling problem in this age group can be reconditioned.

3. Dogs Ten Months Old and Older who growl and possibly bite are much more difficult to recondition. Sometimes they cannot be changed. *Once a dog is past ten months of age and has a growling, snarling, or biting problem, he can cause serious injuries and therefore requires professional evaluation.*

Please read all entries listed under "Biting" for dealing with the problem of growling. Everything written about biting problems applies to dogs who growl, including the environmental and reconditioning solutions for all dogs under ten months of age.

GUILT

Guilt is an intellectually conceived idea about an emotion. It is often a symptom of psychological or emotional disturbance in human beings. When this term is applied to dogs, it inaccurately attributes human thoughts, feelings, and actions to an animal that actually has its own species-specific behavior. The behavior of canids, especially that of domestic dogs, is unlike that of human beings in most respects. Behavior resulting from feelings of guilt cannot be accurately assigned to dogs.

When a dog lowers its ears, furrows its eyebrows, drops its tail, and slinks away, it is not because of guilt. This behavior can be caused only by anticipation of disapproval, punishment, or abuse. Because of the inherited need to maintain social contact in a pack structure, the domestic dog craves approval and acceptance. If the dog has a behavior problem for which it has been punished, it will appear to look "guilty." But in reality it is simply in a state of fear or depression associated with the anticipation of more punishment or disapproval.

The only relief for such a dog comes when his owner understands the problem in terms

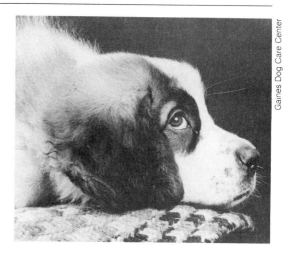

Gaines Dog Care Center

of dog behavior and attempts to solve it with teaching and reconditioning techniques. Use this directory of problems for that purpose.

HOUSEBREAKING "MISTAKES"

Housebreaking problems alter the relationship between dogs and their owners. Those new to housebreaking problems feel betrayed by their alleged "best friend" and come to view him as a pay-toilet running amok. There goes the carpeting, the permanently waxed floor coverings, the throw rugs, the natural-finish hardwood floors, the terra-cotta tiles. If something is not done quickly, there goes the dog. Housebreaking is as necessary as deodorants and indoor plumbing. We can live without them, but who wants to?

The definition of housebreaking is . . . teaching your dog to relieve himself outside, in the street or backyard. He must *never* be allowed to go in the house. Housebreaking must not be confused with paper training, which teaches the dog to relieve himself in the house, on paper spread on the floor. (See

"Housebreaking and Paper Training.") Nor should any housebreaking problem be confused with the problem of excessive wetting (listed as a separate entry, "Excessive Wetting").

Some dogs who have had a measure of housebreaking training continue to have "accidents" and minor failures. This entry is meant to deal with those deficiencies. If your dog has never had the benefit of such training please refer to "Housebreaking: A Five-Part Program" on page 165. There, you will find a complete training course. When dealing with previously housebroken dogs with problems it is sometimes advisable to start over from the beginning. Consider using the five-part housebreaking program for this purpose.

There are two types of housebreaking problems. The first has to do with a dog that has no concept of what you expect or demand of him. He must be taught to use the outdoors instead of your floors. The second type of housebreaking problem has to do with a dog that was once trained and is now making mistakes. It is possible that a previously housebroken dog making mistakes was never taught properly in the first place. A frequently used solution for housebreaking problems is to start at the beginning of the housebreaking procedure, as described in this article, and do it properly. However, one should first make an attempt to discover the specific cause of the problem and solve it on that basis. How to do that will be dealt with later.

Here are some key pointers if you are trying to solve the problems of a previously housebroken dog. Try to figure out why the dog has had an accident. Was it a physical disorder or a lapse in memory? Was the dog housebroken properly? Was there something in the dog's environment that caused the problem? Many housebreaking mistakes are made because of a change in the dog's feeding/walking schedule. Emotional upset caused by some change in the dog's life is a common reason for housebreaking mistakes. You must investigate the situation like a detective, isolate the problem, and then decide on a solution.

Do not get angry at the dog or abusive in any way. For the same reason that you would not hit or yell at a six-month-old baby, you must not react harshly to a dog. Contrary to what you might have heard or read elsewhere, dogs are not spiteful. *They do not punish their owners for any reason by soiling the floor or the furniture or anything else.* Many people mistakenly believe that their dogs mess in the house for revenge after having been left alone. It is impossible. These problems develop because of anxiety, fear, nervousness . . . or because the dog was never housebroken properly.

Most dogs make housebreaking mistakes because of confusion about relieving themselves indoors. As puppies, most of them have been placed on newspapers, indoors, and encouraged to eliminate on the floor in the presence of their human caretakers. It is the most common mistake dog owners make. There is no need to paper-train a dog before teaching him to go outdoors. Once a dog has been paper-trained, he has been praised for relieving himself on your floor, in your presence. A month later he is trained to go outside, but he comes indoors and continues to defecate on the floor because he was indoctrinated to do it. There are good reasons for paper training but you cannot have both housebreaking and paper training without creating confusion in the dog's mind. If your dog was taught to go on newspapers and now has problems, you must start at the beginning of housebreaking and go through the five-part housebreaking program offered on page 165. Dogs can be housebroken in three days or three weeks. It depends on the dog and the owner.

Origins of the Problem

There are three aspects of natural dog behavior that make housebreaking possible. The first is the dog's need to mark one or more places with his body's waste matter and continue to do so. The second is the dog's instinct and the third is behavior learned from the mother, to keep his eating and sleeping place free of urine and feces.

If you have ever walked a dog, you will notice that he sniffs and sniffs until he finds a special spot on the ground or on some vertical object. Once his interest has been aroused, he will urinate or defecate (or both) on that particular spot. It is a *scent post* from another dog's elimination and has attracted your dog as a territorial marker, a sexual message, or simply a communiqué announcing the presence of one more dog in the neighborhood. "Scent posting" or "marking" is common to wolves and all dogs, wild or domestic. It is an important fact for dog owners who wish to housebreak their dogs. Once you allow your dog to establish his own scent posts outdoors, he will always return to them to eliminate. *However, once the dog establishes them indoors, he will always return to those, too.* A dog's ability to smell this scent is so great that ordinary soap and water will not remove the scent even if humans no longer smell it.

In the first three weeks of a puppy's life the development of his sensory capacities and motor functions is limited to breathing independently, seeking warmth, seeking his mother's teat, and feeding. During this period all puppies are blind, deaf, and unable to walk (although they do crawl or "swim"). They do not possess the capacity to pass the body's digestive waste matter independently. It is removed from the body with the help of the mother. For reasons we can only guess, the mother is concerned with the cleanliness of the nest. She does not want her puppies' body waste contaminating their eating and resting place. To stimulate the elimination reflexes of the puppies, she systematically rolls each one over on its back and licks it. First she licks the belly to promote elimination and then she licks the body openings to remove the waste (which she ingests).

By the end of the third week the puppies

begin to see and hear. Shortly afterward, they are able to crawl and then walk away and eliminate independently, away from the nest. At first the puppy leaves the nest to eliminate anywhere. During the eighth week the puppy begins to use specific areas for elimination. The concept of never soiling the nest is reinforced as instinctive/learned behavior by the mother, who continues to lick the puppies clean, although they no longer require her stimulation. At the end of the eighth week, puppies begin to seek out specific scent posts on which to eliminate. At this age they are capable of controlling their need to eliminate for at least six hours a night without soiling their sleeping area. However, they will urinate and defecate frequently during the day if stimulated by the activities surrounding them. Puppies in this age group will eliminate at least every hour and will attempt to do so as far from the nest as possible. However, they make no attempt to wait until they are taken outdoors. This behavior can be seen in grown dogs with housebreaking problems. Some dogs will dig into a carpet as though trying to bury their stool or cover it with newspapers or whatever is handy. This behavior has nothing to do with trying to "hide the evidence," as is often supposed. The dog is following its instincts to remove the offending mess if it is too close to the "nest." It is a rare dog that will soil his eating or sleeping area unless he is confined there and cannot control himself. The instinct to keep the nest clean is probably for avoiding detection by predators and territorial intruders.

Reasons for the Problem

Too Much Water. If dogs being housebroken have access to water all day and night, they will drink many times and urinate often. When a dog spends the entire day in a yard and has access to water one hour before coming indoors for the evening he will have urination "accidents" through the night. The same is true if he drinks from the family swimming pool or open toilet bowl without anyone's knowledge. Too much water added to his ration can upset the feeding and walking schedules of the five-part housebreaking program offered on page 166, because it will cause excessive urination. If the intake of water is not scheduled, the dog will have many "accidents."

Medical Reasons. A dog with kidney problems, diabetes, bladder infection, internal parasites (worms), colitis, pancreatic disease, et cetera, will be unable to participate in a housebreaking program. It is difficult if not impossible for an unhealthy dog to control his body eliminations.

Improper Diet. Dogs cannot maintain their housebreaking controls if they eat dog food that does not agree with them, eat many between-meal snacks, are overfed, or are fed human food indiscriminately from the table. Any change from the scheduled diet can and most likely will cause diarrhea. To housebreak a dog properly, you must place him on a feeding schedule (see the five-part housebreaking program on page 166). Feeding a dog more times than his schedule calls for will cause "accidents." It will defeat the purpose of the feeding schedule and prevent his being housebroken.

Changing Diets. If you change from one dog food to another, the change will cause stomach upset leading to diarrhea. It is impossible to housebreak a dog successfully when he is not in control of his elimination.

Improper Feeding Time. Housebreaking problems arise if the dog is fed first thing in the morning *before* he is taken for his first walk. If you feed your dog late in the evening he will need to defecate at two, three, or four in the morning, since six to eight hours are required for food to leave the body. Dogs not fed at the scheduled feeding times suggested in the five-part housebreaking program on page 166 will not develop proper housebreaking control of their bodies. Lack of consistency in feeding times is the downfall of most housebreaking efforts.

Evening Stimulation. If a dog is exercised late in the evening during his last walk, he will drink when he is finished. This can cause urination "accidents" through the night. Rawhide or other chew toys given late in the evening can cause diarrhea and defeat the dog's housebreaking training.

Not Eliminating Urine or Defecation Odor. Because dogs always return to the same spot they soiled before, housebreaking cannot be accomplished without first removing their scent markings.

Use of Paper. It is impossible for a dog to maintain his housebreaking discipline if he is also introduced to soiling on newspapers indoors, so you must make a choice for one or the other and stick to it. (See "Paper Training," page 170.)

Those from the East or Midwest who buy a puppy during the winter months often paper-train him because it is too cold to take him outdoors. By the time the weather is warm the dog is totally paper-trained and it becomes difficult to maintain housebreaking discipline.

Housebreaking mistakes indoors can be caused by paper training at the puppy's last residence. Some breeders and pet shops have puppies relieve themselves on newspaper, a practice that makes housebreaking difficult.

Lack of Confinement. Puppies and dogs being housebroken cannot maintain body discipline if they are given the freedom to wander all over the house when they are left alone. They cannot be expected to control themselves if they are free to wander without supervision even when someone is home. Because dogs do not like to soil their own area, they will go to another part of the house to eliminate, negating your housebreaking efforts.

Improper Confinement. Dogs that are confined behind a closed door, cut off from the rest of the house, will become upset, nervous, or anxiety-ridden and lose control of their body discipline. Inevitably they will soil the floor.

Great Expectations. It is useless to expect absolute housebreaking control from young puppies. They do not develop complete control of the sphincters controlling the opening and closing of the bladder and the rectum until after the fourth month.

Who Is the Culprit? If there is more than one dog living in the house it is difficult to tell which dog is having "accidents." If one dog messes on the floor the other may follow soon after with his own "accident."

Moving. The odor of a previous dog in your new house may cause your dog to have "accidents." Your dog may simply be marking his new territory. This is not really a housebreaking problem unless it becomes a habit.

Separation Anxiety. If a dog is urinating and defecating in the house, the cause could be separation anxiety, which is the fear of being alone or separated from the owner. Dogs suffering with this emotional problem will pace or whine once they suspect that they are going to be left alone. When the owner leaves, they immediately urinate and defecate on the floor.

Being Left Alone Too Long. A puppy cannot control his body functions for eight hours. He must be walked every three or four hours, every day. The age and the size of the dog determine how often he must be walked.

Size, Age, and Breed. Housebreaking is influenced by these factors. For example, toy breeds are more difficult to housebreak than some of the larger, working breeds. Toy breeds take longer to develop physical control. They have a more difficult time being left alone. As a rule, older dogs are more difficult to housebreak than younger dogs, although a dog as old as ten years can also be housebroken.

Solutions (Environmental)

A Doggie Door. Install a miniature door in your front or back door that allows your dog to go in and out at his leisure. (Such doors are manufactured and advertised in leading dog magazines. A housebroken dog will then follow his urges and eliminate out-doors. This is recommended only if you have an enclosed yard.

A Fenced Yard. People who live in houses rather than apartments and must be away from home most of the day will benefit greatly by building a fence around the backyard. The dog can then be kept outdoors until the family comes home from work.

Outdoor Confinement. When you are solving housebreaking problems, it can be useful to confine the dog outdoors when no one is at home to watch him or walk him frequently.

You may buy a portable dog run, which is an easy-to-install chain-link enclosure. They are sold at hardware stores and fence companies. Attach a long clothesline to a tree and the side of your house. Run the line through the loop of your dog's leash and hook him to it. This becomes a trolley run with a pulley effect, allowing the dog to be outdoors although still confined.

Rid the Dog and the Environment of Parasites. Some housebreaking problems are caused by medical problems stemming from parasites such as fleas, ticks, roundworms, whipworms, hookworms, or tapeworms. Veterinary treatment is necessary along with extermination.

A professional exterminator is required to rid your house and grounds of parasites. Fleas are difficult to remove. They are the major cause of tapeworm in dogs and cats and must be eliminated.

Maintain thorough sanitation of your dog's area. Remove all stools from the ground daily. Keep your grass short and watered only when necessary. If your dog occupies a cement-slab dog run, keep it hosed down and cleaned often with hot water and disinfectant. Keep gravel clean and free of stools. Lime, salt, or borax will kill the eggs and larvae of parasites living in gravel.

Dogs that are allowed to roam may kill and then eat mice and other dead animals. These can be a serious source of tapeworm A dog infested with tapeworm will have diarrhea and be unable to maintain any semblance of housebreaking.

Water Intake. The dog's last water should be at 7:30 P.M. each evening until his problem is solved. A thirsty dog may be given a couple of ice cubes in the evening. Do not allow access to water at night such as the toilet or the swimming pool. During the day attach a commercial device to an outside faucet called Lixit. This allows the outside dog fresh water, all day long.

Solutions (Reconditioning)

Five-Part Housebreaking Program. The most significant reconditioning solution available is the housebreaking program offered on page 165. All five elements are designed to help the dog owner create a completely housebroken dog in a short period of time.

Frequent Walks. A dog learning to be housebroken or a dog with housebreaking problems must be walked no less often than every three hours. If you work, hire someone to walk the dog. In large cities there are such services listed in the *Yellow Pages* under "Pets" or "Animals."

A dog should be taken out for his first walk of the day early in the morning, before his first feeding and watering. He then should be fed and watered and then walked again. Walk your dog no less than fifteen minutes each time and longer if possible.

Puppies should be walked the minute they awake from a nap no matter what time of the day or evening.

When Housebroken Dogs Do Bad Things

It is rare that a dog who has been *properly* housebroken makes mistakes after several years of good behavior. However, it does happen. The first thing to suspect is a medical problem. Have the dog examined by a veterinarian. As stated earlier, housebreaking "accidents" can be symptoms of any number of medical problems. If the dog has a clean bill of health from the veterinarian, you must determine the cause of the problem if you are going to solve it. Investigate the situation like a professional.

The most useful tool for learning about your dog's problem is the Holmes and Watson Chart. Like Sherlock Holmes you must doggedly follow the facts to wherever they lead. This simple chart will show you the pattern of your dog's mistakes and help you understand the nature of the problem. You will then be in a good position to choose the correct solution.

The chart is very easy to use. Each day, record the important information about your dog's housebreaking mistakes. When do they happen? Where do they happen? What is the nature of the accident (urine or defecation)? Why did it happen (was the dog left alone too long, given too much water, et cetera)? Who did it (if there is more than one dog involved)? Keep this chart for one week

The Holmes and Watson Chart
for Housebreaking Sleuths

	When	Where	What	Who	Why
Monday					
Tuesday					
Wednesday					
Thursday					
Friday					
Saturday					
Sunday					

and you will see a pattern of behavior develop. The mistakes may all happen in the morning or in the afternoon or overnight. All the information you record will help you isolate the problem and determine for yourself what can be done to solve it. The most common solution found as a result of making this chart is readjusting the dog's feeding-watering-walking schedule as suggested in the five-part housebreaking program found on page 166. It is exactly what professional dog trainers do. The solutions become obvious.

Your dog's housebreaking mistakes fall into three types: urination problems, defecation problems, and urination *and* defecation problems.

Urination Problems. These problems are often caused by allowing the dog to drink too much water. Do not allow water to be left down all day. Place the dog on a water schedule just as you did when you first housebroke him. Do not allow the dog to sneak water from the swimming pool or toilet bowl. Use ice cubes to satisfy his off-schedule thirst.

• If the dog is exercised late at night and then allowed to drink, it could cause a urination problem. Do not give a dog with urination problems any water one hour before he goes to bed for the evening.
• The odor must be eliminated with an odor neutralizer or a shampoo done by a pro-

fessional rug cleaner. Try denying the dog access to the area he continually marks with urine. Cover the spot with a large piece of furniture. If that does not work, try confining the dog as you did in the original housebreaking program. Check all areas, including curtains and other vertical objects, for urine stains and odors. The urine stain from a small dog can fade from sight within one hour, and only the dog will find it.

- If your older dog is unable to maintain his housebreaking, he may not have a housebreaking problem. It may be a medical problem. Have him examined by a veterinarian. If there is no medical problem, then you will have to confine the dog to one area and tolerate his physical condition.
- Do not add additional water to the dog's food. It could cause a urination problem.
- Be certain the problem is not excessive wetting (see page 102).
- Is the feeding-watering-walking schedule, as outlined in the five part housebreaking program, still being followed conscientiously? Once you have established such a pattern, it is essential to stick to it as much as possible throughout the life of the dog. Otherwise, housebreaking mistakes will occur.
- There is always the possibility that the dog was never properly housebroken, in which case we suggest you start over at the beginning.

Defecation Problems. These problems are mostly caused by too much food. Do not leave food down all day for the dog to eat. You may be feeding your dog too many snacks between meals. Have a veterinarian determine a proper diet for your dog and stick to it. Quantities should be established.

- If your dog is mature enough for one meal a day feed him in the morning. Do not feed any dog, no matter how young, after 6:00 P.M. The food requires only six hours to pass through his system.
- When a dog makes defecation mistakes in the house, a common cause of the problem is that his scheduled walks are not long enough. Your dog may need to relieve himself two or three times each walk, and that must be taken into account when taking him out.
- A dog should not defecate more than three to four times a day. Any more than that indicates a possibility of internal parasites, such as roundworms. See a veterinarian.
- An old dog may lose physical control of his elimination function. Once a veterinarian determines there is no medical problem other than old age, all you can do is confine the dog to one area and be understanding.

Urination and Defecation Problems. Any or all elements in the above two categories may cause this problem. Keep a chart on your dog's elimination mistakes for one week and isolate the problem.

These are often the problems of an outside dog's being allowed indoors. If a dog is left outside during the day and then allowed to come inside at night, he will probably make mistakes indoors. It is especially true if he drinks excessively before coming in. Eliminate all water one hour before bringing him in and feed him his daily meal in the morning.

If the solutions offered here do not solve

the problem start the five-part housebreaking program from the beginning. See page 165.

Prevention Tips

When to Get a Dog. Do not buy a puppy unless the weather is warm enough so that housebreaking can begin immediately. Don't take a young dog outdoors in the dead of winter for housebreaking without a sweater.

Bring a new dog into the house when you begin a vacation from work or when the children are on their vacation. In that way you can devote the first week or so to housebreaking the dog on a full-time basis. If it is not possible, then bring the new dog into the house on Friday so you can take the entire weekend setting up a proper schedule.

Training Consistency. If you are going to housebreak your dog, do not first paper-train him or use newspapers as a temporary toileting measure. This is an important decision. Paper training only confuses a dog when switching to housebreaking.

Your Dog's Background. Get a thorough background history of your dog. Where did he come from? What was his life-style? What was his schedule? Did he have any prior housebreaking problems? The more information you have on your dog's background, the greater will be your ability to anticipate and cope with his problems.

Patience. Some dogs take longer than others to housebreak. Be patient. Do not take out anger, frustration, or rage on the dog. It is inhumane and counterproductive. If you frighten your dog, you will only create more problems than you started with and prevent

him from being successfully housebroken. Never hit a dog.

The Leash. Housebreaking cannot be accomplished if your dog cannot be walked. Help a young dog or puppy adjust quickly to walking on a leash so he can begin a feeding-watering-walking schedule right away. (See "Leash Rejection" in this directory.)

Get Rid of the Odor. If you have just moved to a new home, thoroughly clean the premises of any odors from previous pets. Use an odor neutralizer concentrate in carpet shampoos, with detergents and all cleaning materials and products.

The Floor. Do not confine your dog on a carpet. Be certain his "accidents" happen on linoleum or some other moisture- and stain-resistant floor covering. This will eliminate the need to use newspapers, which ultimately confuse the dog.

Whose Job Is It? Please bear in mind that housebreaking is the owner's responsibility and not the dog's. He is satisfied with how he relieves himself. But if you want the dog to eliminate according to your needs and sensibilities, then you must be the one who makes *all* the effort. Your dog will then do the best he can. Be satisfied.

JEALOUSY

Accepting jealousy as a canine response depends on how the term is defined and then applied. Can a dog be resentful or bitter in a rivalry or envious of someone? Probably not. Can a dog be fearful or wary of being supplanted, apprehensive of loss of position or affection? These ideas are too abstract. Dogs do not exist on abstract levels of thought and emotion. Dogs may experience jealousy-like feelings as a response to the most simple and direct threat to their needs and desires.

To imagine that they will plot and scheme to harm a newborn baby or a new pet because they feel jealous is to assign human thoughts and feelings to dogs. Natural dog behavior tells us that pack integrity is the real issue when there is a change in the family structure. In the wild state, unless the wolves and dogs of a pack are fully aware of the pregnancy and whelping of a litter, the cubs are regarded as strangers and interlopers and treated with suspicion. Any animal, including one of the same species, is rejected if it is not recognized as a pack member. These are instincts that are genetically programmed and are thought to be connected with population control in relation to how much food a territory can provide. However, don't expect a dog to understand his own behavior. He is just a creature of instinct and habit.

Another aspect of negative behavior that appears to be jealousy has to do with social rank. When a new dog or a baby or a cat enters the household, the dog may become upset or even aggressive. The behavior is not a sign of jealousy but an attempt to reaffirm the order of dominance and subordination.

It is a fact that some dogs develop close emotional ties with other dogs, cats, and humans and protect those relationships with suspicion, hostility, or assertiveness. Most behavior that appears to be jealousy has to do with a dog's fear of losing his own source of personal attention. Whether such a dog is afraid of losing affection, attention, or just

the elements of survival is anyone's guess. When canine behavior appears to stem from jealousy, the best solution is reassurance and added attention to the "jealous" dog. If the dog's behavior becomes annoying, aggressive, or destructive, use the Margolis Maneuver as a correction tool. (See part Two, "Some Essential Tools and Techniques for Problem Solving.")

JUMPING FENCES

Some dogs jump fences (or dig their way out from the bottom like prisoners escaping from Alcatraz. The problems with a dog on the loose are the trouble he will cause and

the danger he places himself in. Dogs on their own have a short life expectancy. Dogs' one natural enemy, the automobile, is a steel-hearted predator killing them by the thousands. A dog who leaps over the wall will find more than freedom on the other side. He's sure to find a car with his name on it. The answer? Prevent his escape.

Origins of the Problem

There are various aspects of natural dog behavior linked to jumping over or digging under fences to get out. It is not enough to say that the dog wants to be free. One must understand that all animals have a high degree of curiosity and a desire to satisfy it. The dog's senses of smell, sight, and hearing are extremely keen and constantly stimulate his curiosity. If given an opportunity, any dog will venture out of his domain to look around.

The mechanism of sexual attraction can stimulate a male dog to attempt escape in the most extreme manner. Dogs have been known to climb fences, jump fences, dig under fences, and even tear through fences to get to a female in estrus (heat). During that time, the female gives off an odor that arouses and provokes male dogs and completely takes over their behavior. When this happens, male dogs may behave in ways that are out of character for them.

Jumping fences is often connected to the dog's highly developed social instincts. Wolves, wild dogs, and domestic dogs are all highly social creatures with a well-developed sense of pack integrity. There are some house dogs that will go to the trouble of jumping over a fence just to be with another dog or person.

The instinct to reaffirm or defend territory is strong in some dogs. They will work themselves into a frenzy in the presence of interlopers if they are thwarted by a fence. A dog's aggressiveness, stamina, and determination will provide the needed adrenaline to give him the necessary energy to make it over a fence, even a high one.

Reasons for the Problem

Outside Distractions. Dogs jump over fences to get to the other side because that's where the action is. They may want to get to a playful dog, a challenging dog, a dog in heat, or any animal they see or hear, including a cat, raccoon, rodent, or a bird.

Other noises are also enticing, such as sirens, human voices, children at play, and the barking of other dogs.

Smells are another reason why dogs hop over the fence. An open garbage can, a neighbor's barbecue, and burning rubbish are all elements that will arouse a dog's wanderlust.

Low Fences. Many fences are only five feet high or lower, not high enough to keep the average dog in his own backyard. Having a low fence is like opening a door for a dog. If the fence is low enough, it becomes a challenge for the dog to attempt a high jump.

Improper Fence. A dog will be tempted to leave the premises if the fencing material can be climbed. Be certain your fence has nothing on it that allows the dog to climb it or boost himself up. Many dogs get away by crawling under the fence because there was no barrier. Others may dig their way out from the bottom if the fence is sitting over dirt.

Boosting Out. If you place an object close to the fence the dog can use it to boost himself out. A tall trash can with a lid, or a bench or table will serve a dog nicely for vaulting his way to freedom. Almost any object close to the fence will give a dog the added boost he needs to jump clear.

Nervousness or Insecurity. Temperament is an important reason why dogs try to get away. If something frightens a nervous or insecure dog he will make a break for it.

Separation Anxiety. An emotionally troubled dog that cannot bear to be separated from its owner, even for a few hours, will make every effort to jump over a fence if given the opportunity.

Stray Dogs. Dogs that have a history of living on their own are candidates for jumping fences and running away even if they seem to like their new homes.

Fear of Loud Noises. An auto backfire, a gunshot, thunder, or even the hiss of a truck's air brakes is enough to get a dog to jump over the fence. Any loud sound will do it.

Teasing. Fenced-in dogs that are teased by neighborhood children or tradesmen get nervous and then aggressive and want to go after their tormenters. Teasing will inspire a dog to jump the fence.

Lack of Exercise. A dog too restricted and too confined will want to get out and release his pent-up energy.

Breed. Some breeds are more likely than others to jump fences. Sporting breeds, hounds, and terrier breeds are facile jump-ers, as are some of the Working Group breeds, such as the German Shepherd Dog and the Doberman Pinscher.

Aggressiveness. Dogs that display hostile, aggressive, or territorial behavior toward people and other dogs will try hard to jump a fence to attack someone or something.

Solutions (Environmental)

Make Higher Fences. If your fence is too low, you can raise the height by nailing 2″ x 4″ posts every 24 inches along the top and then attaching chicken wire to the posts. First determine how much higher the fence should be, and cut the posts to the correct size. It is economical and easier to do than it sounds. For those who have carpentry skills it is best to slant the posts into the yard so the dog cannot go over no matter how high he can jump or climb. Although this measure is not pleasing to look at, it has proven to be effective. It is a temporary structure that can be removed once the problem is solved. Extending the height of your fence also serves as a reconditioning solution for your dog's fence-jumping behavior. Remember, if the fence is not six feet high or higher, it will not effectively keep an average dog in. If you are going to have a chain-link fence placed around your yard or lawn, have the workmen place at least six inches of the fence below the dirt, at the bottom. Doing this keeps the dog from digging beneath it.

Prevent the Dog in Other Ways From Digging His Way Out. An effective way to keep a dog from digging beneath an already-built fence is to set bricks at the bottom, side by side firmly wedged next to each other. The same results can be achieved by digging a narrow trench at the bottom of the fence and laying in it long boards on their sides so that they serve as a strong barrier or wall. You may also use loosely placed rocks in the same manner along the lower fence line. Prevention can even be accomplished with short posts and chicken wire laid into the ground. It is another way of extending the fence beneath the surface of the ground. These preventive measures also work as reconditioning solutions.

Secure Outdoor Confinement. Buy a portable dog run at a hardware store or fence company. This is a small chain-link fence unit, easy to install and easily taken down and moved to a new home, if necessary. Again, place it six inches below the dirt and be certain it is high enough to prevent your dog from jumping over.

You may buy a tie-out stake that installs into the ground like a large corkscrew and enables you to hook the dog to it and keep him in a restricted area.

A clothesline trolley can be rigged between the side of the house and a tree, elevated off the ground by six to seven feet. Run the line through the loop of the leash and hook the dog to the leash. This gives him an improvised dog run when you are confining him outdoors to the limits of your property. Be sure the dog has enough slack on the leash so that he can sit or lie down. These confinement techniques also serve as reconditioning solutions.

Install a Doghouse. In warm, sunny environments dogs may continually jump the fence because they are bothered by the hot sun. A cool, insulated doghouse placed in a shady area may be the ideal solution to the problem. Doghouses may be built with lumber and insulating materials or bought ready-made from a mail order catalogue, a hardware store, or pet supply outlet.

A dog crate with a canvas tarpaulin or strip of sailcloth on top can serve well as a doghouse, providing the door is always taped open. If you use a dog crate as a doghouse, do not use it to confine the dog outdoors. It is too small an area of confinement considering all the distractions outdoors that provoke a dog's curiosity. Outdoor confinement should give a dog ample room to walk around and stretch out.

Solutions (Reconditioning)

Create an Aversion to the Fence. Blow up several balloons and pop them with a needle close to the dog's face. This should create in the dog's mind an aversion to the balloons. Place a string of blown-up balloons on the top or bottom of the fence. They should make a jumper hesitate and then move away from the fence. The biggest, most aggressive dogs will pause before a string of balloons if the dogs have an aversion to them.

Another way to create an aversion to the fence is to place a long, heavy piece of wood on top of it. When the dog jumps, his front paws will knock the loosely placed wood off the top. It will probably startle him and begin to create an aversion to the fence. Keep placing the wood on the top of the fence until the dog discontinues his fence-jumping behavior. The point is to create an aversion to the fence in addition to using a self-correcting reconditioning technique.

Use the Margolis Maneuver. Attach a thirty-foot training lead (or clothesline) to the dog's slip collar. Place the end of the lead

Bob Wortham

Use balloons to create an aversion to the fence top.

sive to a shake can. If the dog is not sufficiently startled by the shake can, try throwing it to the ground, close to him. Do not throw it close enough to hit him with it. The idea is to correct the dog by communicating your disapproval, not to abuse or punish him in any way.

The Water Hose. You can use a water hose to correct a dog who jumps fences. The principle is the same as that of the Margolis Maneuver except that a surprise blast from a water hose instead of a jerk of the leash corrects the dog.

The Wooden Necklace. Here is a solution for an extreme case. It is designed for a big

Bob Wortham

This technique may save your dog's life.

close to the door nearest the dog. Conceal yourself and wait for the dog to start jumping. Once he has made his first leap, rush out, grab the end of the lead, and give it a hard jerk saying "NO, NO, NO" in a loud, harsh tone of voice. Immediately praise him for responding to your correction. Continue this technique until the problem no longer exists.

If it is impossible to work with a thirty-foot lead, use the shake can technique instead of the Margolis Maneuver. When the dog begins to jump, rush out, rattling the shake can vigorously and saying "NO, NO, NO" in a loud, harsh tone of voice. Doing this will work providing the dog is respon-

dog that jumps the fence when no one is home. Attach a heavy stick of wood (size and weight depending upon the individual dog) to a rope. You can use a short length of 2″ x 4″ or part of an old broomstick. Suspend it from the dog's neck so that it hangs just above his legs. When he jumps, the wood will hit his front feet and correct him. It works well and discourages the dog from jumping.

Drill two holes into the exact center of the stick and run the rope through them. Tie the rope securely to the stick and place it around the dog's neck so that it hangs like a neck-lace. If the necklace is too low, he will be able to remove it. If it is too high on his neck, it will not interfere with his jumping. The loop around his neck must have just enough slack to allow his head to slip out easily if he accidentally catches it on something. The wooden necklace should add enough weight to make it hard work to jump in addition to making jumping clumsy and awkward.

Use the necklace as long as it is necessary to solve the problem. It could be solved in about one week. Once you are certain the dog will not jump, you may remove the stick, but keep the rope necklace around him as a reminder for a short period afterward.

Prevention Tips

High Fences. Jumping problems cannot get started if the fence is too high for the dog to jump over. Extend the height of existing fences with vertical posts and chicken wire.

Dogs That Cannot Get Over a Fence. If you have not yet acquired a dog, you might wish to consider a smaller breed. If your dog is going to remain in your backyard, look at the breeds that are the right size for the height of your fence.

Proper Confinement. Install a dog run, a portable dog run, a tie-out stake, or a clothesline trolley. See "*Secure outdoor confinement*" above in "Solutions (Environmental)."

The height of your fence makes the difference. If your dog is a jumper, make it difficult for him to climb out.

JUMPING ON FURNITURE

Some dogs lying on the furniture look as if they belong there like the crown jewels on a

Mordecai Siegal

With or without your permission.

satin pillow. Others seem human as they lean against the arm of a chair. All that's missing is a pair of glasses and a newspaper. How can a dog watch his favorite TV game shows unless he's propped up on his favorite settee? All dogs love the furniture and sleep on it with or without your permission. When you yell at your dog for sleeping on your bed, he thinks he is not allowed to be there only when you are at home. If your dog is a couch potato, you can count on his sleeping on the couch after you leave. Feel the cushion when you get home. Chances are it's still warm.

The question is whether you consider a dog on the furniture suitable for your lifestyle. Dogs that are allowed on couches and chairs sometimes stain them with saliva and any other body fluids that run, drip, or flow. A frightened, anxiety-ridden dog may chew whatever is handy as he goes through his emotional twists and turns. He just might chew the edge of a cushion or the arm of a sofa. After you leave for work, a dog allowed on the couch may decide to snack as he ponders whatever it is that dogs ponder. You might come home to a sofa full of kibble crumbs and canned-dog-food stains. And of course his favorite toy might slide down the back of the chair, causing him to dig for it. Suede, velvet, or silk upholstery will not survive the great bone expedition. Many dogs will claim their favorite piece of furniture as their exclusive territory and become nasty about being shoved off it.

It is necessary to decide whether your dog is allowed on the furniture or not. If you consider his being there a problem, you must do something about solving it. Be consistent about it. Your dog cannot be taught to use the furniture on some occasions and not on others. He is either allowed on the furniture or he is not. The choice is yours.

Origins of the Problem

Most dogs prefer to lounge on something soft and warm, but not necessarily for the most obvious reasons. Dogs of northern breeds, such as Alaskan Malamutes and Siberian Huskies, prefer a cold, hard floor to a carpet, and Great Danes fancy a large bed rather than a sofa.

When a dog takes over a piece of your furniture, several drives are in operation. It is not enough to say that he wants to be comfortable. The question is what makes him comfortable. There is more to his comfort than the softness of the upholstery. Probably the most satisfying reason for being on the furniture is the height. When dogs or wolves create a den, it is usually on a bluff or under a crest of rocks. The idea is to have a solid wall behind them (to prevent unforeseen attacks) and to be as high as possible. A commanding view is always desirable.

The instinct to create an individual den or

nesting place is present in all dogs. Females do it as an expression of maternal instinct, whether they are pregnant or not. When you consider that most wolves mate for life (pair bond), it is easy to understand that the male helps create the den for whelping newborns. Wolves that have pair-bonded share their den and remain close to one another throughout their lives. A variation of this behavior is seen in domestic dogs, with humans (sometimes just one person) becoming the one with whom the dog has bonded. When the humans leave the house, the dog is attracted to the place that has their scent on it. Human scent is found on beds, sofas, chairs, carpets, pillows, and kitchen chairs. It is comforting and reassuring to the dog to station himself on top of the scent of the humans in the "pack." All dogs prefer the comfort of a soft chair or couch if given a choice.

Reasons for the Problem

Prior Use. The most common reason for dogs to use the furniture is because they were brought up onto it as puppies. This custom allows the young dog to claim these areas as territory and use them when no one is home. Even if a dog is chased from a chair hundreds of times, he believes that he is only forbidden to use it when the family is home.

Sleeping in Bed. If a dog is permitted to sleep with a human, the practice teaches him to use the furniture. It is hard to teach a dog the difference between a bed, a sofa, or an upholstered chair. To the dog it is all one thing. When a dog is allowed to sleep on a bed, he is certain to use the rest of the furniture.

Warmth. There are times when the floor is too cold and drafty and the dog seeks the warmth and comfort of a bed or sofa.

Noises. When a dog hears outside noises he will use the couch, the table, or anything else to elevate himself and satisfy his curiosity.

Solutions (Environmental)

Restrict the Areas in the House. The most obvious means of keeping a dog off your furniture is to keep him in the kitchen (with a puppy gate) or in the backyard when no one is home.

Solutions (Reconditioning)

Use the Margolis Maneuver. Place the leash and slip collar on the dog and leave the room. Try to observe his activities without being noticed. If you can catch him in the act of going up on the furniture, grab the leash and jerk it hard. Say "NO, NO, NO." Praise the dog immediately afterward. Then take him to the place where you would prefer him to take his naps, saying "Go to your place," in a friendly tone of voice. If the dog is obedience-trained say "Down," and praise him. Then say "Stay," using the correct hand signal (the flat of your hand blocking his vision for two seconds), and praise him. If the dog is not obedience-trained, then do the same things anyway, but teach the dog to lie down on your command. (See part Two, "Some Essential Tools and Techniques for Problem Solving.") Buy an obedience-training book for this purpose.

If the dog's favorite place is your bed (with you in it) bait him with the help of another person. Place the leash and slip collar on him and then lie down on the bed. When the dog gets into bed with you, have the second person enter the room, take hold of the leash, and administer the Margolis Maneuver.

Use the Shake Can. Do everything outlined above in the Margolis Maneuver *without using the leash and slip collar.* Instead, use the shake can, several of which can be located throughout the house, since they are economical and easy to make. When you catch the dog in the act, rattle the shake can loudly and say "NO, NO, NO." Follow the rest of the procedure as outlined above. The objective is to let the dog know it is wrong to be on the furniture by correcting him and then showing him where he belongs.

Create an Aversion to the Furniture. It does no good to punish or scold or correct your dog unless you catch him in the act. If you come home and feel the dog's body warmth on the cushion, it will have no teaching effect to correct him. It is too late. The most effective reconditioning technique

The next time you leave the house, blow up five or six balloons and tape them to his favorite piece of furniture.

is to create in your dog's mind an aversion to the furniture.

Blow up several balloons and burst them with a pin close to the dog. If the balloons are fully blown, they will startle the dog when popped. The next time you leave the house, blow up five or six balloons and tape them to his favorite piece of furniture. The dog will probably associate the balloons with the unpleasant noise and avoid going near them.

A variation of this technique is to use mousetraps. Set four or five of them on the furniture and cover them with several sheets of newspapers. Tape them down. When the dog jumps on the couch, the traps will go off with a loud snapping sound as they hit the paper and will startle him. He should jump down and stay away from the couch.

Another method for creating an aversion to furniture is to spread aluminum foil on the surface of the furniture. The sound of it under your dog's paws is surprising and unpleasant. So is the slippery feeling.

String a piece of rope across the furniture like a barrier. You can even tie shake cans on it at ten-inch intervals. It might discourage the dog if he has to climb over or under the rope to get to his favorite resting place.

Teach Your Dog the Command "Place." Another way to condition your dog to stay off the furniture is to teach him this command. "Place" gives the dog an area of his own and demands that he use it when he wants to rest, sleep, or quietly watch what is going on. Select his favorite corner of the house and make that his place. Create a pleasant, cozy environment with some toys, a dog bed, a blanket, a bit of carpet, or an old pillow. Once he uses it, his own scent will become embedded in the area, making it his own territory.

Having chosen the place, put the leash and slip collar on the dog and take him to the new area. Kneeling in front of the dog say "Down," and pull his front paws forward so that he lies on the floor in some comfortable position. Tell him he's a good boy. Place your flattened hand in front of his eyes (without touching them) and say "Stay." Praise him again. Then say "Place." Praise him again, drop the leash, and walk away. If he gets up to go with you, take hold of the leash and repeat the process. The sequence is "Down," praise; "Stay," praise; and "Place," praise. Repeat this technique many times, at least until the dog begins to absorb it. Take the dog to various areas of the house and go through the entire routine, always ending at his designated "Place." Soon you will be able to command the dog from across the room, without a leash and collar, and expect him to go to his place, lie down, and stay there . . . off your furniture.

Electronic Correction. It is possible to correct a dog on a general basis with the use of a tape recorder if you know what time of the day he jumps on the furniture. If you have a video tape recorder and camera, you can get this information and correct the dog by remote control. Set up the camera on a tripod and aim it at the dog's favorite piece of furniture. Turn it on and leave. Use a four-to-eight-hour tape. If you do this several days in a row, you can see the dog's furniture-jumping pattern develop.

With this information in mind, make an audio or video recording saying "NO" as you rattle a shake can every thirty seconds. If the dog consistently goes to the couch one hour after you leave, set your tape machine on a timer to start up in one hour. Leave. Your electronic correction may have a good effect. This new and somewhat outlandish technique has been used with success in professional training situations.

Prevention Tips

Consistency. If you do not want your dog on the furniture, then keep him off from puppyhood to old age. You cannot make exceptions to this rule. Do not pick up a puppy and sit with him and then expect him to stay off the furniture as a grown dog. When you want to hold the dog or play with him or simply express your affection, do it on the floor.

Off the Bed. Do not allow your dog to sleep with you on the bed.

JUMPING ON PEOPLE

There are dogs who love to play kissee-facee and will slurp your lips whenever they can. Unfortunately, they do not tap you on the shoulder politely first. With boundless energy a people-jumper springs without warning and climbs the length of your body like a television wrestler about to pounce on your bones. If he's a big dog, he will make it to your shoulders with both paws. Where a smaller dog lands depends on his size and character. Some people consider this behavior a problem, especially if the dog knocks them down, muddies their clean clothes, nips their lips, or humps their legs.

Dogs who jump on people can hurt them, frighten them, and then add them to the growing ranks of dog haters. The naive dog owner may tolerate this behavior, may even enjoy it, but to the non-dog-owning jumpee

Marybeth Eubank

Playing kissee-face is a problem. Most people do not appreciate a large dog jumping on them.

it can be a loathsome experience. Many children are terrified of dogs who jump on them, whether they are knocked to the ground or not. Even the smallest dogs can be annoying to anyone when they jump on legs and relate to the human body as if it were a jungle gym.

Solving this problem is not difficult but requires time and effort. One must not resort to the techniques of the Gestapo or the Spanish Inquisition. Kneeing a dog in the chest or stepping on his back toes to stop him from jumping on people is inhumane and destructive to one's relationship with a house pet. Unfortunately, this is the advice all too often given to the dog owner trying to solve this problem. Here is a better way.

Origins of the Problem

One form of play behavior in dogs and wolves is standing on their hind legs and jumping on one another as though they were boxing. This movement is sometimes called the "play leap." It closely resembles the position of a dog jumping on a human. It begins with a leap triggered by a direct stare when the first contact is made. Play behavior in animals is a release of energy and a test of motor skills in an endless variety of twists, turns, and movements. Often play results in learning new skills as the dog practices older ones. Puppies, adolescents, and occasionally older dogs indulge in play as an experiment with their own capacities.

In the wild or natural setting the jumping of wolves on other wolves can have sexual meanings. Before the female is receptive to the male, an extended canid version of courtship takes place. Part of the pattern of sexual courtship for male and female is the placing of their front legs around each other's necks. This sexual hug looks like play-fighting or wrestling and gets both animals up on their hind legs.

Another aspect of jumping has to do with fighting behavior, where the combatants may paw each other as they stand on their back legs like two stallions. Wolves and wild dogs fight among themselves over such issues as mating, feeding, and dominance.

The claim for dominance is expressed when a dog stands on his hind legs and places both front paws on top of the opposing dog's back. In this situation the dominant dog may growl, display an erect tail, bite the other dog's neck, and even attempt to mount him. The behavior is often seen among puppies and adolescent dogs, not necessarily in the context of dangerous or excessively aggressive behavior. When dogs jump on humans, it is usually a bold but friendly gesture. Such dogs are enthusiastic about people whom they greet and may even be expressing love. However, when they jump on someone, they assert a dominant attitude. It is extremely difficult to train or control a dog that feels dominant to his owner.

Reasons for the Problem

Owner Encouragement and Puppy Indulgence. Puppies jump on their owners many times a day; it is one of their endearing gestures. There isn't an owner alive who doesn't think it is cute. There are those who live with grown dogs who also enjoy having their dogs jump up on them ... when the owners are wearing old or casual clothes. Of course, they get upset when their dog splatters a muddy paw trail across their freshly cleaned and pressed clothes.

Most people allow their puppies to jump on them but fail to see the connection when their adult dog does it. Even allowing a puppy to sit on your lap is a form of teaching him (or at least encouraging him) to jump on you later in life when jumping is undesirable.

Your Voice. When a dog owner speaks enthusiastically to his or her dog or speaks in a high-pitched, baby-like tone of voice, it delights the dog. The problem is that it encourages him to jump up to the source of pleasure. The problem of jumping on people frequently begins here.

Excitement. If the owners are gone for several hours, the dog becomes excited when they first come home. The first thing he does is to jump on them. If that happens frequently, it becomes a generalized form of behavior. Nervous dogs with excessive energy behave this way.

Allowed Other Forms of Jumping. When dogs are allowed to jump onto furniture, this behavior carries over to people. It is not reasonable to allow a dog to jump on furniture and then expect him to refrain from jumping on people. It is too inconsistent.

Teaching the Dog to Jump. Often dog owners teach their dog to jump on them without knowing they are doing it. If they throw balls or toys in the air or offer food from their hands, encouraging their dogs to reach up for it, they are, in effect, teaching their dogs to jump. Anything held high for the dog to reach for teaches him to jump up on people.

Solutions (Reconditioning)

The Margolis Maneuver. Teaching a dog not to jump on people is an easy problem to solve. It simply requires a correction whenever the dog jumps. If applied properly, the Margolis Maneuver solves the problem. (See "The Margolis Maneuver" in part Two, "Some Essential Tools and Techniques for Problem Solving.")

Place the leash and slip collar on the dog. Take him into a situation where you know he will jump on someone. Have one of his favorite people greet him. Dogs usually jump on their owners when they come home. Set up a similar situation where one member of the household comes home and another is ready to grab the leash. When the dog jumps on the home-comer, the helper should jerk the leash firmly to the right, using both hands, and say "NO," in a firm tone of voice. Praise the dog immediately for responding to the correction (even if his response was not too good). Repeat this technique three or

Marybeth Eubank

The Margolis Maneuver is the most effective method for reconditioning a dog that will jump on people whether they like it or not.

four times, and the problem will diminish. If you cannot find anyone to help you correct the dog, do it yourself. With the leash and collar on the dog, jump up and down and get the dog excited. Talk to him with enthusiasm until he starts to jump on you. With the leash in your hand, jerk the dog and say "NO." Praise him immediately afterward. Bear in mind that you must not ask the dog to jump on you. You must re-create the conditions in which he demonstrates his annoying behavior so that you can teach him to stop. Correct the dog every time he jumps on you until he stops doing it.

Emphasize the firmness in your voice when saying "NO" so he will eventually respond to the word without a tug of the leash. The point of the correction is not to use the

leash to pull the dog off the person he is jumping on, but to communicate to him that he is doing the wrong thing. Since a frail person may have difficulty pulling a large dog off someone, it is far more effective to condition the dog to respond to a demanding tone of voice. Most dogs find their owners' disapproval unbearable and will work for the owners' praise. How hard to jerk a dog depends on his age, temperament and size. (See part Three, "Your Dog's Personality.")

The Shake Can. This is essentially the same technique as the Margolis Maneuver as described above, substituting the shake can for the correction from the leash and slip collar. When the dog jumps on someone, rattle the shake can loudly and say "NO," in a loud, firm tone of voice. Praise the dog immediately for responding to your correction. How loud to make the noise depends on the dog's age, temperament, and size. (See part Three, "Your Dog's Personality.") If you are too far from the dog to correct him by shaking the can you may throw it to the floor close to him and shout "NO." That will startle him and communicate your correction effectively.

Have a shake can positioned near the door, inside your house. When you come home, correct the dog if he jumps on you. Correction is even more effective if you walk in with the shake can already in your hand. Take it with you when you leave and have it ready for action as you walk through the door.

A Whistle. This technique is carried out like the Margolis Maneuver, substituting a loudly blown whistle as a correction instead of a jerk of the leash. Always say "NO," in a firm tone of voice after blowing the whistle and then give the dog praise for responding to the correction.

Exercise. Nervous, hyperactive dogs may jump on people because of an excess of energy. The more exercise you can give a dog, the less active he will be between times. A vigorous exercise session has a calming effect.

Obedience Training. If your dog is obedience trained, give him the command "Sit" everytime someone comes to your front door. This command is also useful on the street when the dog looks as if he were about to jump on someone.

Prevention Tips

Getting Down To The Dog's Level. When dealing with puppies, adolescents, and hyperactive dogs, do not encourage them in any way, at any time, under any circumstances to jump on you. If you are going to offer a snack or a toy or just say hello, kneel to the dog's eye level and relate to him there.

Consistency. Decide whether the dog is allowed to jump on people and then be consistent about it. If the dog is not allowed to jump on you or other people, he must also not be allowed on the furniture. Puppies and older dogs must not sit on your lap. The problem of jumping on people comes about because the dog was allowed or encouraged to do it as a puppy. If you do not want the dog to jump on people, then everyone in your family must agree to these conditions and prohibitions from the beginning, or the problem will develop and then continue. If one member of the family indulges the dog, the unwanted behavior will continue and eventually get the dog in trouble. Not letting the dog jump must be a family decision.

LEASH REJECTION

There are dogs who never accept the idea of walking with their owners when attached to a leash. They twist, turn, pull, push, paw and bite the leash to avoid the control over them that it represents. The leash is a dog's best friend, even if he never understands why. It

Dogs who reject the leash show their displeasure in various ways.

is a life-assurance policy and must be seen in exactly those terms by the caring dog owner. *Pet dogs must not be allowed to reject a leash. Their lives depend on its constant and proper use.*

Reasons For the Problem

Lack of Leash Experience. Few dogs are comfortable wearing a leash the first time. Puppies and grown dogs who have never worn a leash and collar are usually unhappy and confused when first hooked up. Many are suspicious and doubtful, although some dogs regard the strange objects as a new toy.

City Dog/Country Dog. Most city dogs are introduced to a leash and collar when they enter a new home. Leash laws, traffic, and fear of theft are the principal reasons. In the country, many dogs are "at large" and free to come and go as they please. Many rural communities have no leash laws because the communities accept the concept of dogs on the loose. (However, some rural communities have strict "deer-chasing" laws, allowing wardens to shoot after the third offense.) Few people realize that more dogs are killed on country roads by speeding traffic than on city streets.

Some country dogs live in backyards, behind tall fences, all their lives and have never been walked on a leash. Occasionally country dogs move to the city and must learn leash behavior. It can be a terrific struggle and only the dominant personality wins.

Frightening Association with the Leash. If a leash was forced on a scared puppy and then pulled too hard because of his re-

sistance, he may have developed a fear of it. Negative associations with a leash represent a difficult problem.

The Leash Itself. Depending on the age and size of the dog, the leash may have been too large or too heavy when he was first introduced to it.

Rock-a-Bye, Doggie. For some people, small dogs are irresistible, and they carry them around much of the day as if they were human babies. Some of the Toy breeds, such as the Maltese, Yorkshire Terrier, Shih Tzu, or Chihuahua are carried around from the moment they enter the human household. The idea of a leash seems irrelevant throughout puppyhood because these dogs are rarely taken outdoors. Sooner or later the dog must be taken outdoors, and then the rejection of the leash becomes apparent.

Excessive Leash Force. If a dog is constantly pulled on the leash because the owner didn't know what else to do to make him obey, the dog will fight a leash every time one is put on.

Solutions (Reconditioning)

How to Leash-Break a Puppy (or Some Older Dogs). Attach a lightweight leash (depending on the size and age of the dog) to a comfortable collar that fits well and allow the dog to walk around the house with the leash and collar on. The dog should never be left alone with the leash attached. The most irritating factor will be the weight of the leash. Puppies are unaccustomed to anything hanging from their necks, and heavy leashes bother them. It is really a matter of adjustment. You must keep an eye on the dog if he is going to walk around the house for hours wearing a leash attached to his collar. When first placing the leash on the collar, try to make it a happy experience. Talk to the dog with enthusiasm and give him some tender loving care. The idea is to create a joyful association with the leash.

The dog may make his adjustment in one to seven days. When he does, you can switch to a conventional, heavier leash (a 6-foot, ⅝-inch-wide leash, preferably made of leather) and allow him to adjust to that. If he chews the heavier leash or bites at it, you must correct him by saying "NO" in a firm tone of voice, pulling the leash out of his mouth, and then praising him for responding to your correction. Leash-breaking a dog is similar to saddle-breaking a horse. It is really a matter of adjustment and acceptance.

When you are leash-breaking a grown dog, the same techniques apply, except that you will need more patience. *When the light-weight leash is attached, the dog must not be left alone.* He must be watched carefully as he drags it around. It is important that he not be permitted to chew or bite on it. It is medically dangerous for dogs to swallow nylon or other synthetic materials that the light-weight leashes are made of.

During this period of adjustment (for grown dogs or puppies) be casual when you first pick up the leash, whether it is the light-weight or normal one. *Place no tension on it, and allow as much slack as possible.* Once the dog is happily dragging the leash behind, pick it up in your hand and act as if the dog were walking you. Take him outside if he'll go, and remain on a grassy surface. If he tends to dig in his heels and refuses to walk, at least his paws will not be injured. A dog that refuses to walk on a leash will always

be behind you. A leash-broken dog will walk closer to you, but will eventually start pulling. Let him pull you. The pulling can be corrected when the dog is taught the obedience command "Heel" (walking by your side), which is much easier than dealing with a dog who does not want to be on a leash. (Hire a professional dog trainer or buy a dog-training book and do it yourself.) Do not use the leash as a negative tool. Let the dog pull you until you are ready to have him obedience trained.

Prevention Tips

Walk Your Puppy. Even if your dog lives outdoors in a backyard, take him out for scheduled walks using a leash and collar.

Introduce the Leash Early. Using the techniques described above in "How to leash-break a puppy," begin as soon as possible, the sooner the better.

Maintain a Positive Attitude About the Leash. Never use it as an instrument of punishment.

Do Not Carry the Dog. Even toy breeds require exercise, and nothing gives better exercise than a walk three times a day. Try to avoid carrying the dog around indoors as if it were a newborn baby. Do not allow small dogs to become too dependent upon human help for everything.

Make Your Voice Enthusiastic. Make the idea of going out for a walk (attached to a leash and collar) as much fun as possible. Be exuberant and use a happy tone of voice when getting ready to go out.

Be a walkee-talkee. The dog should always associate the leash with a happy experience.

Use Patience. Understand that the dog is dealing with something new and strange. Impatience, frustration, or anger only stresses the dog and delays achieving the desired results. Place yourself in his position.

PULLING ON THE LEASH

The right arm of a new dog owner is always longer than the left. That's because the owner is yanked down the street three times a day by an exuberant dog who is so thrilled to be outside that he can hardly control himself. New dogs strain at the ends of their leashes; do not respond to the walking command "Heel"; and will not walk by their owners' sides. It is comical to see a dog pulling a bedraggled owner down the street. Who is walking whom? People don't laugh if it's their arms that are being stretched by a dog out of control. Pulling on a leash is a solvable problem.

Origins of the Problem

Domestic dogs have the same behavior patterns as wolves and wild dogs (although the

"Mush!"

patterns are somewhat modified from many generations of domesticity). When walking a dog for the first time we see in him the universal canid, with his youthful curiosity and unquenchable thirst for new things to examine. Beyond that is the tremendous drive to find a territory and claim it for his pack and for himself. It is inherited behavior in all canids. Wolves and dogs live in packs and hunt for their food together. Without a territory to hunt in there can be no pack. A territory or range varies from twenty to five hundred miles for a food-hunting pack in the wild. For domestic dogs it can be an apartment, a yard, a city block, or an entire neighborhood. Some pet dogs living in the country will claim several miles for themselves. Because domestic dogs eat at home, the entire notion of territory is unnecessary and without purpose. However, the instinct for territoriality remains.

Your dog's cousin the wolf is capable of running twenty-eight miles an hour when chasing a prey animal and can maintain a slow chase for fifty miles in one day. Wolves have enough daily energy to follow a herd of deer for a long distance, chase one animal at a fast speed, and then attack it with many leaps until it is down.

When walking a young dog try to see the bright new world through his eyes. From his perspective you are a member of his pack and the two of you are out claiming a territory by marking it, learning its ins and outs by sniffing it, and making mental maps for future reference. It is not enough to say a dog wants to be free. Free for what? To claim territory and then explore it and to find a mate. Young dogs experience the same drives and desires as their wild relatives. Your energetic dog, pulling you down the street, has not yet learned that he is a pet and is going to be taken care of for the rest of his life.

Reasons for the Problem

Lack of Training.   Few dogs walk properly with their owners without obedience training. The command "Heel" is an important ingredient in a basic obedience course. It teaches a dog to walk on your left side with his head next to your thigh. He walks when you walk and stops when you do. A dog walking in "Heel" never leaves your side.

Outside Distractions.   Other dogs, interesting smells, new people are all exciting to a young dog. He will pull the person on the other end of the leash as hard as he can to satisfy his curiosity and desire to see it all. An untrained dog does not understand that he should remain at your side.

Dominance. A dog that pulls on the leash is essentially a dog that has not yet been sorted out in the pack structure. He may believe he is an Alpha wolf, or pack leader.

Breed Tendency.   Pulling can be instinctive in some breeds and must be expected. All Nordic-type dogs, including the Akita, Alaskan Malamute, Eskimo Dog, Norwegian Elkhound, Samoyed, and Siberian Husky, fall into this group. The size and strength of the dog determines how hard he will pull on the leash.

Previous Teaching.   Every dog responds to being pulled by pulling back in the opposite direction. It is a reflex action and is seen when dogs are tied up for long periods of time or are constantly pulled on the leash away from where they want to go. When a dog owner constantly pulls on his dog's leash, he is conditioning the dog to pull.

Solutions (Reconditioning)

Teach the Command "Heel." The obedience command "Heel" is a series of right turns and right U-turns made by the owner when the dog is held by three feet of a six-foot leash attached to a slip collar. Whenever the dog runs ahead or lags behind, the owner jerks the leash firmly but nonabusively, makes a sharp right turn, and walks briskly in another direction without pausing

Teaching the command "Heel."

or allowing the dog to hesitate even if he is caught off-guard. By having the leash jerked (as you would in a correction), hearing, "Tootsie, Heel," being taken in a right U-turn, and being walked briskly in the opposite direction, the dog comes to accept you as his leader and begins to learn what you expect of him on his walks.

Teaching a dog the obedience command "Heel" is beyond the scope of this book. This command requires more technique than the brief summary given above. Please refer to any of the many fine dog training books available. *Good Dog, Bad Dog* (Signet Books) by Mordecai Siegal and Matthew Margolis is recommended.

Consistent Walking Behavior. Always place the dog on your left side. Use a six-foot

Bob Wortham

leather leash attached to a slip collar. Hold the leash in your right hand, allowing two or three feet of slack to drape across your knees. This keeps the dog close to your side. Do not allow the dog to pull you. If he pulls, jerk the leash firmly and make a right turn, walking in the opposite direction. Do not allow the dog to go to the end of the leash unless it is to relieve himself.

Prevention Tips

The Slip Collar. If the slip collar is not attached properly, it can choke the dog, causing him to pull. (See part Two, "Some Essential Tools and Techniques for Problem Solving.") The slip collar must form the letter "P" with the end hanging from the dog's right side. The slip collar must be worn properly to be effective. Some dogs react negatively to a slip collar, in which case use a conventional leather collar or a dog harness.

MOUNTING

Mounting, an upsetting problem, is what happens when a dog jumps, places his paws around an adult's leg, a child's body, or the vertical portion of a piece of furniture and simulates sexual intercourse. Although some dog owners are amused at the sight of this behavior, the majority become upset and justifiably concerned. Some children become frightened to the point of terror if they are the dog's objective. A panicked child could easily get bitten. It is a potentially dangerous situation.

The human issues involved are modesty, sexual attitudes, good taste, bewilderment, fear, and possible injury. The canine issues are dominance, control (over the dog's behavior), and sexual confusion. Because mounting can lead to injury, it should be considered a serious problem and dealt with immediately.

Origins of the Problem

The birth rate of wolves, coyotes and other wild canids is restricted by several natural limitations. Most wolves and coyotes pair bond and live out a monogamous existence. Females experience only one estrus cycle a year throughout maturity. Males do not usually produce sperm except when females are ready for mating, which creates only one breeding season per year. Sexual activity is almost never engaged in except during that one mating season. Sexual maturity in wolves and coyotes is reached after two years of age. These conditions reduce the quantity of offspring, which helps to keep a balanced ecology, since a territory has its limitations and provides food and shelter for a measurable number of animals. If the animal population becomes too dense for one area, it is reduced by hunger, sickness, death, and migration. These are the natural conditions of life for wild dogs and their cousins. Predictable sexual behavior is part of the delicate balance.

Domestic dogs are different because they are not subjected to all the restraints of nature. After hundreds of years of artificial breeding and selection, their sexual process and behavior have changed along with their appearance. The domestic dogs' birth rate is unnaturally high and completely out of proportion to their ability to survive without human help. Domestic dogs are sexually mature after six months of age. The female estrus cycle is experienced two and sometimes three times a year, allowing for that many matings. Male dogs are capable of producing sperm all year long during their normal adult lives. And, significantly, domestic dogs do not mate for life or pair bond as their canid cousins do. Matings are based on random chance or by prearrangement between breeders of pure-bred dogs. The delicate balance of nature has been removed as a factor, altering the domestic dog's sexual behavior. Like human sexual behavior, it is no longer linked exclusively to procreation. Sexual behavior in pet dogs is varied and unpredictable. A subordinate dog will not be sexually active unless encouraged and supported by the correct conditions

for mating. Sexual expression in domestic dogs is often an indication of a dominant personality.

Reasons for the Problem

Puberty. Young male dogs may engage in mounting behavior at the first sexual stirrings and express their appetite with humans.

Temperament. Dogs with nervous or excitable personalities tend to mount humans and objects.

Unintentional Teaching. When dog owners encourage their pets to jump on them in play, they may be inadvertently encouraging them to mount. Dogs invited onto human laps or allowed to place their paws on shoulders or chests are being set up for the problem of jumping, which could lead to mounting.

Menstrual Cycle in Women. Some dogs are stimulated by close contact with women experiencing menstruation.

Estrus in Dogs. Male dogs are stimulated by the scent of a female dog in heat. A female in estrus can be detected by a male for many miles.

Frustration. Male dogs that have had sexual experience sometimes mount out of a desire for further sexual contacts.

Hypersexuality. Some dogs have greater sex drive than others. Such dogs are usually more dominant, aggressive, and easily stimulated.

Solutions (Environmental)

Neutering the Dog. Sexually aggressive and dominant dogs with this problem may be cured with the help of surgical sterilization. It takes about six weeks for the male hormone testosterone to leave the dog's body completely after surgery. Although surgical neutering is likely to end the problem of mounting, there can be no guarantee. Consult a veterinarian.

Solutions (Reconditioning)

The Margolis Maneuver. The problem of mounting can be solved in most dogs by consistently correcting them with the use of a leash and slip collar. Set up the conditions under which the dog mounts. Place a slip collar on the dog and attach a leash to it. Do not invite the dog to engage in this behavior, because he may then become confused when you correct him. Allow it to happen. When the dog mounts, jerk the leash and say "NO, NO, NO" in a loud, firm tone of voice. Praise the dog for responding to your correction. (See "The Margolis Maneuver" in part Two, "Some Essential Tools and Techniques for Problem Solving.")

Shake Can. This is simply another form of correction, substituting a shake can for the Margolis Maneuver. When the dog mounts rattle the can loudly. Say "NO, NO, NO" in a loud tone of voice. Praise the dog for responding to your correction.

Water Gun (or Squirt Bottle). These are alternate correction tools. Squirt the dog in the face with a spray of water when he mounts. Say "NO, NO, NO" in a loud tone of voice. Praise the dog for responding to your correction.

Exercise. Allow your dog to work off some of his sexual energy by running, playing with you with a ball or Frisbee, or jogging with you. Teaching your dog obedience training and then putting him through his paces on a daily basis has a good effect.

Prevention Tips

Adjustment of Your Behavior. Do not play roughly with dogs who mount; doing so can arouse them. With such dogs, eliminate all interaction that involves jumping or the placing of paws on the legs, chest, or shoulders. If mounting behavior is considered a problem, it must not be tolerated at any time. It cannot be allowed in one set of circumstances and forbidden in another. The dog cannot distinguish when it is acceptable and when it is not.

NIPPING AND MOUTHING

A nip is a diminutive bite. When a puppy or grown dog nips someone, he essentially bites with his twelve front teeth. The bite is a quick pinch without full pressure. A puppy nip can be more painful than a nip from a grown dog because puppy teeth are needle-like and sharp. Unfortunately, nipping is not often taken seriously by dog owners because small dogs seem cute when they try to do what grown dogs do. When a nipper turns into a biter, it is already too late.

Mouthing is a similar problem that often leads to biting. When a puppy *mouths* he constantly puts his mouth on your hand, your arm, your leg, or anything that belongs to you, including your shoes, socks, and sweaters. If you own one of the breeds of dog that are excessive droolers, such as the Bulldog, St. Bernard, or Basset Hound, then mouthing can be especially unpleasant. Some owners tolerate this behavior, but most others simply are confused and not sure what to do. Do not stand in the shadow of indecision. Nipping and mouthing lead to more serious problems and should be dealt with right away.

Origins of the Problem

(See "Biting.")

Reasons for the Problem

Teething. Puppies, like human babies, are born without teeth. The puppy's first teeth push their way through the gums between three and four weeks of age. The last of these baby teeth erupt during the sixth week. Permanent teeth replace the first set at about four or five months of age and continue to do so for several months.

The first (deciduous) teeth fall out and are traded for adult teeth. In dogs, the roots of the baby teeth become part of the new, permanent set. As in humans, the entire process is called teething and is characterized by soreness and itching of the gums, along with some slight bleeding and drooling. Occasionally, also as in humans, teething is accompanied by slightly elevated body temperature, vomiting, and even diarrhea. When puppies and young dogs teethe they are uncomfortable and even listless, because of pain. All of their energy and concentration are focused on the discomfort in their gums. Chewing, nipping, and mouthing become compulsive activities offering some relief.

Breed Characteristics. Most hunting breeds use their mouths for work. Retrievers and other bird dogs are especially fixated on oral activities.

Communication. Dogs communicate a great deal with their mouths. They bark, they lick, they chew, nip, and mouth. Nipping can be an expression of aggression, defensiveness, playfulness, frustration, or anger. Mouthing can be an expression of fear, insecurity, or playfulness.

Owner-Induced Behavior. Nipping and mouthing can come about because of the way some humans relate to their dogs. Playing rough, aggressive games such as tug-of-war encourages this negative behavior. Boxing with the dog and roughhousing are ways of teaching this behavior. Placing your fingers in the dog's mouth is practically an invitation to nip or mouth. Hitting a dog can induce him to "fight back" with his teeth. Pushing the dog away with your hands can also cause the problem. When you are grooming the dog or administering medicine, he will nip or mouth if you hurt him. What you do with your hands can cause pain or discomfort to your pet and create the habit of nipping or mouthing.

Solutions (Environmental)

Soothe His Teething Pain. Because teething pain and discomfort are major causes of nipping and mouthing in puppies, it is important to deal with them therapeutically. Soak six washcloths in cold water. Twist them and put them in the freezer of your refrigerator. When they are frozen, give them to the puppy one at a time. Each one will stay cold for about one and a half hours. As he chews each one, the coldness will numb his gums and ease the pain of teething. Although it does not stop the chewing, nipping, and mouthing, it diverts it to an acceptable place.

Use ice cubes in the same therapeutic manner as the frozen, twisted washcloths.

Chewing toys have the same good effect. Use hard rubber toys, rawhide bones, toy bones made of nylon.

Solutions (Reconditioning)

The Margolis Maneuver. This is the simplest and most effective reconditioning technique for this problem. It is easy to set up the nipping situation so that the puppy can be corrected. Place a leash and slip collar on the dog. Hold the leash in your right hand, allowing two feet of slack, and kneel. Play with the dog in your usual manner. Pet him and offer your hand. If he nips or mouths it, jerk the leash to the dog's right side and say "NO" in a loud and firm tone of voice. How hard to jerk the leash depends on the size and age of the dog. (See part Three, "Your Dog's Personality.") Instead of taking your hand away, leave it in place. Let him draw away. That is the only way to know if he is responding properly to the correction. If you jerk the leash and pull your hand away, you are not teaching the dog anything. Play with him again and put your hand near his face again. If he starts to mouth or nip, jerk the leash again, saying "NO." Keep your hand in place. Eventually he will turn his head away as you keep your hand near his face. Praise him lavishly for responding properly to your corrections. Repeat the process and give him great praise every time he responds properly.

When using this corrective technique on a dog that is teething, give him an acceptable chew toy after praising him for responding properly to the correction. See "Easing his teething pain" above in "Solutions (Environmental)."

Shake Can. Use the same techniques as in the Margolis Maneuver, substituting the shake can for the leash and slip collar. Hold the shake can behind your back. Give it a quick, vigorous shake when the dog nips or mouths, say "NO" in a loud tone of voice. Leave your hand in front of him. When he stops nipping or mouthing, praise him.

Water Gun or Squirt Bottle. Use the same techniques as in the Margolis Maneuver using a squirt in the face instead of a jerk of the leash.

Prevention Tips

Keep Your Hands Away From the Dog's Mouth. Your hands should never be in his mouth unless you are going to medicate him.

Never Hit Your Dog. Hitting may cause him to nip or bite you.

Play Gently. Be loving and affectionate in all play activity. The dog should associate your hands with love and affection rather than negative treatment, which will lead to nipping and mouthing.

PAPER TRAINING "MISTAKES"

In this, the age of the throw-away society, the disposable dog toilet is a great convenience. For all its usefulness, paper training is not without its problems and can puzzle many dog owners, newcomers and old hands alike. Those with new dogs are always angered and befuddled when their puppy uses the floor for a toilet, even though they spread newspapers all over the house. And they feel especially betrayed when the dog makes an utter mess of the carpet after the breeder told them that their new puppy was paper-trained.

There is nothing more confusing in dog ownership than paper training. Dogs are not born with the desire or instinct to relieve themselves on newspapers. It is a demanding form of conditioned dog behavior that requires information, determination, and patience from the dog owner. Paper training involves a set of simple but effective techniques. Without them the dog owner will always be frustrated looking at the too-late edition lying neatly on the floor, next to a puddle and a pile on the carpet.

To clear up the confusion, here is a definition of paper training that must be understood and accepted in its unchanged form. *Dogs that are paper-trained urinate and defecate on newspapers spread on the floor in one location in your home. Never move the papers to any other location once the paper area has been established. The dog must always eliminate indoors at the set location.*

Paper training is an alternative to housebreaking. It is a different concept. Do not attempt to use both techniques. Doing that will lead to failure. Decide whether to paper-train or housebreak your dog and stick with whichever one you opt for. Consider paper training your dog if (1) you live in an area with severe weather conditions; (2) your dog is small (paper training is not good for large dogs); (3) your dog is a female (most male dogs lift a hind leg to urinate and could stain a wall); (4) you are at an advanced age; (5) you are in poor health; (6) you have difficulty climbing stairs or using an elevator to take your dog out; (7) you dislike walking your dog at night; (8) you are a working person and cannot get home in the early evening.

Should you decide to paper-train your dog, refer to page 170 for a complete training program, "How to Paper-Train Your Dog." If your dog has already been paper-trained but is experiencing failures on a regular basis, you may be helped by the remainder of this entry. However, it may be necessary to start over, from the beginning, with the help of the complete training program on page 170.

Origins of the Problem

(See HOUSEBREAKING)

Reasons for the Problem

Improper Technique. Most people believe that a dog will know what to do if they simply lay a piece of paper on the floor. Many place newspapers all over the house, in many different areas (the bathroom, the kitchen, the foyer, the dining room) and then fail to understand why their dog uses the floor once the papers are put down. Simply placing newspaper on the floor is not paper training.

Housebreaking and Paper Training. This is too much of an inconsistency for any dog. If a dog is first paper-trained and then housebroken, he is likely to use the floor with or without newspapers. Paper training teaches a dog that it is desirable to relieve himself indoors, on the floor.

Time of the Year. Many puppies are bought as Christmas presents when it's cold outside. Consequently, the new owner paper-trains the little dog in order to avoid taking him out in the cold weather. In the spring, the dog is then housebroken and taught to use the street. But by then it's too late. The dog has been taught to use the floor and is confused between housebreaking and using the floor.

Failure to Remove the Scent. Because dogs always return to the same spot they soiled, paper training cannot be accomplished without first removing the scent markings (from urine and feces) that are present around the house, though they are detected only by the dog's keen nose.

Old Odors. If you have recently moved into a new home and you know that another dog lived there before you came, clean the floors and baseboards with an odor neutralizer. It is important to obliterate these subtle odors left by the previous dog. All dogs are attracted to old urine and defecation odors, whether from other dogs or themselves. A dog's incredible sense of smell will detect the urine scent of another dog even though a human cannot. It will stimulate him to eliminate on top of it.

Lack of Confinement. Puppies and dogs being paper-trained cannot maintain body discipline if they are given the freedom to wander all over the house when they are left alone. In fact, they cannot be expected to control themselves if they are free to wander

without supervision even when someone is home.

Improper Confinement. Dogs that are confined behind a closed door, cut off from the rest of the house, will become upset, nervous, or anxiety-ridden and lose control of their body discipline. Inevitably they will soil the floor.

Too Much Water. If young dogs and puppies being paper-trained have access to water all day and night, they will drink many times and urinate all day and night. If the intake of water is not scheduled, the dog will have many "accidents."

Improper Diet. Dogs cannot control their elimination habits if they eat dog food that does not agree with them, eat many between-meal snacks, are overfed, or are fed human food indiscriminately from the table. Any change from the established diet can and most likely will cause diarrhea. To paper train a dog properly, you must place him on a feeding schedule. See "How to Paper-Train Your Dog" on page 170. Feeding a dog more times than his schedule calls for will cause "accidents." The purpose of the feeding schedule will be defeated and his being paper-trained will be prevented.

Evening Stimulation. If a dog is exercised late in the evening during his last walk, he will drink when he is finished. The water he drinks then will cause urination "accidents" through the night. Giving him rawhide or other chew toys late in the evening can cause diarrhea and defeat the dog's paper training.

A Second Dog. Paper-trained dogs may make "mistakes" when a new puppy or older second dog is added to the household. In this situation the "mistakes" are the result of emotional stress.

Great Expectations. It is useless to expect absolute paper training control from young puppies. They do not develop complete control of the sphincter muscles controlling the opening and closing of the bladder and the rectum until after the fourth month.

Solutions (Reconditioning)

The problems connected with paper training have to do with improper training, confusion about the location of the papers, human inconsistencies, and regression. These can all be solved by starting over and teaching paper training properly. See page 170, "How to Paper-Train Your Dog." However, if you have already paper-trained your dog and he is making infrequent "mistakes" the problem may not require starting over. It may be of a temporary nature and the following solutions will help.

Odor Neutralizer. If your dog fails to use the papers or is missing them and soiling the floor, it is necessary to obliterate the odor. This odor, imperceptible to human smell, draws the dog back to the same spot and elicits his instinct to "mark" it with new urine or defecation. Buy an odor neutralizer concentrate at a pharmacy or pet supply store and use it according to the instructions on the label. Odor neutralizers do not mask the smells; they alter them. Spread more papers over a wider area and always use one sheet with the scent of the dog's previous use on the exact spot you want him to use.

Confine the Dog. Until you can determine if your dog has had a total regression of training or not, keep him confined to one area with the help of a puppy gate or dog crate. The dog must be confined overnight or when no one is home to watch him. Pay careful attention to his feeding and walking schedule (see page 170, "How to Paper-Train Your Dog") and make the proper adjustments. That may be the solution. If the problem is temporary it is unnecessary to keep the dog confined. Otherwise, begin training over again.

Correct the Dog. If you catch the dog in the act of urinating or defecating off the papers say, "NO! NO! NO!" in a firm tone of voice. If available, rattle a shake can.

Same Spot. Sometimes a dog becomes fixated on one spot and constantly relieves himself there. Besides using an odor neutralizer you could cover the location with a piece of furniture. If the dog soils the furniture it is time to begin paper training over again, from the beginning. See page 170, "How to Paper-Train Your Dog."

Prevention Tips

Decide. Owners whose dogs are house soiling must make a training decision. Housebreaking teaches a dog to relieve himself outdoors and *never* indoors. Paper training teaches a dog to relieve himself indoors, on the floor, on top of newspapers. Decide whether to housebreak your dog or paper-train him, and stick with your decision. One program contradicts the other. To implement both will set up the conditions for failure. To housebreak your dog, see page 165. To paper-train your dog, see page 170.

PHOBIAS

There is nothing funny about a dog experiencing emotional pain. And yet party chitchat often includes the latest story about the antics of a humanlike dog who is considered a neurotic reflection of its owner. It may be true that dogs living with humans have acquired some of their abnormal behaviors and psychological quirks. But few realize that phobic reactions to ordinary situations involve anxiety, hysteria, and aching from within. It's not much to laugh about.

The word *phobia* is derived from the Greek word *phobos,* meaning dread, a strong fear, a fear-determined aversion. When dogs or people have a phobia, they are consistently afraid of an object, a situation, or of certain persons. Their fear is persistent, real but inappropriate. The feelings of dread and panic are totally out of proportion to the reality that causes the fear because phobias really stem from sources deep within the personality. The objects, situations, or persons that create this intense fear in humans are usually symbols for something too painful to acknowledge. The phobic reaction occurs shortly after a traumatic event and recurs for years afterward. Sometimes the untreated phobia lasts a lifetime.

In dogs, phobias spring from an association with a feared object, a group of persons, or a situation that involved a terrifying incident, or they are the result of an inherited personality distortion. No one knows for sure. When a puppy is exposed to the sound of a gunshot, he may thereafter fear any similar noise. The fear may become *generalized* and develop into a fear of all noises, from the slam of a door to the starting up of

a refrigerator motor. There is an endless list of different phobias dogs and people develop. The most common human phobias are fear of falling, of heights, of open spaces, of closed spaces, of cats, of other people, of lightning, of dogs, of horses, of dirt, of germs, of darkness, of fire, and of animals of every description. The most serious (and frequently found) phobias in dogs are fear of closed places, fear of strangers or other people and fear of noises. These are the phobias dealt with in this entry of the directory. The solutions offered have had a high rate of success with these types of problems. Dogs with severe phobia problems are extremely difficult to change. Consult an animal behaviorist who is a trained psychologist specializing in animal behavior.

Origins of the Problem

It is likely that wolves and wild dogs, as well as domestic dogs, develop phobic reactions to objects and events that are associated with powerful experiences. One can speculate that a wolf standing next to a tree hit by lightning might fear electrical storms and the threat of them for the rest of his life. He might even develop a tree phobia.

At the beginning of the third week of life a puppy or wolf cub begins to develop a primitive fear response to his environment. Loud noises are heard and responded to with fright. Pain is felt for the first time. Anything that produces fear or pain creates behavioral inhibitions in the young animal. Some researchers have found that dogs in the five-to-six-week age group were quick to recover from emotionally frightening events. But dogs in the eight-to-nine-week age group had a much slower recovery rate.

A seven-week-old puppy will be somewhat hesitant with humans it has met for the first time. A fourteen-week-old puppy that has never been handled by humans will experience intense fear, suspicion, and a need to escape when confronted by them for the first time. All dogs that are isolated or denied access to new people and situations for a long period develop avoidance behavior and become extremely suspicious.

Older puppies have a much greater memory development than younger ones and therefore may cling to traumatic events (and the fear they produced) for a greater period of time. Perhaps there is one period in a young dog's life when he is more likely to develop a phobia than at any other time. There are dogs who have suffered extreme injury from cars but did not develop a phobic reaction to them. And yet, who can explain why one dog will become hysterical at the slightest rumble of thunder and another will not? All dogs experience fear. They may cower, hide, or run away. But the phobic dog will tremble with terror to the point of hysteria. He may defecate, cry, howl, whine, bark uncontrollably, bite, or slam into walls or doors and inadvertently destroy his environment. Phobic behavior in dogs is abnormal behavior, and, for the most part, unexplainable because the dogs cannot tell us why they associate fear and pain with the person, place, or situation that upsets them. For that matter, few humans can, either.

FEAR OF CONFINEMENT

The phobic reaction to being closed in is frightening to watch. Dog trainers refer to it as the *escape syndrome*. Dogs with this phobia are so frightened when closed in they will howl and bark and dig at the walls and doors to escape. They are destructive to themselves and to human property. This phobia can be seen in various degrees. A closed-in dog may simply pace and whine or he may hysterically try to dig his way out.

Reasons for the Problem

Inherited Behavior. Phobic behavior can begin with a genetic problem. A dog born with a shy or nervous personality is more likely to develop a phobia than any other type.

Negative Experience. Negative experiences can be harmful to any dog but especially to a nervous, timid, or shy dog. If such a dog were confined behind a door, in the dark, and a loud noise frightened him, he would desperately want to run. However, his confinement would prevent him from escaping. Depending on how long he was forced to endure the fearful stimulation, a dog in that situation could become phobic.

The same is true of a tethered dog that becomes entangled in his leash and trapped for a long time in a state of panic.

Incidents associated with automobiles can lead to claustrophobia. A dog confined to a car with no way to escape may become phobic after hours of fright. Being constantly teased or baited while confined in a car can deeply disturb a dog. An injury sustained when riding in a car, or a trip to veterinarian producing pain, can create an intense emotional aversion to confinement in cars, which could generalize into a fear of all confinement.

Punishment.   Being punished in a particular room could create a phobic reaction to the room, which could then generalize into a fear of confinement.

Personality.   A nervous or shy dog is more likely to become phobic than any other personality type.

Unknown Past.   It is possible that a new owner of a phobic dog is dealing with past trauma.

Solutions (Environmental)

Make a Chart.   Make a list of all the closed-in areas that create a phobic response in your dog. It is possible that it will be a long list. Write down every known place that frightens the dog. Once the list is complete, number the items in the order of their intensity. The bathroom may be number one and the kitchen number two, with the basement number three, for example. This list may help you find the original source or incident that created the phobia, so you can undo the damage. It will also help you determine where to begin modifying the dog's behavior with *desensitization* (see "Modifying your dog's behavior").

Use a Puppy Gate.   Do not place any dog behind a closed door. This prohibition is especially important in dealing with dogs that are claustrophobic. Instead, use a puppy gate in the doorway, giving the dog a good field of vision beyond his confinement.

Create a Reassuring Environment.
When leaving a dog alone, leave the lights on with a radio or TV playing. The claustrophobic dog might feel better if he hears a tape recording of his owner's voice. Tape-record long conversations, monologues, and dialogues from the dinner table. Try to develop a one-, two-, or even three-hour tape and play it when you leave.

Provide a blanket or sheet with your scent on it for the dog to sleep on. It could be comforting.

Use a Dog Run.   Either build a dog run made of chain-link fence sitting on a slab of concrete or buy a portable dog run at a pet supply store, hardware store, or a fence company. One of these is an important alternative to indoor confinement for a claustrophobic dog. Although confined, a claustrophobic dog may respond well to being left outdoors. He has a *sense* of freedom.

Tie-Out Stake.   An acceptable way to confine a dog outdoors is to buy a tie-out stake, a device that screws deep into the ground. Attach one end of a chain or strong rope to the dog's leather collar and the other end to the metal top of the tie-out stake. Most of these stakes swivel, giving the dog the ability to move around without twisting the tether. His movements are limited by the length of the tether.

Clothesline Trolley.   Attach a clothesline 8 to 10 feet off the ground from the side of your house to a tree. Run the clothesline through the loop of a leash. Be sure the leash is long enough to allow the dog to lie down. This homemade device allows the dog to run back and forth but keeps him confined. However, never use a slip collar or any other training equipment with an overhead line.

Exercise. Claustrophobic dogs feel better and accept *proper* confinement with greater comfort when they have used up their excess energy in exercise. Before leaving, walk your dog for fifteen to thirty minutes and have as long and vigorous a play period as possible. Toss a ball or Frisbee and run the dog.

Solutions (Reconditioning)

Solve the Secondary Problem. If you must confine a dog with an aversion to confinement, ... solve the problem that makes confinement necessary. It could be chewing, housebreaking, running away, or something else. Find that problem entry in this directory and work on it. Eliminate the problem, and you eliminate the need for confinement.

Avoid Punishment Areas. Avoid placing the dog in areas where he has been punished. Do not confine a claustrophobic dog in an area he associates with punishment.

Modify Your Dog's Behavior. There are two important approaches to eliminating phobic behavior in dogs (or at least lessening its emotional effect). They are based on the theories of Ivan Pavlov, B. F. Skinner, and J. Wolpe. The first approach, *desensitization,* is to re-create gradually the conditions of the negative experience (in small degrees) and introduce positive associations and reinforcements at the same time. It is a basic form of learning in which a new response is acquired as a result of satisfying a dog's need. The positive associations should be a combination of love, praise, and reassurance accompanied with special food treats. Bring

the dog into the confinement area but do not close it off. Offer him small but favored tidbits such as slivers of cheese, cooked chicken, or liver. Pet the dog, hug him, talk to him, and offer lavish praise. This can be a slow, drawn-out process, taking weeks or even months. In the beginning, introduce the confinement area for short periods of time and simultaneously offer large measures of love, praise, and food treats. As time progresses, extend the period in the confinement area until you feel that the dog might tolerate being gated in the room alone.

The second approach to modifying your dog's behavior is to get him to relax when confronting the object of his fear. This idea is called *counterconditioning.* The theory is that an animal cannot generate intense anxiety when it is in a state of relaxation. Eating is one known way to relax a dog. Feeding him in the confinement area may begin to ease his anxiety about being there. Start out slowly by calling him into the area and offering him an enticing morsel, a hug, and a great deal of praise. Take him out of the area right away. If all went well, then repeat the process as often as the dog will tolerate it. Eventually you may feed him his complete meal set down on the floor in the room that frightens him. You know you have made progress if you can call the dog into the confinement area, feed him a complete meal, and leave him there after closing the gate.

Apply Obedience Training. Hire a professional dog trainer or buy a training book such as *Good Dog, Bad Dog* by Siegal and Margolis and begin obedience training. Dog training calms a dog because it organizes his responses, establishes in his mind that you are his leader, and helps him try to please you. An obedience-trained dog has a much easier time coping with his phobic responses by concentrating on your commands and not on his fear. Obedience training is relaxing and aids in counterconditioning (see "Modify your dog's behavior").

Add Another Pet.   Sometimes introducing another pet has a positive influence. If another dog or cat enters the feared room, the troubled dog may follow.

Use the Kennel Method.   There are boarding and training kennels that will introduce your phobic dog to a new environment with new people to observe him, relate to him, train him, and gradually desensitize him by re-creating the negative situation with positive reinforcements. Getting the dog away from the specific confinement locations at home and desensitizing him with the help of a different confinement area has been a successful therapy. Other dogs and other people have a good effect on problem dogs.

FEAR OF NOISES

Thunder is the first thought we have when considering the dog who is terrified of noise. But there are other more common noises that create phobic reactions in dogs. The sudden loudness of a TV when it is first turned on, firecrackers, fallen objects, street traffic, horns, high winds, screeching tires, and sirens are all sounds that will cause a phobic dog to quake with fear, yelp, run away, or display the most intense escape behavior. It is sad and painful to watch a dog you love experience such emotional suffering. Something should be done about it.

Reasons for the Problem

Isolated Environment.   When a puppy is raised in a rural area where there are peace, quiet, and few people, he may become traumatized when moved to the loud, noisy city. The grinding sound of garbage trucks or even the boisterous sounds of kids horsing around could frighten the dog. At first the dog may act timid or shy but later he may exhibit all the terror symptoms of a phobic dog afraid of noises and their sources.

Bad Experience with a Car.   Screeching tires, backfires, sudden horn honking, engine revving, or even slammed doors could begin the dog's phobic reaction to noise.

Firecrackers.   Only the most experienced (and sensitive) dog owners realize how difficult firecrackers are for dogs. The constant explosions are regarded by many dogs as warfare and terrorize them. Many a phobia was started on the explosive Fourth of July.

Abuse.   Some dogs are the victims of abuse from children who deliberately try to frighten them with noise. Dogs that are teased or hurt or yelled at by unfriendly neighbors can be scared into the beginning of a phobic response to noise.

Inherited Behavior.   Bad breeding has resulted in many phobic dogs. Dogs born shy or nervous or timid can become phobic, but the phobias are really symptoms of the underlying problem, their inherited shyness or nervousness.

Noises in the Home. Without realizing it, many dog owners generate so much noise in their homes that they create a phobic response in their dogs. People who constantly argue and shout may scare their dogs (and everyone else, including their children). In some homes dog owners bang on things with their hands, swat rolled-up newspapers in their hands for the frightening effect (thinking the noise has something to do with dog training), throw cans and pots around, and slam doors continuously. Some people yell and scream at their puppies from the first day the dogs come into the house.

Kennel Raising. If a dog spent the first five or six months of his life in a kennel, he would have some difficulty adjusting to a home environment with everyday noises. A poor adjustment could be the beginning of a phobic response to noise.

Solutions (Environmental)

Make a Chart. List all the noise sources that create a phobic response in your dog. It is possible that it will be a long list. Write down every known noise that frightens the dog. Once the list is complete, number the items in the order of intensity. Thunder may be number one and fire engines number two, with rifle shots number three, for example. This list may help you find the original noise source or incident that created the phobia. It will also help you determine where to begin modifying his behavior with *desensitization* (see ''Modify Your Dog's Behavior'').

Create a Reassuring Environment. When leaving a dog alone, leave the lights on with a radio or TV playing, as suggested above.

The dog who fears loud noise might feel better if he hears a tape recording of his owner's voice. Tape-record conversations, monologues, and dialogues, as described above. Try to develop a one-, two-, or even three-hour tape and play it when you leave. Do not play the tapes too loudly.

As suggested above, a blanket or sheet with your scent on it could be comforting for the dog to sleep on.

Provide Exercise. Nervous or shy dogs who fear noise feel better after using up their excess energy in exercise. Before leaving, walk the dog for fifteen to thirty minutes and have as long and vigorous a play period as possible. Toss a ball or Frisbee and run the dog.

Solutions (Reconditioning)

Use Obedience Training. Hire a professional dog trainer or buy a training book such as *Good Dog, Bad Dog* by Siegal and Margolis and begin obedience training. Dog training calms a dog because it organizes his responses, establishes in his mind that you are his leader, and helps him try to please you . An obedience-trained dog has a much easier time coping with his phobic responses by concentrating on your commands and not on his fear. It is relaxing and aids in counterconditioning. (See ''Modify Your Dog's Behavior.'')

Modify Your Dog's Behavior. Desensitization and counterconditioning, two important approaches to eliminating phobic behavior in dogs, are discussed on page 149. To use desensitization to alter a noise-phobic dog's behavior, refer to your chart, selecting the number-one noise source on the list. Make a tape recording of the noise. Introduce the recording to the dog at a volume high enough to be heard but low enough not to frighten the dog. Feed the dog a food treat that he enjoys, such as bits of cooked chicken, liver, or cheese. Pet him, hug him, talk to him lovingly, and praise him for listening to the recording. In the beginning, introduce the noise for short periods of time, but bring the volume up slightly at each new session. Offer large measures of love, praise, and food treats as you introduce the recording of the noise source. As time goes on, extend each session until you feel the dog can tolerate the noise at a loudness that simulates it in reality.

The second approach to modifying your dog's behavior is to use counterconditioning and to get him to relax when confronting the object of his fear. The theory is that an animal cannot be anxious when it is in a state of relaxation. Since eating is one known way to relax a dog, feed him as you expose him to the noise source. Start out slowly by calling him to you and offering him an enticing morsel, a hug, and a great deal of praise. Play a recording of the noise source at a moderate level. If all went well, then repeat the process as often as the dog will tolerate it, but feed him more of his meal each time. Eventually you may feed him his complete meal, set down on the floor, while you play the noise recording at full volume. You know you have made progress if you can call the dog to you and feed him a complete meal as a recording of the noise plays at a loud volume.

Try the Kennel Method. There are boarding and training kennels that will introduce your phobic dog to a new environ-

ment with new people to observe him, relate to him, train him, and gradually desensitize him by recreating the negative situation with positive reinforcements. Getting away from the specific noise locations at home and desensitizing the dog with the help of a different noise location has been a successful therapy.

FEAR OF PEOPLE

Nearly all phobias in dogs begin with a frightening experience. The exception is *fear of people*. The most common cause of this phobia has to do with living conditions during the earliest part of the dog's life. There is a critical period for puppies that influences the development of their behavior. It starts at the end of the second week or the beginning of the third week of puppyhood and continues to the seventh or eighth week. During this time a puppy must be socialized

Among many kennel-raised puppies, fear of people and close contact is very common.

by human beings to adapt to living with them. The puppies should be handled in a loving, gentle way at least once a day throughout this critical period to become capable of achieving their full potential as pet dogs. Unfortunately, some dogs have little or no contact with humans throughout puppyhood and as a result grow up as shy, nervous dogs, uneasy with most people. In extreme cases they develop a phobic response to anyone other than the one or two persons they live with. The fear of strangers all too often begins with an alienated puppyhood.

Reasons for the Problem

Inherited Behavior. Although no dog is known to be born phobic, some have inherited shy or nervous behavior. Shy and nervous dogs are more easily made phobic than other personality types.

Lack of Socialization. See the introduction to this section.

Lack of Human Contact. A perfectly socialized dog can develop a fear of people if he is constantly isolated from humans other than the person who feeds him. Dogs kept in a kennel for the first six months of life may have limited outside contact with humans. Such a dog could have been bullied by his littermates. Some kennel dogs are afraid of men if they have known only women (or the reverse). Some dogs in kennels relate only to other dogs, and some are overprotected. These dogs will be hesitant with most people. They are the perfect candidates for a phobic response to people.

Punishment. There are persons who constantly hit dogs thinking they are train-

ing them to be protective. The idea is to make the dogs vicious toward strangers but loving and protective toward their owners. This treatment, however, often results in creating dogs that have a phobic response to most people and are too alienated to be pets.

Solutions (Environmental)

Make a Chart. List all the people who create a phobic response in your dog. It is possible that it will be a long list. Make another list of every person the dog tolerates without fear or hesitation. Once the lists are complete, number each person in the first list by order of the intensity of the dog's fear. The mailman may be number one, or a delivery boy on a bicycle. Try to determine if those on the fear list can be classified into types. Some dogs, for example, are frightened of people walking with a limp or men with a package, et cetera. This list may help you find the original source or incident that created the phobia, which will help when trying to undo the damage. The types the dog is most frightened of are the ones to work with the most when trying to modify his behavior with *desensitization*.

Take the Dog Out. Begin a program of walking the dog at every opportunity. The dog should begin a socialization process involving new places and people. Go to parks, shopping centers, and malls. Introduce the dog to as many new people as possible.

Solutions (Reconditioning)

The Kennel Method. There are boarding and training kennels that will introduce your phobic dog to a new environment with new people to observe him, relate to him, train

Taking frequent walks with your dog can be an important part of his socialization training.

him, groom him, love him, and gradually desensitize him by re-creating the negative situation but with positive reinforcements. Getting away from the home environment and desensitizing the dog with the help of different people in another atmosphere has been a successful therapy. When a child goes to a sleep-away camp for the summer, he or she comes back healthier and more mature, with a greater ability to cope with new people and new situations. A brief interlude of separation is usually stimulating and psychologically rewarding. The same can be true for problem dogs. Other dogs and other people have a good effect on them.

Modifying Your Dog's Behavior. One approach is to try to desensitize your dog. Bring the dog into an area inside your home where he is most relaxed. Have someone on your fear list walk into the house where the dog can see him. The person chosen should be the least feared on the list. Have him or her maintain a great distance from the dog so that he does not experience a phobic response. Offer him small but favored tidbits such as slivers of cheese, small cubes of cooked chicken, or liver. Pet the dog, hug him, talk to him, and offer lavish praise. Invite the "stranger" to step a little closer. Each time he or she does, reward the dog with loving praise and a food treat. Continue doing this until the dog reaches the limits of his tolerance, and then end the session. You may repeat this an hour later or a day later. As the dog indicates a tolerance for the "stranger," introduce someone else higher on the fear list. With diligence and patience, it is possible to end your dog's phobic behavior toward people.

The second approach is *counterconditioning* described more fully on page 149. Eating is one known way to relax a dog. Massage is another. Feeding the dog when "strangers" are present may begin to ease his anxiety about being there. Start out slowly by calling him into an area he feels good about and offering him an enticing morsel, a hug, and much praise. As in the above technique, have someone from the bottom of the fear list enter the premises, maintaining a great distance. Place the dog's food bowl on the floor with a small portion of his meal in it. As the dog begins to eat, invite the "stranger" to step in closer. Pet the dog and offer him loving reassurance. Have the "stranger" come as close as possible without triggering the phobic response. If all went well, then repeat the process at his next feeding time. Eventually you may feed him his complete meal set down on the floor with all sorts of people present. You know you have made progress if you can feed him a complete meal and leave him there with another person in the room.

Obedience Training. Hire a professional dog trainer or buy a basic training book and begin obedience training. Dog training calms a dog because it organizes his responses, establishes in his mind that you are his leader, and helps him try to please you. An obedience-trained dog has a much easier time coping with his phobic responses by concentrating on your commands and not his fear. It is relaxing and aids in counterconditioning. (See "Modify your dog's behavior.")

Prevention Tips

Puppy Selection. Select a good source from which to get your new dog. Consult the American Kennel Club or any of the popular dog magazines. Talk to a neighbor who owns a dog you admire. When buying a dog from a breeder, ask if the puppy has been socialized and how the process was done. Do not buy a puppy that has not been exposed to and handled by various types of people throughout its life. Find out as much as possible about the dog's background. Was it handled mostly by a man or by a woman? Where was it raised, in the home or backyard? Were there children involved? Was the dog ever punished, and how? The answers to these questions will tell you if you want the puppy.

Test the puppies for behavior. Look at each one separately, not all as a group, and watch how they relate to you. If you bend down and the little dog runs away from you, he is afraid of people. A puppy may be fine with the breeder but frightened of anyone else. Do not buy a puppy that exhibits shy behavior. Shyness is a problem that will never be overcome. It could get better, but it cannot be eliminated. Look at the puppy's mother and father, if possible, and see if they are of sound, even temperament.

Many People. Introduce the puppy to as many people as possible. Do not isolate dogs of any age and keep them from being with people. Take them for long, pleasurable walks so they can see new places and people.

Eye Level. Have people relate to the dog by kneeling down to his eye level. Towering over a small dog intimidates him.

Play. Play with the dog as much as possible and show your affection for him. Making the dog feel good about his life goes a long way to prevent phobias.

Punishment. Learn the difference between punishment and correction. If your dog misbehaves or makes a mistake, correct him (see part Two, "Some Tools and Techniques for Problem Solving"); do not punish him. Punishment is a form of revenge. It is destructive to the dog's personality. A dog can be made shy by smacking him constantly or hitting him with a rolled-up newspaper or pointing your finger at him and saying "Bad dog. What did you do?" If your dog has a behavior problem like chewing, barking, or lack of housebreaking, then solve the problem with the help of this directory and stop hitting the dog.

Overprotective Behavior. Do not carry your dog around with you all the time or allow him to sleep with you if he is timid or shy. Permit your dog to mature and not be frightened of people. If you smother him with protective behavior, he will never learn to adjust to new people.

Indoor/Outdoor Dog. If your dog is kept outdoors, allow him inside the home as much as possible so that when visitors arrive he can relate to them. This will teach him to enjoy new people and situations instead of becoming frightened of them.

RUNNING AWAY

Dogs that dash out the door should have a bus painted on their sides. They go faster than the cross-country express. When we think of running away, it conjures up the image of a youngster packing his possessions into a bundle and slinging them on the end of a stick. Do dogs really run away from home? Not intentionally. Dogs simply run. It isn't until they are lost that they realize they've gone too far. Every dog has a bit of the Tom Sawyer about him and is willing to go rafting down the Mississippi playing pirate if given half the opportunity. Most dogs are innocent mischief-makers who will get themselves into serious trouble if their best interests are not looked after. An open door, an unlatched gate, or an experiment off-leash is all it takes for Fido Fleetfeet to trip the light fantastic and chase that big burger in the sky, three traffic lights down, past the quick-food palace. Some dogs would never dream of leav-

An open door, an unlatched gate, and thou . . .

ing the couch and the bowl, but others just ache to see the exact spot where the sky meets the land. The trick is to turn your innerspringer into a home-setter.

Origins of the Problem

The heart and soul of a wolf lies within every pet dog. Wolves and wild dogs spend half their lives on the move. From early spring to autumn they settle into their territories, hunt, eat, mate, and whelp their young. With the frost and the wind comes the need to follow the great herds of deer, elk, caribou, and other prey animals: the movable feast. The canine nomads spend autumn, all winter, and part of spring moving south with the game, spreading across hundreds of miles each year, only to return in the warm months. It is a natural urge for all canids to leave the comfort of the den and move to another place. But they always return to the home territory if fate allows it.

The wolf is a long-distance runner and enjoys the advantage of endurance over his prey. The dog's desire to run is based on his hunting instincts. His leg muscles itch to expand and contract in a leaping-style gallop like the gazehounds and the Doberman Pinschers, who are among the fastest dogs in the world. It could be a fast-moving object crossing a dog's sight line or a distant butterfly that sets him in motion. A faraway howl or a sweet smell in the air will make some dogs run to the tundra if you open the door and step aside.

Reasons for the Problem

The Open Door. Most dogs will run out an open door if they are not restrained. Why shouldn't they?

Other Animals. If a dog sees, smells, or hears another animal he will run away if he finds the opportunity.

Nervousness. An uneasy dog, insecure in his home, will bolt the instant the door opens.

Lack of Training. An untrained dog may or may not jump a fence or run out a door or front gate if it is open. Dogs that have been trained have sorted out their position in the pack. They will hesitate and look to the pack leader (you) for permission before running out. Even if they do not hesitate, the command "No" or "Stay" will keep them in check.

The Smell of Food. Aromas of food or even garbage cans inspire a dog to leave.

Females in Heat. Male dogs can easily detect a female in estrus (heat) and will do all in their power to find her.

Fright. Any loud noise such as an auto backfire could startle a dog and make him run in panic.

Unlocked Gates. If a gate is unlatched or a door unlocked, it could open when a medium-to-large dog places his weight on it.

Children. Children often fail to close the door or yard gate behind them. If the timing is right the dog will run out.

Solutions (Environmental)

Proper Locks. Buy self-locking devices for gates and doors. They automatically close and lock when released.

Garbage. Keep all garbage and trash containers sealed and put away, if possible, to avoid attracting the dog.

Solutions (Reconditioning)

Obedience Training. Have your dog obedience-trained by a professional trainer or do it yourself with a book. The commands "Sit" and "Down-Stay" are the most useful if the dog attempts to run out an open door. A trained dog given one of these commands would not leave.

The Margolis Maneuver. See part Two, "Some Essential Tools and Techniques for Problem Solving" for implementing this solution. Place a slip collar and leash on your

Recondition the runaway dog with the help of the Margolis Maneuver.

dog. Open the door and allow him to start for it. Jerk the leash to the right firmly and say "NO" in a harsh tone of voice. How hard to jerk the leash depends on the size, age, and personality of your dog. (See part Three, "Your Dog's Personality.")

Praise the dog for responding (even though you made him stop) and say "Sit." With your left hand push the dog's haunches down into a sitting position as you pull the leash upward, above his head. Praise him. Then place your flattened left hand across the dog's eyes and say "Stay." If the dog moves say "NO," and correct him with a quick but gentle tug of the leash. Praise him. Repeat this procedure ten times, twice a day,

until the dog understands what you mean with the verbal command alone. Buy a dog training book and give the dog a complete obedience course.

The Shake Can. After working with the leash and collar to your satisfaction (as described above) you may use the shake can as a convenient "brush-up" tool. Look up "Shake Can" in part Two, "Some Essential Tools and Techniques For Problem Solving," for more information.

Have one or more shake cans placed near the front door or gate. If the dog attempts to run out, rattle the can loudly and say "NO," in a loud, firm tone of voice.

Bob Wortham

Prevention Tips

Puppy Training. If your dog is still a puppy, begin obedience training right away. It is much easier when the dog is young. It is possible to begin training a dog when he is eight weeks old.

Close the Door . . . and keep it closed.

SPITE

If your dog gets into your closet and eats five shoes, a chemise, a designer suit from Lord & Taylor, and all the undeveloped film from your trip to Paris, it was not done to get even

. . . no matter what you did. Dogs do not operate out of spite.

Spite is a concept that someone deliberately did something to harm you. When a person acts out of spite, he or she holds a grudge against you and behaves with malicious bitterness in a desire to punish you or to enjoy feelings of revenge. Spite is the shortened version of *despite,* originally meaning *contemptuous defiance* and is derived from the Latin *despolicere,* meaning *to despise.* Dogs do not think or feel in this manner. They respond to situations simply, in their own, unique manner, which we sometimes consider problem behavior. A dog may behave aggressively or in an overly subordinate or overly dominant manner. But dogs never behave with malice.

When you leave a dog alone for eight hours, he may become bored, have excess energy that must be expressed, or suffer with anxiety. His destructive behavior may be an emotional release or a crying out for your attention. He may have been frightened. How does a dog know that you are ever coming back, once you leave? The result could be any form of destructive behavior, such as chewing, house soiling, or howling. Dogs may mess on a bed in a hotel room because they are claiming it as territory, delivering a message (in their own unique way) and asking you to return, or because they have an urgent need to defecate. No one understanding *natural* dog behavior can believe the canine mind capable of punishing a human being out of spite. To believe dogs behave this way is to endow them with sophisticated mental processes requiring reasoning and judgmental abilities equal to those of human beings. It is to anthropomorphize or apply human characteristics to an animal that is brilliant but is brilliant in its own way.

Dogs do not understand the expression *forgive and forget but first get even.* If your dog exhibits problem behavior, look up the behavior in this directory of problems. Read the entire article entry dealing with the problem and try to solve the problem with understanding, teaching, and reconditioning techniques. Your own behavior may well be a factor, but not because the dog is out to get you. Spite does not make right.

STEALING FOOD

Dogs live by the philosophy, "I don't have to do this for a living; I could always starve to death." If you fed your dog an adequate daily ration of a premium commercial dog food or cooked meals with the proper balance of protein, carbohydrates, fat, water, vitamins, and minerals, your dog would still gulp down your steak if given the chance. Never leave your dog alone in the room with a Beef Wellington (or an open can of sardines, for that matter). A dog cannot be trusted unless it has been trained not to steal food. Even a trained dog can make a disaster of a dinner party. Don't get caught with your glass raised, toasting "Here's to good company, good wine, and . . . good grief!"

Origins of the Problem

Dogs are not hungry all the time. But they will eat at every opportunity if the food is from your plate, because the human diet has mainly meat, fowl, fish, or cheese in it. These are important protein sources for a dog, too. In the wild a dog's hunting instincts show

Bob Wortham

A lovable dog will steal your heart and your birthday cake too if you let him.

him the way to the food by sight, smell, and sound. After a long chase he may have to fight it, kill it, and eat it raw. He will probably have to share it with others. In the home your cooking sends the aroma of the food into the air and stimulates his sensitive smell mechanism. It is much easier to snatch the food than fight for it. But from the dog's point of view he must have it.

In the wild, wolves and dogs are successful at catching what they hunt less than 10 percent of the time. They have been known to go seventeen days without a meal. The average wolf can consume from nine to twenty pounds of food at one sitting, and 95 percent of his diet is meat. After a kill made by the entire pack, the leaders eat first. First they devour the organ meat and the contents of the stomach, which will be grass, leaves, and other plant matter. The rest of the pack eats when the leaders allow it. Under such conditions it is not hard to understand why it is instinctive for all canids to eat at every opportunity.

When your house dogs steal food from the table, it does not seem to them to be incorrect behavior even though you feed them regularly. If they were living out a natural existence in a dog pack, they would have to snatch food when it was available or else starve to death. Dogs will gorge themselves because their instincts tell them they cannot be certain where the next meal is coming from or when. The genetic programming of dog behavior does not take into account the glorious array of pet food at the supermarket. To your dog the food chain bears no relationship to the A&P.

Reasons for the Problem

Hunger. Some really are hungry. Consult a veterinarian for a proper diet based on your dog's age, weight, and health.

Improper Feeding Schedule. A sensible feeding schedule is essential for maintaining your dog's health and establishing good eating habits.

Cooking. Cooked food is enticing because it transports the stimulating aroma through the air to the dog's nose and sets his instincts in gear.

Height. If a dog is tall enough he will reach up and take what is available.

Table Feeding. When dogs are fed from the table it is a logical progression to steal food when possible. From the dog's point of view, it is not so much stealing but doing what must be done.

Leftovers. Dogs that are fed leftovers from the humans' food supply are encouraged to take what they can, when they can.

Availability. One must assume that a dog will take food from a plate or kitchen counter if the opportunity is made available.

Solutions (Environmental)

Establish a Feeding Place. Feed your dog in one place only and nowhere else. Discourage your dog every time he attempts to bring his food away from the established feeding place. This will help recondition the dog from stealing food.

Feeding Schedule. Place your dog on a sensible feeding schedule and stay with it until his age or state of health requires a change. It is best to consult a veterinarian about this. Puppies from three to six months old usually eat three times a day, with the last meal in the late afternoon or early evening. Dogs six months to one year old should eat twice a day, with the last meal in the late afternoon. Dogs one year and older eat once a day, in the morning. After housebreaking or paper training, fresh water should be available at all times.

Solutions (Reconditioning)

The Setup. In all the reconditioning techniques the dog must be "baited" or set up. In other words, the conditions for stealing food must be created by you so that the dog can be caught in the act and immediately corrected. If a dog is not corrected as he does the bad thing, he cannot associate the correction with the misdeed.

The Margolis Maneuver.   This technique will solve the problem in most cases. (See "The Margolis Maneuver" in part Two, "Some Essential Tools and Techniques for Problem Solving.") Place a leash and slip collar on the dog. Put some freshly cooked meat on the table. When the dog goes for it (and he surely will), jerk the leash to the right and say "NO," in a loud, firm tone of voice. Praise him for responding properly. Give the dog another opportunity to take the food. Repeat the correction procedure if he goes for it. Always praise the dog after a correction to reassure him and to reward him for responding properly. Set up the situation many times. Repeat the corrective technique until the dog refuses to touch the meat. Test him for several days.

The Shake Can.   Once you have used the Margolis Maneuver to your satisfaction, place several shake cans at easy-to-reach locations in the kitchen and dining area. (See "Shake Can" in part Two, "Some Essential Tools and Techniques for Problem Solving.") If the dog attempts to steal food rattle the shake can loudly and say "NO," in a loud firm tone of voice. Always praise him after any correction. The shake can permits you to correct the dog without having to use the leash and slip collar.

Leave several shake cans in a row on the counters and table surfaces when you are not home. If the dog jumps up, one or more

Shake, rattle and roll the shake can to stop a dog from taking the food out of your mouth.

will fall to the floor and startle him. It has a self-correcting effect.

Balloons.   Inflate several balloons and puncture them with a pin close to the dog. The sound will create an aversion to the sight of the balloons. Before you leave the house, tape six inflated balloons in a row to the counter or table surface. Because of the aversion to the balloons, the dog is likely to stay away from them.

Obedience Training.   Have your dog obedience-trained by a professional trainer or buy a training book and do it yourself. Use the commands "Down," "Stay," or "Place."

Prevention Tips

Do Not Make Food Available to the Dog. This seems so obvious, but it needs stating. If the food is not available to the dog, he cannot steal it. When you bring a meal to the table, remove him from the scene.

Do Not Feed the Dog From the Table. When you do, you are allowing him to jump to conclusions ... not to mention to your food.

Do Not Feed Your Dog Leftovers. When you feed your dog human food, you are not only teaching him to like it; you are teaching him to eat off your plates. It is the wrong thing to do if stealing food bothers you.

Housebreaking and Paper Training

A FIVE-PART HOUSEBREAKING PROGRAM

All dogs can and should be housebroken. Only those with a medical problem cannot achieve success with the program given here. And they, too, can be housebroken when the condition is corrected. A puppy of eight weeks and older can begin this program and be housebroken within one week. Depending upon the dog, the owners, and consistent adherence to the program, the average dog can be housebroken between three days and three weeks. Young puppies will still require confinement after they have been housebroken until they are proven reliable, which will be at four or five months of age.

The elements of this housebreaking program are (1) Feed-Water-Walk Schedule, (2) How to Feed Your Dog, (3) Removing Old Odors, (4) Confinement, and (5) Proper Correction. These elements will work only when they are used together. To leave any one or more of them out during the housebreaking process will ensure failure. *Once your dog's house training is successfully completed, it will no longer be necessary to confine him as before.* All other aspects of the five-part program are valid for the life of the dog.

1. Feed-Water-Walk Schedule

Dogs living indoors benefit most from this approach. The objective is to condition the dog's mind and body to eliminating body waste at specific times of the day and night. Daily repetition of feeding, drinking, and walking at the same times creates in the dog's mind and body an alarm clock that will last a lifetime. Depending upon the size of the dog, his age, the amount he eats, and his house training, it will take three to six hours after feeding for food to travel through his digestive system and leave his body. Obviously, puppies digest food much sooner than grown dogs. Most dogs relieve themselves immediately after eating. By learning your dog's digestion time, you can predict when he must relieve himself. The schedule must be adjusted to suit other physical needs, as well. For example, puppies, with smaller bladders and stomachs and less sphincter control, must be walked more frequently than mature dogs. Consult your veterinarian for your dog's digestion time.

By always feeding, watering, and walking your dog at the same times every day, you teach him to create an inner schedule consistent with your schedule. This inner schedule will continue after the housebreaking program is finished. He becomes motivated to control his need to eliminate because his body clock anticipates walks at specific times every day.

Please bear in mind that a dog's age determines the type of schedule you create for him. A young dog must be fed more often than a fully grown dog. During the major growth period (three to ten months of age), puppies require more food per pound of body weight than older dogs do. They should not eat their whole daily requirement at one meal. They need to eliminate more frequently, and that means more walks. Young puppies should be walked according to the schedule below.

Large dogs do not need as many walks (for the purpose of elimination) as small dogs. They can control their need to relieve themselves for much longer periods of time.

When you are setting up a Feed-Water-Walk Schedule, the time for the first walk of the day should be determined by how many hours have passed since the dog was last walked. *There must not be a nighttime interval longer than eight hours.* If your dog's last walk is at 11:00 P.M., his first walk the next morning should be at 7:00 A.M. Here are some suggested schedules that can be used exactly as they are or adjusted to take into account the needs of your dog or your family.

Schedule for Puppies
Three to Six Months Old

7:00 A.M. — Walk the dog.

7:30 A.M. — Feed, water, and walk.

11:30 A.M. — Feed, water, and walk.

4:30 P.M. — Feed, water, and walk.

7:30 P.M. — Water and walk (last water of the day).

11:00 P.M. — Walk the dog.

Schedule for Dogs
Six Months to One Year Old

7:00 A.M. — Walk the dog.

7:30 A.M. — Feed, water, and walk.

12:30 P.M. — Water and walk.

4:30 P.M. — Feed, water, and walk.

7:30 P.M. — Water and walk (last water of the day).

11:00 P.M. — Walk the dog.

Schedule for Dogs
One Year Old and Older

7:00 A.M. — Walk the dog.

7:30 A.M. — Feed, water, and walk.

4:30 P.M. — Water and walk.

7:30 P.M. — Water and walk (last water of the day).

11:00 P.M. — Walk the dog.

First thing in the morning — Walk the dog.

Before leaving for work — Feed, water, and walk.

Midday — Have a neighbor or hired walker feed, water, and walk a puppy (only water and walk a grown dog).

Home from work — Walk the dog.

Immediately after walk — Feed, water and walk a puppy or dog under one year old (only *water* and *walk* a grown dog).

Early evening — Water and walk (last water of the day).

Before going to bed — Walk the dog.

When walking your new dog or puppy for the first time remember his need to "scent post." (See page 111, "Origins of the Problem.") This instinct works to your advantage. Allow your dog to seek out the "scent marks" of other dogs and eliminate over them. These will become permanent stations along the path of your dog's daily walks. Congratulate and praise your dog every time he relieves himself any place outdoors. An important part of the teaching process is to praise him for doing the right thing and correct him when he does the wrong thing.

2. Feeding Your Dog During Housebreaking

Meeting your dog's nutritional requirements should always be the first consideration when selecting a proper diet. However, during the housebreaking period there is another equally important goal. It is essential that the dog's digestion be in perfect order,

or the housebreaking program will fail. If your dog develops loose stools, diarrhea, or the need to urinate excessively, it will be impossible for him to follow any of the Feed-Water-Walk schedules and he will not become trained.

Feed your dog a mixture of meat-based canned dog food and dry cereal dog food. One part canned meat combined with three parts moistened dry cereal dog food should maintain a firm stool and allow for successful housebreaking. Do not overfeed your dog. However, puppies must be able to eat as much as they want for growth. If your dog leaves food in the bowl or is defecating excessively, you are feeding him too much. Reduce his food portion. Do not feed your dog *anything* from the table and stay away from between-meal snacks. Stick to the feeding schedule with great consistency.

Your dog's stomach is sensitive. Any sudden changes in his diet will cause diarrhea. If you are going to change your dog's diet, do not make the switch suddenly. Hold off on housebreaking until the change is completed. Over a four-day period, add some of the new food to the old food, increasing the amount each time as you decrease the old food. Once you have settled all the questions about your dog's diet, you may begin the housebreaking program.

3. Removing Odors of Past Mistakes

A dog's scenting ability is the greatest of all his senses. Picture the human nose and then compare it to the canine snout. Inside each is a fine lining called the smell membrane containing thousands of smell receptors (in humans) and millions of receptors (in dogs). In humans this area is less than one inch long. In dogs it can be four inches long. Smells trigger electric impulses to the olfactory center in the brain, arriving there as raw information to be evaluated. Dogs use their noses more than their eyes and maintain a memory storage in the brain based on smells. The canine sense of smell is extraordinary.

It is impossible to housebreak a dog unless you obliterate all past odors of his own urine and defecation. This includes past mistakes on the carpet and areas of the floor where he was permitted to use newspapers as a toilet. Every time the dog relieves himself on the floor, an odor remains no matter how well you may scrub it away. This remaining odor draws the dog back to that spot and triggers his instinct to "mark" on top of it. It is a continuing cycle that can be ended only when the dog's scent of urine is eliminated. This explains why dogs with housebreaking problems always seem to relieve themselves in the same locations. Although the odor may not be evident to the human nose, it is perceptible to the intricate smell mechanism of a dog's nose. Buy an *odor neutralizer concentrate* at a pharmacy or pet supply store and use it according to instructions. This type of product is the only means available to obliterate previous scent posts in your house successfully. Ammonia, bleach, vinegar, and other household products do not remove these odors from the dog's keen sense of smell. Odor neutralizers do not mask the smells; they alter them.

4. Confinement

Unhousebroken puppies will relieve themselves about every hour (depending on their activity level and water intake) and will do it on the floor, in front of you. Adolescent and mature dogs who have experienced your displeasure have greater sphincter control and will wait until you leave before letting go on the carpet. It is not defiance, arrogance, spite work, or stupidity that makes them behave this way. They are simply unhousebroken dogs who are caught in the crossfire between human demands and their natural inclinations. Their bodies have not been regulated and they have not been taught (in a manner they can understand) what you expect of them.

Restricting your dog's indoor movements (especially when no one is home) is a key factor for a successful housebreaking program. During the housebreaking program, confine your dog or puppy if you do not have time to watch for the signs that tell you he is going to relieve himself. (Dogs and puppies sniff close to the ground, whimper and whine, make gagging sounds, turn in circles, and even head for the door when they must eliminate.) If you are going to leave the house, it is essential that the dog in the housebreaking program be confined to one small area until your return.

As described in "Origins of the Problem," dogs are born with the instinct not to soil their eating and sleeping area. They are also taught this by their mothers. When you confine your dog, he quickly realizes that he will be forced to remain in the same area with his urine and defecation if he lets go. Sometimes a dog cannot help himself and soils his own area anyway. However, he did not soil the entire house, creating more aggravation (and scent posts to return to).

Do not mistake "confinement" for imprisonment or tying the dog down someplace. Simply confine the dog in a small but comfortable area adequate for his physical and psychological needs. Leave him in the selected confinement area with his food, water, toys, and bedding. A puppy gate installed in the doorway will keep him there. The kitchen is the most commonly chosen confinement site because of the size, location, and floor covering. Linoleum or floor tiles will withstand your dog's "accidents" better than any other covering. This is the ideal situation. You may also use a bathroom or small hallway for this purpose. The area should be large enough for the dog to walk around without feeling punished, and he should be able to see other parts of the house and family activities. Never confine your dog or puppy behind a closed door. This is psychologically harmful and counterproductive. Some owners have successfully housebroken their dogs using wire dog crates for confinement purposes. Many breeders recommend them, although they are not necessary for housebreaking unless you have no other practical area for confinement.

During the housebreaking program confine your dog when you leave the house or do not have time to watch for his mistakes. *Unless you plan to paper-train your dog, do not lay any newspapers down on the floor in the confinement area.* If the dog has an accident on the floor, take him outside and praise him lavishly if he eliminates there. Clean up the mess from the floor, get rid of the scent with an odor neutralizer, and continue the program as outlined. Using newspapers on the floor only teaches the dog to use the floor and prevents the successful conclusion to housebreaking.

It is good for the dog to run around loose as much as possible. Release him from confinement when you get home. The dog should be allowed to run around in the house, provided that someone watches him for signs that he has to relieve himself.

5. Correction and Praise

This is the fifth element of housebreaking, the most important part of the program. If your dog relieves himself inside the house in front of you, rattle a shake can vigorously and say "NO" in a loud, firm voice to impress him with your displeasure. The manner in which you say "No" should be based on your dog's personality. A puppy or a sensitive or shy dog cannot tolerate an overbearing manner. (See part Three, "Your Dog's Personality," to learn how to correct dogs of various personality types.)

Your dog will probably stop eliminating if your correction was firm enough. Place a leash and slip collar on him and quickly take him outside to the place where he is permitted to relieve himself. Praise him the minute you get there, whether he relieves himself or not. If he continues to eliminate in the correct area, lavish him with tremendous praise. This praise and correction is the most important element of this teaching process. Place several shake cans around the house for warning and keep the dog's leash and slip collar handy. If you cannot reach a shake can in time say "NO" in a loud, firm tone of voice and then take the dog out. Praise him afterward.

The only language that communicates between dogs and humans is the one of positive and negative messages. It is precisely how dogs communicate between themselves. Dogs thrive on acceptance and praise. When these are denied and negative messages are substituted, all dogs correct their behavior. It is the only known teaching process available for domestic dogs.

The most common misconception that dog owners have is the meaning of the terms "correction" or "negative messages." They are often confused with the word "punishment." Punishment is an act of retaliation against a dog for doing something offensive to a human being. It is based on emotion and motivated by revenge. Punishing a dog for destructive behavior may offer a temporary emotional release, but be assured that it teaches a dog absolutely nothing. The most important thing about dogs this book can impart to you is *punishment is not teaching*. If your dog behaves badly, your objective should be to solve the problem, not to punish the dog. These are two different matters.

Corrections or *negative messages* are simple, humane techniques for communicating to a dog that he has just done the wrong thing. The Margolis Maneuver is the most effective and frequently used correction technique available to dog owners. It delivers a mild, negative sensation with the use of a leash and slip collar. It does not hurt. The reason why dogs interpret it as a negative message is because it is always accompanied with the verbal reprimand "No." The jerk of the leash and the tightening of the slip collar (for an instant) are associated with the owner's criticism and lack of approval. The correction is part of the teaching process.

Praise is a reward. It motivates a dog to do whatever it is that you expect of him. You should always praise him for his efforts. If he misbehaves or fails to execute a command, correct him (using the Margolis Maneuver, a shake can, or a firm "NO"). *After*

every correction it is essential that you immediately praise your dog. It reassures him and rewards him for trying to do the right thing.

Do not correct your dog for messing in the house unless you catch him in the act. Your dog has no way of associating your correction with a misdeed if the "accident" happened more than ten seconds ago. Correcting him later would be useless and cruel. Forget all about yelling, hitting, swatting with a newspaper, or rubbing the dog's nose in his own mess. You would not hit a small child for making a mistake when you were teaching him or her something new. Do not slap a newspaper against your hand as a correction. It threatens the dog and is simply another form of punishment. The objective is not to frighten the dog but to tell him that he has just done something wrong. The next step is to teach him the correct thing to do.

HOW TO PAPER-TRAIN YOUR DOG

1. Papering

Select a convenient place in your home as the dog's papering area. The basement, bathroom, hall, or kitchen is suitable. Do not select an area with a hardwood floor unless it is sealed and bonded with varnish or polyurethane. A linoleum floor is best.

Accumulate a tall stack of newspapers and a pile of plastic garbage bags.

Spread newspapers over the entire floor of the selected area, three to five sheets thick (depending on the size of the dog and the quantity of urine produced). When the dog eliminates on this floor, he will have no choice but to do it on paper.

Always place one sheet of soiled paper under the fresh paper in the area of the floor the dog favors. He will be drawn to that spot by the slight scent of urine and will eliminate on it. Leave the papers on the floor twenty-four hours a day. Change them immediately after each use. Do this for five days.

On the sixth day begin to decrease the papered area from the outer edge so that the bare floor shows like a border. For the next three to five days, gradually reduce the papered area of the floor. Do this until paper covers only a small portion of the floor. You should have to paper only the spot the dog has chosen to use. If he misses the paper, spread more paper down and try to work your way back to as small an area as necessary.

2. Feeding and Watering Schedule

Most dog owners feed and water their dogs in the same confinement area used for papering. Take the food and water out of the area after the dog has eaten and drunk from his bowl. When papering the dog (as indicated in the following schedules) allow him ten minutes to use the papers. When the dog uses the papers, lavish praise on him. It will encourage him to use the papers all the time.

Use the following schedules to regulate the dog's digestive system and modify his behavior.

Schedule for Puppies
Three to Six Months Old

7:00 A.M. — Paper the dog.
7:30 A.M. — Feed, water, and paper the dog.

11:30 A.M. — Feed, water and paper the dog.
4:30 P.M. — Feed, water, and paper the dog.
7:30 P.M. — Water and paper the dog (last water of the day).
11:00 P.M. — Confine the dog in the paper area for the night.

Schedule for Dogs
Six Months to One Year Old

7:00 A.M. — Paper the dog.
7:30 A.M. — Feed, water, and paper the dog.
12:30 P.M. — Water and paper the dog.
4:30 P.M. — Feed, water, and paper the dog.
7:30 P.M. — Water and paper the dog (last water of the day).
11:00 P.M. — Confine the dog in the paper area for the night.

Schedule for Dogs
One Year and Older

7:00 A.M. — Paper the dog.
7:30 A.M. — Feed, water, and paper the dog.
4:30 P.M. — Water and paper the dog.
7:30 P.M. — Water and paper the dog (last water of the day).
11:00 P.M. — Confine the dog in the paper area for the night.

Schedule for Those
Who Go to Work

First thing in the morning: Paper the dog.
Before leaving for work: Feed, water, and paper the dog.
Midday: Have a neighbor or hired person feed, water, and paper a puppy (only water and paper a grown dog).
Home from work: Feed, water, and paper a puppy or dog under one year old (only water and walk a grown dog).
Early evening: Water and paper the dog (last water of the day).

Before going to bed: Confine the dog in the paper area for the night.

When the paper training is completed, continue to feed the dog according to the times established in the feeding and watering schedules. Water may then be made available at all times and confinement should not be necessary. If the dog regresses, adjust the feeding and watering schedules and confine him until he is back to normal.

3. Diet

Meeting your dog's nutritional requirements should always be the first consideration when selecting a diet. During paper training try to maintain normal digestion and avoid loose stools, diarrhea, or the need to urinate excessively. Feed your dog a mixture of canned dog food and dry dog food. One part canned food combined with three parts moistened dry dog food should maintain a firm stool and allow for successful paper training.

4. Removing Odors

It is impossible to paper-train a dog unless you obliterate all past odors of his urine and defecation mistakes in the places where he is not papered. Every time the dog relieves himself on the floor, an odor remains, no matter how well you may scrub it away. This remaining odor draws the dog back to that spot and triggers his instinct to "mark" on top of it. It is a continuing cycle that can be ended only when the dog's scent is eliminated. This explains why dogs with paper training problems always seem to relieve themselves in the same locations.

Buy an odor neutralizer concentrate at a pharmacy or pet supply store and use it according to the instructions on the label. This type of product is the only means available that will successfully obliterate previous scent posts in your house. Odor neutralizers do not mask the smells; they alter them.

5. Confinement

Restricting your dog's indoor movements (especially when no one is home) is a key factor to a successful paper training program. During the training, confine your dog or your puppy if you do not have time to watch for the signs that tell you he is going to relieve himself. (Dogs and puppies sniff close to the ground, whimper and whine, make gagging sounds and turn in circles when they must eliminate.) If you are going to leave the house, the dog must be confined to one small area until your return.

Confine the dog in the papering area with a clean set of papers on the floor. A puppy gate installed in the doorway will keep him there. The kitchen is the most commonly chosen confinement site because of the size, location, and floor covering. The area should be large enough for the dog to walk around without feeling punished, and he should be able to see other parts of the house and family activities. Never confine your dog or puppy behind a closed door. This is psychologically harmful and counterproductive. Some owners have successfully used a wire dog crate for confinement purposes. Many breeders recommend them, although they are not necessary for paper training unless there is no other practical area for confinement.

It is good for the dog to run around loose as much as possible. Release him from confinement when you get home. The dog should be allowed to run around the house, providing someone watches him for signs that he has to relieve himself.

6. Correction and Praise

If your dog relieves himself on the uncovered floor, out of his papering area, rattle a shake can loudly and say "NO" in a loud, firm tone of voice to impress him with your displeasure. The manner in which you say "No" is based on your dog's personality. A puppy or a sensitive or shy dog cannot tolerate an overbearing manner. (See part Three, "Your Dog's Personality," to learn how to correct dogs of various personality types.)

Your dog will probably stop eliminating if your correction was firm enough. Quickly remove him from the room and carry him to the papering area. If he is too large to carry, hold him by the collar and briskly walk him there. Praise him the minute you get him there, whether he relieves himself or not. If he continues to eliminate in the papering area, lavish praise on him. Praise is the most important element of the teaching process. Place several shake cans around the house for this purpose. (See "Shake Can" in part Two," Some Essential Tools and Techniques for Problem Solving.") If you cannot reach a shake can in time, say "NO," and take the dog to the papering area. Praise him afterward.

A correction is a negative message telling the dog he has done something wrong. When you rattle the shake can and say "NO" in a loud voice, you are correcting the dog.

Praise is a reward. It motivates a dog to do whatever it is that you expect of him. One should always praise him for his efforts. If he misbehaves or fails to execute a command, correct him (using the Margolis Maneuver, a shake can, or a firm "NO"). *After every correction, immediately praise your dog.* Your praise reassures him and rewards him for trying to do the right thing.

Do not correct your dog for messing away from the papering area unless you catch him in the act. That would be useless and cruel. Your dog has no way of associating your correction with a misdeed if it happened more than ten seconds ago.

When good dogs do good things.

Acknowledgments

The authors wish to thank Victoria Siegal for her tireless efforts. Without her sharp pencil, keen eye, good taste, and sound judgment this book would never have reached a satisfactory state of completion.

We gratefully acknowledge the skills and generosity of those who made the photographs possible. Those pictures depicting problems and their solutions were all taken by Bob Wortham in Los Angeles, except for six by Marybeth Eubanks of the National Institute of Dog Training. Most other photographs were taken by Mordecai Siegal. We wish to thank the Dog Museum of America, Gaines Dog Care Center, Sporting Dog Specialties, Inc., and *Pedigrees* (*The Pet Catalog*) of Spencerport, New York, for lending us one or more photographs.

The problems-and-solutions photos would not have been possible without the help and cooperation of those who so graciously "recreated" those situations for our cameras. A tip of the Siegal-Margolis hat to those who performed for us. The dogs in the pictures: "Duke" Nathan, a black Labrador Retriever–Pit Bull mix; "Baron," a German Shepherd Dog; "Kiwi," a German Shepherd Dog; "Ralph" Margolis, a Maltese; "Emily" Margolis, a German Shepherd Dog; "Love" Watson, a Beagle; Am. & Mex. Ch. Golden Rule's Earth Wind N' Fire, C.D., P.C. (call name "Winner"), a Golden Retriever; Sun-Fax Synchronicity "Timmy," a Golden Retriever; "Gus" Hirsch, a Doberman Pinscher; "Nugget" Misel, a Yellow Labrador Retriever; and "Sweet Pea," a Pomeranian.

The people in the pictures: Matthew Margolis, Christine Plantenga, Ken Anthony, Jr., Philip Nathan, Wendy Agustin, Lisa Bleecker, and Jack Craig.

A large debt of gratitude is owed to several members of the staff of the National Institute of Dog Training in Los Angeles. Without their devoted assistance, the photography sessions would have been impossible. Many thanks to Kris Frainie, office manager; Lori Delgado, kennel supervisor; Glen Allison, assistant kennel supervisor; Kenneth Sunada, assistant kennel supervisor; trainers Wendy Agustin, Lisa Bleecker, Jack Craig, Christine Plantenga; and special thanks to Ken Anthony, Jr., executive director of NIDT.

It is with special pleasure that we acknowledge the important help of Sherry Davis, director of training, NIDT, for her tireless efforts in organizing and coordinating the photo sessions. She selected the dogs, dealt with the trainers, and made a difficult task work smoothly. We are also appreciative of the efforts of Philip Nathan, director of marketing, NIDT, who did everything for the photo sessions from handling dogs to driving cars to digging holes and making props. Thanks, guys. We couldn't have done it without you.

Samuel Johnson said, "Knowledge is of two kinds. We know a subject ourselves, or we know where we can find information upon it." He was right. The authors went outside their own experience and information to learn more from the many knowledgeable dog people who so generously shared the wealth of their learning. *Although this book does not deal with specific breeds, it is hoped that the information extracted from the treasure trove generously given by the supporters of the breeds mentioned below will be useful to all dogs and their hopeful owners everywhere.* We are thankful to Barbara L. Henderson, V.M.D., American Whippet Club; Gloria Cronin, American Shetland Sheepdog Association;

Natalie D. Carlton, the Rhodesian Ridgeback Club of the United States; Leslie J. Benis, Puli Club of Southern California; Camille La Bree, Norwegian Elkhound Association of America; Irene Reasons, the Pekingese Club of America; Pamela K. Warner, the Papillon Club of America; Robert M. Brown, D.V.M.; Elsie S. Neustadt, Greyhound Club of America; Helen Gleason, German Shepherd Dog Club of America; Mrs. Dennis A. Ronyak, English Setter Association of America; Mrs. Betty C. Floyd, Cardigan Welsh Corgi Club of America; Margaret G. Thomas, Pembroke Welsh Corgi Club of America; Walter M. Jones, Dachshund Club of America; Mrs. K. D. Romanski, the English Cocker Spaniel Club of America; Ann Filetti, Borzoi Club of America; Marcy Spalding, the Belgian Sheepdog Club of America; Edward Kilby, the American Bloodhound Club; Sylvia Thomas, the Akita Club of America; Karen Armistead, Afghan Hound Club of America; Nell N. Fox, the Australian Terrier Club of America; Karen B. Dorsch, the American Bullmastiff Association; Randie C. Meyer, the American Belgian Tervuren Club; Mrs. Jean Sheehy, the Basset Hound Club of America; Jill Farley, Weimaraner owner; Gale S. Studeny, Weimaraner owner; Martha Kuhn, Weimaraner Club of America; Chris Jones, the American Shih Tzu Club; Bardi McLennan, Welsh Terrier Club of America; Karen B. Dorsch, Bullmastiff Club of America; Robert M. Brown, D. V. M., Great Pyrenees Club of America; Cynthia Morse and Allan Vargo, the Bull Terrier Club of America; Lynn S. Urban, Mastiff Club of America; and Mrs. Roger S. Foster, Jr., Newfoundland Club of America; the Briard Club of America; and the Chow Chow Club, Inc.

It is a pleasure to work with such a talented editor as Mary E. Tondorf-Dick, Managing Editor of Little, Brown and Company, and her assistant, Sarah Dewey Pence. No problems there, only solutions.

A nod, a wink, and a hug to Mel Berger of the William Morris Agency. Diamonds are not an agent's *only* best friend. And to Gladys Katz and Bernice Hess, who make that agency a nice place to visit, many thanks.

Index